THE FLIGHT OF THE BLACK NECKED SWANS

MILTON PEÑA VÁSQUEZ

Milton Peña

Typeset in Minion Pro

Design, typesetting and publishing by UK Book Publishing

UK Book Publishing is a trading name of Consilience Media

www.ukbookpublishing.com

ISBN: 978-1-910223-64-2

Cover illustration: © Milton Peña Vásquez

Back cover photographs

Top right: Nurse taking a patient's blood pressure

From left:

Coup of September 11, 1973. Bombing of La Moneda (presidential palace)
https://commons.wikimedia.org/wiki/File:Golpe_de_Estado_1973.jpg – Attribution 3.0 Chile

Milton Peña (centre) on top of Mount Kilimanjaro

Milton Peña in theatre with his team

Recollections, Diaries And Letters Of A Refugee Surgeon From Chile

Escape From Fascism

Life In Exile

A twelve-year quest for better and safer patient care at a National Health Service hospital in Greater Manchester, England

&

A campaign for legislation concerning mandatory nurse and midwife to patient staffing ratios in England

For my family of black necked swans

DEDICATION

- To the victims of the fascist repression that followed the *coup d'état* in Chile in 1973.
- To those who, throughout the world, suffer political persecution.
- To the British people, who welcomed hundreds of Chilean refugees after the *coup.*
- To my patients, their parents and relatives, who trusted me.
- To nurses and midwives, wherever in the world they work.
- To the employees at Tameside Hospital, and the patients and members of the public, who supported my efforts and offered encouragement.
- To my mentors for their teaching and guidance, over long years of education and training.
- To those who, over the years, have campaigned to improve standards of care in the National Health Service (NHS) and for legislation on nurse and midwife to patient ratios.
- To all whistle-blowers who put their careers and reputations on the line in the pursuit of truth and fairness.

FOREWORD

Dr Milton Peña's journey to Britain from strife torn Chile in the 1970s, as an asylum seeker, is presented in this book. The narrative is presented in historical detail and you are made aware of an epic struggle to overcome adversity, in escaping a fascist political regime in Chile, in learning to become fluent in English and to become a consultant orthopaedic surgeon, in the National Health Service in Lancashire, England.

His detailed record keeping using his diary shows the adverse effect on patient care, that can result when patient services are subordinated to health economics, by health service managers, without due diligence from the Management Board. This resulted in an excess mortality despite the valiant efforts of the dwindling numbers of medical and nursing staff.

It was a reduction of nursing numbers on his orthopaedic wards, which led to substandard care that prompted attempted corrective measures, to no avail. The junior doctors of Tameside Hospital themselves drew up a Junior Doctors Charter in an effort to improve the delivery of medical services; the Charter was accepted by the Trust but was not acted upon adequately.

It was Milton Peña's determination to seek the truth and improve the quality of care for the patients themselves, [at some personal sacrifice as a whistleblower] that was a factor in the eventual demise of the managerial regime who must bear the major responsibility for the poor clinical outcomes resulting by overly concentrating on balancing the books! His love of nature and mountaineering are without doubt factors that helped in giving him fortitude to deal with the setbacks he experienced. By his determination in speaking out against the aforesaid management systems methods, he has helped to improve the health service delivery of the patients present and in the future in Tameside Hospital and hopefully other NHS trusts in England.

Nicholas O'Mullane – *Retired Consultant Physician*

CONTENTS

PREFACE

The idea of writing this book came to me in early 2012. During the preceding seven years, working as a hospital doctor, I had become known in the local community as a campaigner on issues surrounding the care of patients, activities that brought me into repeated conflict with my employers. I slowly began to feel the need to put pen to paper – or, more accurately, to reach out for my laptop – to explain to the public my concerns about issues such as the inadequate nurse staffing levels on the wards, the avoidable deaths that inevitably occur as a result, and the harm caused by elevating financial considerations above the needs of patients. The project, however, developed in a way not originally intended and led me to return to my roots which lay in Chile, where I was born, in order to explain who I was and why, entirely by fortuitous circumstances, I ended up living in Britain.

A *coup d'état* took place in Chile in September 1973. Hundreds of citizens were arrested and summarily executed within twenty four hours. Others were killed after undergoing weeks of horrific and unimaginable torture. Hundreds were captured and were never seen again. Many died in armed clashes, trying to resist the brutal dictatorship that followed, which lasted seventeen years.

After escaping to Argentina with my family, we sought political asylum in various countries. The United Kingdom was the first to respond. Thus, in July 1974, we entered Britain as political refugees.

Writing about the events of that time – more than forty years ago – has been difficult, because it brought back the feelings of guilt that I had survived, and that after settling in England I had concentrated almost exclusively on my family and my career. At the same time, however, re-living those horrendous experiences, and committing them to print, has been good because it has allowed me to free long-repressed emotions. Writing about this period of my life has given me the opportunity to pay due tribute to the thousands of victims of the dictatorship.

I could quite easily have written a book concerned only with my experience at Tameside Hospital and, indeed, this thought has crossed my mind many times. In the end, I decided to place that later episode in my life in its broader context but divided the book into three parts which, to some extent, stand alone and can be read separately. Part 1 covers the period before I moved to Tameside Hospital.

In the first chapter I begin with a brief introduction to Chile's geography; I make a plea for its unique native forest which, regrettably, is being destroyed at an alarming rate and for the Mapuche, the aboriginal people that inhabited central and southern Chile, who continue to suffer intolerable discrimination, exclusion and repression. I introduce the black necked swans, reminisce a little about of my parents and the university that formed me as a person and explain why I chose to study medicine.

The second chapter is dedicated to the memories of President Salvador Allende, lovingly known to his friends as 'Chicho', for his curly reddish hair, and Dr Miguel Enriquez, who was the leader of the Movement of the Revolutionary Left (MIR) at the time of the *coup*, to name just two of the many heroes that made the ultimate sacrifice. It is also written to honour General René Schneider, who was shot during an earlier botched Central Intelligence Agency (CIA)-led coup; General Carlos Prats who was killed by detonation of a bomb under his car; and Brigadier General Rodolfo Bachelet, who died as a result of torture. These three generals paid the ultimate price for their loyalty to the President. Not least, it has been written to pay a tribute to all those who resisted and fought against the dictator and to all the victims of the atrocities of the dictatorship, from all political groups.

The second chapter relates to political events in Chile between 1970 and 1973. Based on the incontrovertible evidence in historical declassified documents, from the USA Department of State and USA Congress Select Intelligence Committee, among many others, I denounce the war against Chilean democracy by the United States government. My personal experience during those times closes chapter two.

In chapter three I recount our escape to Argentina, with my young family and a friend, where we became refugees.

The next chapters, in Part 1, are perhaps mundane. In them I describe settling in England; language and cultural barriers; restarting my career; training and taking post-graduate examinations; becoming an orthopaedic surgeon; and our first visit to Chile after eighteen years of exile.

In Part 2, with the help of the diaries, the book subsequently covers my quest for safer hospital care since 2002, and my campaign for legislation on nurse and midwife to patient ratios. Writing these chapters has made me reflect on my past, and it has helped me to understand why I feel so passionately about these issues.

My interest in mountains – which began by chance in the French Alps in 2007, and continued with treks to mounts Kilimanjaro, McKinley and Aconcagua – is an integral part of the narrative thereafter. I hope it makes the book less dull and stimulates some of you to take up trekking.

From the outset, I wish to make it absolutely clear that Parts 2 and 3 of this book have not been written and/or published to denigrate the reputation of Tameside Hospital – where I worked for seventeen years – or the National Health Service (NHS), the nation's most cherished institution. On the contrary, I have repeatedly maintained that Tameside Hospital provides a timely and satisfactory – and on many occasions excellent – service to the vast majority of its users.

What happens, however, when 'balancing the books' is placed above everything else year after year in an NHS hospital? The short answer is: a significant minority of patients inevitably suffer and, at worst, avoidable deaths occur. In addition – and this is not always mentioned – workers suffer acute levels of stress; real wages are reduced; terms and conditions of employment are eroded; and jobs are lost.

***

In 2003, I wrote a detailed letter reporting dangerous nurse staffing levels at Tameside Hospital and requested an investigation – a request that was ignored by the regulatory authority. This was in spite of the fact that the hospital's mortality statistics were amongst the worst in the country. In May 2005, I contacted the *Manchester Evening News* with my concerns – reluctantly becoming a whistle-blower – as a result of which I was disciplined. From 2007, I continued to spell out my concerns to successive chairmen of the hospital's Board of Directors, the Chief Executive Officer (CEO) and the regulators.

In October 2010, I sent Andrew Lansley, the Secretary of State for Health, a document entitled 'A Factual Report on the Systemic Failure of Integrated Governance and Leadership of Tameside Hospital Foundation Trust Board'. It was passed to the regulatory bodies – Monitor and the Care Quality Commission. It was comprehensive and in my view had enough evidence to call for an immediate investigation. Alas, no investigation was forthcoming.

In February 2013, however, the Prime Minister, David Cameron, demanded a review of the quality of care being provided by 14 NHS trusts that were persistently showing high mortality rates. Tameside Hospital Foundation Trust was one of them. The Rapid Responsive Review Report, that followed, highlighted some areas of good practice but, overwhelmingly, its detailed findings were a damning indictment of the leadership, governance and quality of care at the hospital.

***

In Part 2 of this book, I praise the employees – in particular the nurses – who work or worked at Tameside Hospital, the great majority of whom were, and are, hardworking, highly professional and caring. I am, however, critical of some of those who held high managerial posts and colluded with the directors to conceal the hospital's failings.

Presently, there are no laws to regulate nurse and midwife to patient ratios in England. In my experience, this permits hospitals to have shifts with staffing levels as low as one qualified nurse for twenty-four patients or worse. Legislation which guarantees minimum staffing levels exists in other developed nations, such as Australia and Canada, and I believe that patient care would benefit enormously by its introduction in this country.

***

Writing Chapter 8 – Tameside Hospital – has allowed me to reflect upon the prolonged and historic under-funding to which it seems to have been subjected. Arguably, in 1948, when the local Workhouse merged with the District Infirmary, to create an NHS hospital, the funding allocated to the Ashton-under-Lyne General Hospital, as it was then called, was probably not sufficient and the initial lack of resources, over time, became serious underfunding by the 1970s. Although the principles, upon which the NHS had been created, had largely been achieved, pay for nurses and support staff had been kept low, the buildings were inadequately maintained and long waiting times for non-urgent hospital treatment existed. Even so, the NHS was still an undoubted success, as health statistics demonstrated, and at a cost – per head of population – less than half that of the USA.

However, instead of simply addressing the long waiting lists, maintenance issues and the like, the in-coming Conservative government, elected in 1979, began to impose its ideological dogma on the NHS, as elsewhere in the public sector. Prime Minister Margaret Thatcher believed that all public bodies were inherently wasteful. In 1983, she commissioned a report from a supermarket manager, Sir Roy Griffiths, and thereafter chief executives and managers supplanted senior doctors in the management of hospitals. The number of senior managers rose from 1,000 in 1986 to 26,000 in 1995. The introduction of the *internal market* in 1991 split the NHS into purchasers and providers, establishing hospital trusts as *financially independent providers* that were required to enter a competitive market with other trusts and the private sector. The internal market never attained the efficiencies it was supposed to achieve. The costs of new buildings constructed under *Private Finance Initiative* deals added to the financial problems of trusts, resulting in the reduction of up to 30 per cent of beds and 25 per cent of the salaries' budget, mainly affecting nursing staff.

***

As with other trusts, for several years at Tameside Hospital, the drive to acquire the subsequently introduced *foundation trust* status became the absolute imperative, the panacea towards which all decisions were subordinated. Failures were covered up, critics silenced and supporters rewarded. The propaganda department grew and publicity techniques were refined. Finally, with the seal of approval of the regulators, foundation status was gained – together with the accompanying responsibilities. The Trust was now on its own. It needed to balance the books, and 'cost improvement programmes' had to be implemented – which were invariably accompanied by only very perfunctory quality impact assessments. The internal market demanded an unprecedented increase in the number of employees at every administrative level: business managers, purchasers and procurers as well as accountancy firms, trouble shooters, turn-around directors, management-consultants and advisers, and the expenses increased exponentially.

***

Parts 2 and 3 of this book denounce the ineffectuality of successive health regulators over the years. It demonstrates the contradictory role of Monitor – the regulatory body responsible for foundation trusts – which effectively penalises trusts that put patients before finances. It is highly critical of the previous board of Tameside Hospital as a corporate body and exposes how a chief executive officer and a small inner circle of directors and key consultants controlled the organization. It shows the feebleness of successive chairmen and non-executive directors who rarely challenged executive decisions in board meetings. It reveals the lengths to which some hospital consultants will go to please their employer, even in circumstances where it is clearly failing to deliver safe care. And it tells of how previous directors of human resources ran their department and instead of doing everything possible to attract doctors and nurses – as the word resources implies – acted mainly as disciplinarian enforcers of the trust's policies, many of them out-dated.

In Part 3, I include a selection of letters and the reports I wrote in 2003 and 2010. They may be of interest to those researching the ever evolving Health Service in England. I apologise for the fact that they are repetitive but that, unfortunately, is unavoidable.

I have omitted the names of the majority of hospital employees except for the CEO, directors, some consultants, senior managers and chairmen.

ACKNOWLEDGEMENTS

I wish to express my gratitude to those who, in many different ways, helped to give this work what merit it has:

To Derek Pattison, for his helpful suggestions during the early stages of the project.

To Steph and Pablo who encouraged me not to give up.

To Julie who patiently proof-read the drafts, and offered constructive advice throughout my book-writing effort.

Special thanks to Nick O'Mullane, retired consultant physician and trusted colleague who, from time to time, reminded me that the book had to be published, not least because the aspects relating to the Trust and the NHS are of public interest.

I am deeply grateful to Rod McCord, campaigner and friend, who has read the book very closely and critically.

Thanks also to Ruth Lunn, from UK Book Publishing, for her help and advice and to Jason Thompson from UK Book Publishing for designing the book.

Part 1

Chapter One

CHILE

'Oh Chile, a long petal of sea and wine and snow'
– Pablo Neruda

Chile is a country shaped like a ribbon 2,672 miles long, and 112 miles in average width. It lies in the south-west quarter of South America, and extends from latitude 17 degrees north to Cape Horn at 54 degrees south, between the Pacific Ocean and the Andes mountains. Not surprisingly, giving its extreme north-south orientation, it has a varied and unique geography and climate.

The 600 miles long Atacama Desert, in the north, is rich in minerals such as silver, copper and lithium. Towards the north-east frontier with Bolivia and Argentina, the desert rises gradually into the Atacama Plateau, reaching an altitude of 4000 m.

The Central Valley is formed by separate valleys such as Aconcagua, Elqui, Maipo, Colchagua, Maule, Casablanca and others; they have their own rivers and micro-climates which are ideal for vineyards and wine production. The Central Valley extends south to the mighty Bio-Bio river which I know well because its forms the southern boundary of the City of Concepción, where I lived for ten years.

Along the length of Chile, the Andes' numerous volcanoes and mountains form a constant backdrop. Chile has about 100 lakes distributed along all its regions. They are all spectacularly beautiful and often some of the snow-covered volcanoes reflect in the waters of the nearby lakes, e.g. the Parinacota volcano in the Chungara lake in the Atacama Plateau, and Osorno volcano mirrored in the Llanquigue waters in the so called Región de los Lagos (Lakes' District), in the south of the country.

Further south there are temperate rain forests, archipelagos with hundreds of islands and glacier fed fjords extending down into Cape Horn, where the Pacific and the Atlantic oceans meet.

The Humboldt Current, originating in the Antarctic Peninsula, moves north along the length of the Chilean coast and thus the water at the numerous Chilean beaches is always cold, as I experienced in Dichato and Pingueral resorts, in Central Chile, a lifetime ago.

A trench exists along two thirds of Chile's northern coast; it is 5 km deep on average, and therefore most of Chile lies at the edge of a profound sea precipice. This is due to the position of the two tectonic plates that a long time ago collided with each other and gave birth to the Andes. These plates continue to move and, from time to time, this causes earthquakes and tsunamis, as happened in July 2010, with devastating consequences.

On a positive note, about 54,000 square miles of Chilean territory (19%) are now protected by the government; they include many national parks, e.g. Torres del Paine in the Magellan's region; national reserves, e.g. Villarica in the Lakes' District; and national monuments, e.g. Cerro Ñielol in the southern city of Temuco. However, most of the protected land is near the Andes and much needs to be done to protect the coastal ranges.

A PLEA FOR THE TEMPERATE FOREST AND THE MAPUCHE

The native forests are so magnificent that the best loved Chilean poet Pablo Neruda once said, '*He who does not know the Chilean forests, does not know the planet*'. He was reflecting on the splendour and uniqueness of its trees such as *alerce, coigue, mañio* and the evergreens *laurel, peumu, luma, belloto, avellano, ulmo* to name but a few. There are more than fifty species of trees and thirty eight are listed as endangered, vulnerable or rare, *alerce and araucaria* (monkey-puzzle) being two of them. Ninety per cent of the temperate forest-dependent species, including the world's smallest deer (the Pudu), can be found only in Chile.

Deforestation by national and trans-national corporations with little regard for the ecology, increased dramatically after 1974, when the dictatorship began its free market reforms. All publicly-owned forests and processing facilities were sold at below-cost prices and the forest industry was privatized. According to the World Wildlife Fund (WWF), from 1985 to 1995 nearly two million hectares of native forest were destroyed for wood chip, with an annual expansion rate of seven to ten per cent, replacing it with radiate pine and eucalyptus, to make pulp for paper.Effluents from newly-created pulp mills polluted precious wetlands with disastrous results for water birds including black necked swans.

Neruda, who won the Nobel Prize for Literature in 1971, also felt deeply for the Mapuche, the generic name for the largest group of aboriginal people inhabiting central and southern Chile for 12,500 years. According to where they lived, they called themselves differently: those in the north *Picunche*, in the valleys *Nagche*, in the forests and coastal lands *Huiliche*, in the Andean elevations *Pehuenche*. Many still speak Mapudungum, a language and part of a culture which they are trying to preserve. The word *mapu* means land and *che* means man.

Proud and fierce warriors, for many years they kept the expansion of the Inca Empire at bay at the river Maule in central Chile. Afterwards, they fought the Conquistadores until a peace treaty was signed in 1641, when the Spanish Crown, having pushed them 150 miles southwards, recognised that the Mapuche were an independent nation. The treaty stipulated that their land extended south of the river Bio-Bio, to the Patagonia and beyond, into lands which are now Argentina. However, the pact was not always respected by the Spanish and battles continued for nearly 300 years.

Between 1860 and 1885, combined armies of Chile and Argentina, which had become independent republics, massacred more than 100,000 Mapuche. They were forced from their lands to live impoverished lives in *reducciones* (reservations) and their territory, five million hectares, appropriated by the state. Soon, a great part of this land was handed over to members of the ruling class and to foreigners. Ever since, the Mapuche have suffered appalling discrimination and many have migrated to cities all over Chile. In total, the territory of the 3,078 reservations, added up to around half a million hectares. Not surprisingly, during the dictatorship, Mapuche, living as communities in reservation land, were forced to divide it into private family plots or *parcelas*, to facilitate its acquisition by forestry companies and hydroelectric corporations; or, worse still, fraudulent claims by wealthy landowners.

For the last 25 years the Mapuche people have been actively campaigning nationally and internationally to regain some of their land. In 2007, a community of Pehuenche, the people living in the araucaria tree forest, were granted 8,900 hectares of land in southern Chile, a mere fraction of their original territory.

THE BLACK NECKED SWANS

These unmistakable swans inhabit the wetlands and other saltwater and freshwater habitats such as swamps, marshes, brackish lagoons, lakes and sheltered coastal areas of southern South America. They are strong fliers capable of long distance migration at speeds of up to fifty miles per hour. When flying, their call is a soft, melodious whistling note, which is different to the loud call of most other swan species. They have an immaculate white body plumage that contrasts sharply with a velvety black neck and head. Their striking eyes are surrounded by a thin white line that reaches the rear of the head. They are special in that both parents carry their young on their backs for the first three weeks of life. In all other species, only the mother carries the cygnets. They can be found in Chile, Argentina, Paraguay, Uruguay, and southern Brazil. Whilst I was researching, I learned that there is a colony of about two hundred, in a lagoon in the Falkland Islands, which migrates between there and the South American continent.

In 2004 and 2005 thousands of black-necked swans, in a nature sanctuary near Valdivia in southern Chile, died or migrated away. Witnesses' accounts tell of swans falling from the sky on houses, cars and everywhere. Autopsies attributed their deaths to high levels of iron and other metals, which had polluted the water of the river feeding the wetlands. Thankfully, the increased rainfalls caused by the *El Niño* weather events have created new wetlands, which these intelligent birds have colonised, and their numbers have recovered.

MY PARENTS

I will say a little about my late parents. Elsa Vásquez Lagos, my mum, was a primary school teacher. Mum was forever encouraging all of us, my two brothers and sister, to read, and I will never forget her smile, the day she presented us with a collection of twenty or so books called *'El Tesoro de la Juventud'* (The Treasures of Youth). Jorge Manuel Peña Muñoz, my dad, worked for the National Railway Company. Mother took a daily train to her Teacher's Training College, in Angol, a small city in southern Chile. Dad was then a ticket inspector and that is how they met and fell in love. Later, dad became a stationmaster and thus, steam locomotives were an integral part of my childhood.When dad was in his thirties, he became a timber merchant and manufacturer. I remember walking by his side in the Chilean forests where he would measure the girth of huge trees, which he would mark and buy, for processing at his timber yard. I have always loved trains, trees, forests and wood because of him.

Mother was apolitical. She adored teaching and her main interests were religion, reading and of course running our home.

My dad was a supporter of the centre-left Radical Party, which years earlier, in December 1938, had taken a visionary man, Pedro Aguirre Cerda, to the presidency under the slogan 'to *govern is to educate'*. The president had graduated first a teacher and later a lawyer, with further studies in Economics and Administration at the Sorbonne, in Paris. Within a short period he had ordered the building of 500 schools. He had created technical-industrial colleges to form the engineers that his plans to industrialize Chile had needed. He had founded CORFO (Corporation for the stimulation of Development and Production) and this had led to the birth of the manufacturing, steel and sugar industries. He had carried out the first agrarian reform and had legalised the Communist and Socialist Parties. He had named Dr Salvador Allende, then 31 years old, as his Health Minister (Secretary of State for Health).[Doctor Allende would recount, many years later, that it had been the defining experience of his political career, which had persuaded him that in Chile it

5

was possible to construct socialism within the existing political institutions.]

President Aguirre, like Dr Allende, thirty years later, had been an under-dog candidate to the presidency and never finished his term because, sadly, he died of tuberculosis in 1941; and like him he had been deeply humanitarian.

Looking back I can see why, Dad, who was educated at a technical-industrial college, was attracted to the Radical Party and why in turn, I was influenced by Dad's ideals and by his involvement in politics.

WHY I CHOSE MEDICINE AS A CAREER

I was about twelve years old when I decided to become a doctor. The greatest motivation was the illness of my younger brother Jorge, who is six years my junior. At the age of two, he contracted an infection of his left thigh bone, *osteomyelitis*. He suffered greatly, had many operations and spent months in hospital until he was ten, when finally he overcame it. I witnessed his pain and our mother's sorrow when we had, occasionally, no other option but to leave him alone in his hospital cot. Every time the infection re-appeared, his little thigh swelled with pus and he became unwell. When this happened, after some unavoidable delays, we would bring him to Concepción, for further operations. This went on for eight years and, in the very wards where I would later train to be a doctor, I promised him that I would one day become one, to cure children. My exposure to sick little ones in those wards, when I was only eight years old and throughout my early adolescence was, without doubt, one of the reasons that motivated me to pursue an orthopaedic career, caring for children as well as adults.

During my teens, I was encouraged to achieve the grades required to gain a place to study medicine, by my parents and by my uncle Jorge, my dad's brother, who was a doctor, a socialist and a good friend of Dr Allende.

I confess that I am an avid reader. Looking back, I think that two books about doctors that I read in my middle teens – *Bodies and Souls* written by the Frenchman Maxence Van der Meersch, and *The Citadel* written by the Englishman J. Cronin – were influential. I mention them here because in my view they are worthy of reading, particularly *The Citadel* which recounts the life and work of a doctor before the creation of the National Health Service.

ALMA MATER

I studied medicine at the University of Concepción, situated in the second largest city in Chile and 270 miles south of Santiago. You have possibly never heard of this university, literally on the other side of the world. Founded in 1919, it ranks amongst the ten best in South America and each year educates more than 23,000 students, including many from abroad. Its motto, 'For the free development of the soul', is fitting. The university's Concepción campus is known as the Ciudad Universitaria (University City), and it is within walking distance of the city centre, and reachable via a diagonal avenue named after President Pedro Aguirre Cerda. The vast campus is set against a backdrop of forested hills and it is unique in having *black necked swans* living in a small lagoon, colloquially known as 'laguna de los patos' (ducks' lagoon) because, as everywhere in the world, ducks and swans happily intermingle.

***

A bloody military *coup* took place in Chile on 11 September 1973, when the elected president Salvador Allende died whilst defending La Moneda, the presidential palace. Martial law was declared. The National Congress, political parties, trade unions, freedom of speech and habeas corpus were all abolished. A military junta initially took power and the blackest period in the history of my country began. Authorities at all universities and hospitals were dismissed, detained or killed [twenty professors were tortured and murdered] and replaced by military officers. Political books were burned by soldiers in the street. The worst atrocities were committed between 1973 and 1977 but unimaginable cruelty and barbarity continued until 1990.

Official reports indicate that at least 3,197 Chileans were murdered, of whom over one thousand remain *desaparecidos* (disappeared). Their names, age, occupation and description of the circumstances of their arrest, torture and assassination or disappearance can be found on the website *Memoria Viva (Living Memory)*. No fewer than 36,948 were tortured for political reasons during the seventeen years long dictatorship. Over 200,000 escaped into exile, among them me and my family.

Chapter Two

SALVADOR ALLENDE'S SACRIFICE

*'Each people is free to choose its own road to socialism, mine is a democratic and peaceful road.' – **Salvador Allende***

On September 4th 1970, Dr Salvador Allende – a founder of the Chilean Socialist Party – headed the presidential poll with 36.3 per cent of the vote against his main opponent, Jorge Alessandri, on 34.9 per cent. He had been the candidate of a coalition of parties called *la Unidad Popular* that included the Socialist, Communist, Social Democratic and Radical parties; and in addition the Action Popular Unity Movement (MAPU), a splinter group of the Christian Democratic party, whose candidate had come third in the poll.

UNITED STATES OF AMERICA WAR AGAINST CHILEAN DEMOCRACY

Henry Kissinger – then assistant for national security affairs to Richard Nixon, President of the United States of America (USA) – was incensed. Mistakenly, he had believed that Dr Allende had little chance of success and thus, he had failed to authorise sufficient funds to the Central Intelligence Agency (CIA), to influence the outcome. The dastardly interference, by the USA government and the CIA, in the previous three presidential elections, in which Salvador Allende had been a candidate, had succeeded in preventing his election, but not this time.

After hearing that Dr Allende headed the poll, Edward Korry, the USA ambassador in Chile, reported to Kissinger *'Not a nut or bolt shall reach Chile. Once Allende comes to power we shall do all within our power to condemn Chile to utmost deprivation and poverty.'* However, for Kissinger and Nixon, it was still possible to stop Dr Allende assuming the presidency on November 4th, by any means.

Nixon's intentions were summarised by William Broe, Chief of Western Hemisphere Division, in a CIA memo labelled 'The Genesis of Project FUBELT' dated September 17, 1970:

> 'The Director [of the CIA] told the group that President Nixon had decided that an Allende regime in Chile was not acceptable to the United States. The President asked the Agency to prevent Allende from coming to power or to unseat him. The President authorized ten million dollars for this purpose, if needed.'

For years, the CIA had been steadily placing and recruiting spies in key positions all over Chile, including the labour and university student movements, the university academia, the media, and the political parties. Its agents were in regular contact with officers of the Chilean armed forces and paramilitary police, and passed regular reports to their controllers.

Of all the armed forces, the navy was notoriously anti-Allende and two of its admirals, one of them José Merino, immediately, after Allende's triumph, threatened to resign, but were persuaded against it. Merino would become one of the main conspirators.

Desperate post-election measures by Edward Korry, acting on Nixon's instructions, to prevent Dr Allende's ratification by the Chilean Congress, failed when the Christian Democratic Party refused to vote against Allende, whereupon Nixon gave instructions to the CIA to proceed to a military *coup*. A cable by the Deputy Director of the Central Intelligence Agency to CIA station chief in Santiago, 16 October 1970, reads:

> 'It is firm and continuing policy that Allende be overthrown by a coup. It is imperative that these actions be implemented clandestinely and securely so that the USG [the U.S. government] and American hand be well hidden.'

CIA agents proceeded to make twenty-one contacts in two weeks, with Chilean military men, and assured them that the United States government would support a *coup*.

THE ASSASSINATION OF GENERAL SCHNEIDER

There was little time to act because the decision of the Congress, to ratify Dr Allende as president, was only weeks away. The primary obstacle to the *coup* was the Commander in Chief of the Army, General René Schneider, an officer loyal to the Chilean Constitution and a strong supporter of the Chilean military's tradition of non-involvement in politics.

A plan was approved by the CIA, which included kidnapping General Schneider as a first step. After two unsuccessful attempts by the plotters – and according to declassified documents – on October 15, 1970, a frustrated Kissinger told President Richard Nixon *'This looks hopeless. I turned it off. Nothing could be worse than an abortive coup.'*

However, a botched third attempt by Roberto Viaux, a rogue retired army general, took place. He was under CIA control but 'disobeyed orders'. It resulted in the killing, on October 22, 1970, of General Schneider. The guns used had been supplied by the CIA, and smuggled into Chile in diplomatic cases; they were later dumped in the sea. General Schneider's assassination shocked the nation and the armed forces, and was widely reported, but it did not lead to a *coup*.

The out-going president, Eduardo Frei, immediately appointed General Carlos Prats, also a constitutionalist, as successor of murdered General Schneider.

NATIONAL CONGRESS RATIFIES DR ALLENDE AS ELECTED PRESIDENT

On October 24, 1970, Salvador Allende was confirmed as president of Chile by the National Congress. At his fourth attempt, Dr Allende had become the first avowed Marxist in the world to be elected president of a nation, after a free election. He had won a plurality vote with the support of just over a third of the electorate; however there had been other Chilean presidents elected with even lower percentage of votes.

In Washington, after hearing the news, an angry Nixon ordered the CIA Director *'Now make the Chilean economy scream.'* At a meeting of the National Security Council, November 6, 1970 he stated:

> Our main concern in Chile is the prospect that he [Dr Allende] can consolidate himself and the picture projected to the world will be his success. If we let the potential leaders in South America think they can move like Chile and have it both ways, we will be in trouble. No impression should be permitted in Latin America that they can get away with this and that it's safe to go this way. I want to work on this and on the military relations—put in more money. On the economic side we want to give him cold turkey.

Soon after assuming the presidency, on November 4th, through the implementation of his mandate, Dr Allende set out to improve the conditions of the twenty per cent of people that lived in extreme poverty. As a trained physician and previous Health Minister, under President Pedro Aguirre Cerda, he knew that measures such as free milk for nursing mothers and school children; improved health care facilities; housing and sanitation; and raising the minimum wage, were much needed and quickly implemented them. Other measures included social security rights for all workers; anti-illiteracy campaigns; land redistribution and rent reductions.

Like his friend, the poet Pablo Neruda, Dr Allende felt deeply for the marginalized Mapuche people, estimated to be around one million, and quickly granted three thousand scholarships, to be distributed among them.

In order to finance such programmes, President Allende gained unanimous congressional approval to accelerate the nationalization of key industries. Two of the three largest copper mines in Chile had been owned for 42 years by Anaconda, an American Company which, after an initial investment of $30 million, had taken out of the country more than $4,000 million in profits. The other mine, owned by Kennecott Copper Corporation, also American, likewise had taken huge amounts of profits.

These companies and the International Telephone and Telegraph company

(ITT), which owned seventy per cent of CHITELCO (Chile's Telephone Co), and many others, played a major role in the destabilisation of the democratically elected government.

In fact ITT involvement had begun in the summer of 1970, when a member of the ITT board of directors, John McCone, contacted the CIA in Washington to offer $1 million in ITT corporate funds for the anti-Allende effort, during the election campaign. ITT-CIA involvement in the campaign was exposed and reported world-wide in 1972 and I can still remember the feelings of anger and frustration that I and my comrades had felt at that time.

THE USA ECONOMIC BLOCKADE AND CIA LED DESTABILISATION OF CHILE

What chances of success did Dr Allende's economic policies have, when faced with the might of US Government and powerful American corporations?

Under pressure from the USA government, international agencies and banks began an economic boycott of Chile. The World Bank, Inter-American Development Bank (IDB), First National City Bank, Chase Manhattan, Agency for International Development (AID), Bank of America and the Export-Import Bank either cut programmes in Chile or cancelled credits. The government continued to pay off old loans from the IDB and the World Bank, but neither made new loans to Chile.

Ambassador Korry's words to Kissinger soon turned to actions, and in order to create unrest and further destabilise Allende's government, the USA imposed a total blockade of goods including medical drugs, spare parts for vehicles and machinery and other such necessities of everyday life.

(In my hospital we ran out of Penicillin and other drugs hitherto exported from the USA and this became a serious problem).

In addition to its role in plotting with the military, and extreme right wing groups such as *Patria y Libertad* (Fatherland and Freedom), which were conducting a terrorist campaign, the CIA extensive web in Chile carried out misinformation campaigns through the media; funded opposition groups;

incited workers strikes and manipulated the parliamentary process.

With CIA funds, the owners of Chile's haulage companies organised a complete stoppage of work in October 1972, and Chile's transport became paralysed, and they repeated this ploy again during late July and August 1973, fatally crippling the country – all part of the conspiracy to justify the *coup.*

Between 1971 and 1973 the CIA regularly ran fake scare stories in 70% of the press and on 90% of radio. [23 CIA journalist-agents from fifteen different countries were operating in Chile, on a campaign of disinformation that included direct mailing of their 'foreign' news articles to selected Chilean military leaders and former president Eduardo Frei.]

The CIA was also very effective in masterminding street protests against the government, by women of the upper classes, rallies that were be well publicised in Chile and abroad. The CIA had done this on previous occasions in Chile and other South-American countries.

The country became divided between President Allende's supporters and his enemies. Dr Allende's foes included most of the media and in particular the newspaper *El Mercurio*, key military men, industrialists, powerful land owners and professional associations. Other declared enemies were the right wing National Party and some of the leaders of the Christian Democratic Party. Combined, these two political organisations had a majority in the Chamber of Deputies and the Chamber of Senators, the two elected parliamentary assemblies, and they played an important role in giving the eventual *coup* a gloss of justification.

Although during the first year and a half of Dr Allende's mandate the economy flourished, and there was an air of optimism, soon after, the colossal forces against him began to take its toll. Thus, a year later the country was exactly the way the US Government-CIA and internal anti-Allende foes had plotted it to be: affected by marked inflation; food and fuel shortages; a roaring black market; CIA organised strikes in the copper mines, steel industry, and haulage and railway companies. Yet, in spite of these and many other opposition-orchestrated obstacles, from abroad and from inside the country, President Allende's popularity increased to 43 per cent, as shown by the results of the congressional elections, held in March 1973.

After two and a half years, the USA government master plan had succeeded in causing profound destabilisation. The CIA led strike of the managers in the copper mines (three per cent of the work force) had paralysed the industry. These employees were violently demonstrating against Allende and causing chaos in the centre of Santiago. In response, on 21 June 1973, a massive rally in favour of the government took place. It was also in answer to anti-government disruptions, in the capital, by neo-Nazi groups, carrying swastika banners, supported by CIA funds.

Left wing revolutionary parties including a section of the Socialist Party believed that a USA-backed military takeover was imminent, and urged the workers and supporters to be ready to defend the government. For months, the workers have been organising 'industrial belts' to be mobilised when the inevitable *coup* came. These were critical times, when demonstrations and rallies to show support for the government were occurring in every major city, against a backdrop of frequent right wing extremist's terrorist actions and daily front page attacks in the CIA controlled papers as well as on television and radio.

Dr Allende tried to broaden his political support by asking respected non-Marxist politicians, including from the Christian Democratic Party, to come into his cabinet, but they all declined. By this time, the leaders of this party, which initially had supported Dr Allende's ratification as president, were giving signals to the conspirators that they were in favour of a military *coup*.

THE TANKS' REGIMENT COUP ATTEMPT

On June 29, 1973, there was a further *putsch* attempt, led by army officers of the Second Armoured Regiment in Santiago. Around 9 a.m. six Sherman tanks and army trucks with 100 soldiers converged upon La Moneda, the presidential palace, and began firing. Pedestrians ran for their lives. The guard of carabineros protecting the presidential palace bravely repealed the attack and soon troops loyal to the government arrived. Fifteen innocent civilians lost their lives in the uprising. Among them was Argentinian camera-man Leonardo Henrichsen, who was callously killed by an army officer whilst filming the mutiny. In fact, he managed to film his executioner just before he was shot nearly point blank. Seven soldiers died and many more were wounded.

Surrender was negotiated by three loyal generals: Pickering, Sepúlveda and Prats and the Minister of Defence, José Tohá. In the background, amongst the officers in the loyal forces, there was an upstart general called Augusto Pinochet. Within minutes of the *coup* the streets of the centre of Santiago filled with thousands of government supporters wanting to show their support, but they were asked to disperse. A massive organised rally in support of the government took place a few days later.

The aborted *coup* was a further symptom of the growing desperation and boldness of conspirators in the armed forces, in collusion with right wing groups and the CIA, aiming to oust the President by force.

The President knew that some of the commanders in the higher echelons of the Armed Forces were loyal, and to shore up his government he appointed army General Carlos Prats as Minister of Defence; air force General César Ruiz as Minister of Public Works and Transport; and Admiral Raúl Montero as Treasury Minister, in July 1973. He was using all the experience he had gained, during 40 years in politics, to allow his government to survive. On the shadows, the CIA, with its budget of $10 million to spend, continued to provide funds and co-ordinated covert assistance for a further *coup d'état* attempt.

A declassified document sent from the CIA chief station in Santiago to the US Department of State, dated July 25, 1973, is astonishingly revealing:

'In the aftermath of the abortive military uprising of 29 June a Council of five [Chilean] flag-rank officers [general and admirals] met to discuss the preparation of a counter-insurgency plan for the Armed Forces. This plan is near completion and lacks only the identification of priority targets and a listing of measures requiring inter-service coordination. Under this plan each of the three branches of the Armed Forces will have its own organization and responsibilities. Nevertheless, there will be inter-service groups set up to coordinate those activities requiring joint efforts.

The plotting officers within the Armed Forces are hoping that the truck owners' strike scheduled for 26 July will be postponed until the council has an opportunity to complete its counter-insurgency plan which could be used as the basis for a coup d'état.

Although the Air Force is not considering any action in conjunction with the truckers, they plan to remain on alert for a crisis that might develop as a result of the strike. In the meantime, Navy and Air Force plotters continue to work closely together on their preparations for a coup d'état and neither is planning a unilateral action.'

THE ASSASSINATION OF COMMANDER ARTURO ARAYA

On 27 July, 1973 Commander Arturo Araya Peeters, the Navy's aide-de-camp to President Allende, was callously assassinated, as part of a wider plot involving a bomb detonation and the commencement of yet another stoppage by the lorry owners. Three members of the right wing terrorist organisation *Patria y Libertad* created a commotion outside his home, with the aim of bringing the commander to his balcony and then, from distance, a marksman shot him fatally in the chest. A few days earlier, Commander Araya had told his family that he had been warned by officers in the Navy that he was a target, and that he might be killed. [Years later Mexican-American CIA agent David Sánchez Morales, a notorious assassin, confessed to have been the perpetrator of the crime.] There can be little doubt that the order to assassinate Commander Araya had come from conspirators within the Navy, who were worried that he would reveal their plans.

On Monday, August 20, 1973, General César Ruiz, who had been unable to resolve the haulage strike, resigned his Ministerial and Commander in Chief posts and was replaced by General Gustavo Leigh, who was a plotter.

General Prats' position soon also became untenable, and he was forced to resign, two days later, when the Council of Generals out-voted him twelve to six.

In the Navy, officers led by Admiral José Merino had been plotting since May and had been in regular contact with the US Navy attaché and the Intelligence Service of the US Navy. In August, he and these officers tried to force the resignation of Admiral Montero, with the excuse that the death of Commander Araya was part of a plot they had 'uncovered', among non-commissioned officers, supposedly to subvert the Navy. Admiral Montero resisted, but his authority had been crucially weakened.

All these events reflected the growing power of the conspirators, encouraged by the knowledge that the USA was on their side, backing their eventual take over by force.

With the successful neutralisation of loyal Admiral Montero, it was treacherous Admiral Merino who, from then on, led the planning for the *coup* and liaised with the schemers in the other branches of the Armed Forces, *Carabineros,* CIA agents and US Navy Intelligence. He brought in the element of coordination, which was lacking on all previous attempts.

Following the resignation of General Carlos Prats, President Allende appointed General Pinochet as Commander-in-Chief of the Army on August 23, 1973, believing that he would be loyal to the constitution.

PINOCHET'S BETRAYAL

General Pinochet was not involved initially in the conspiracy, and he was not informed of it until 7th September 1973, when after thinking about it for one day, at a secret meeting at its own home, decided to turn against Dr Allende, and put his signature to a letter that Merino and Leigh had already signed.

Pinochet was astute and until then he had kept his cards close to his chest. He had succeeded in presenting himself as a constitutionalist and had gained Allende's trust. When the President confided to Pinochet that he was going to speak to the nation on Monday 10th and call for a referendum, the duplicitous traitor effusively congratulated him, and asked Dr Allende to postpone it until Wednesday 12th. He knew that the coup was planned for Tuesday 11th, and that the last card of the President would never be played. Furthermore, on 10th September he attended a pre-arranged routine meeting at the Ministry of Defence, with Minister Orlando Letelier, and – continuing with his deceit – reaffirmed his loyalty to the President.

The night before the coup, officers of the conspirators worked franticly to coordinate the armies at their disposal, contacting the commanders they knew were on their side. Ironically, they did it from the Ministry of Defence, the building which had been their headquarters for weeks, situated in front of La Moneda.

THE DAY OF THE COUP

On 11 September 1973, a *coup d'état* backed by the USA government and facilitated by the CIA and the USA embassy in Santiago, took place in Chile.

By day break, the port city of Valparaiso was taken by the Navy. No resistance was encountered. USA warships were anchored off the coast, with marines ready to disembark and give military support to the plotters, but in the event this was not needed. As I said earlier, workers and government supporters in the *poblaciones* (poor communities) and the countryside, along the length of Chile, had never received arms to fight the might of the Armed Forces.

Admiral Raul Montero, an Allende loyalist, was rendered incommunicado; his telephone service was cut and his cars were sabotaged before the coup d'état, to ensure he could not thwart the conspirators.

César Mendoza, a general of the *Carabineros*, the national paramilitary police force, had agreed to join the traitors – Leigh, Merino and Pinochet. Thus a four man military junta, in control of the Army, Air Force, Navy and *Carabineros* took over power. The plotters had at their command 87,000 men. Many of their officers had been waiting for this moment, having been indoctrinated and trained in counter-insurgency techniques, by personnel of the USA Army School of Americas, in the Panama Canal Zone. (1,100 officers had attended this school, in the seven years before Allende was deposed.)

By 8 a.m. the centre and industrial quarters of the capital Santiago, Concepción and other main cities, were occupied by platoons from regiments of the army and carabineros, supported by tanks, Mowat armoured vehicles and Puma helicopters.

Although he had been made aware that the Navy had mutinied and his government was in great danger, Dr Allende, immediately, decided to go to the presidential palace where at about 7.20 a.m. he was joined by the General in Chief of *Carabineros*, José María Sepúlveda, and the Head of *Investigaciones* (Plain Clothes Police) Alfredo Joignant, both of whom remained loyal. He was also supported by ministers José Tohá, Anibal Palma and Arturo Jirón; Miria Contreras, his secretary; many friends and advisors (among them four doctors); and Patricio Guijón and José Quiroga, two of his personal physicians. His body guards included seventeen members of a group of operatives known as GAP (*Grupo de Amigos Personales del Presidente*) and a few members of *Investigaciones*. He tried to contact General Pinochet, still believing in his loyalty, but the traitor never answered.

Soon afterwards, Dr Allende addressed the people of Chile over the radio: *'Confirmed reports indicate that a sector of the Navy has rebelled and is occupying Valparaíso. Santiago is normal and [the soldiers are] in their barracks. I'm here defending the government that I represent by the will of the people. Be alert and vigilant. I wait for the soldiers of Chile to respond positively and defend the laws and the Constitution. Workers must go to their workplace and wait for new instructions.'*

At 8.32 a.m. he heard the edict of the traitors, demanding his abdication and realised that he did not have the support of the army or *carabineros*. Soon after the Junta's broadcast, the armoured vehicles belonging to *carabineros* at La Moneda abandoned their positions and left. In his office, Allende listened to an offer from the junta, relayed to him by his military aides, that a plane was ready to take him and his family out of the country. But Allende's refusal was categorical: *'The Armed Forces have broken with their tradition. I will not surrender, nor resign.'* He gathered his friends and gave them the options of either staying or leaving. Without exception they all chose to stay. Shortly before 9 a.m. his daughters Isabel, and Beatriz who was pregnant at the time, arrived to support their father.

At 9.10 a.m., amidst the chaos, the President sat by his desk facing a large window, in plain sight of the guns of insurgent soldiers positioned on a roof opposite. Then, serenely, without notes and from his heart, he delivered a moving farewell speech, on the last standing free radio, Radio Magallanes:

My friends,

Surely this will be the last opportunity for me to address you. The Air Force has bombed the towers of Radio Portales and Radio Corporación.

My words do not have bitterness but disappointment. May they be a moral punishment for those who have betrayed their oath: soldiers of Chile, titular commanders in chief, Admiral Merino, who has designated himself Commander of the Navy, and Mr. Mendoza, the despicable general who only yesterday pledged his fidelity and loyalty to the Government, and who also has appointed himself Chief of the Carabineros.

Given these facts, the only thing left for me is to say to workers: I am not going to resign!

Placed in a historic transition, I will pay for loyalty to the people with my life. And I say to them that I am certain that the seed which we have planted in the good conscience of thousands and thousands of Chileans will not be shrivelled forever.

They have strength and will be able to dominate us, but social processes can be arrested neither by crime nor force. History is ours, and people make history.

Workers of my country: I want to thank you for the loyalty that you always had, the confidence that you deposited in a man who was only an interpreter of great yearnings for justice, who gave his word that he would respect the Constitution and the law and did just that. At this definitive moment, the last moment when I can address you, I wish you to take advantage of the lesson: foreign capital, imperialism, together with the reaction, created the climate in which the Armed Forces broke their tradition, the tradition taught by General Schneider and reaffirmed by Commander Araya, victims of the same social sector which will today be in their homes hoping, with foreign assistance, to retake power to continue defending their profits and their privileges.

I address, above all, the modest woman of our land, the 'campesina' who believed in us, the worker who laboured more, and the mother who knew our concern for children. I address professionals of Chile, patriotic professionals; those who days ago continued working against the sedition sponsored by professional associations, class-based associations that also defended the advantages which a capitalist society grants to a few.

I address the youth, those who sang and gave us their joy and their spirit of struggle. I address the man of Chile, the worker, the farmer, the intellectual, those who will be persecuted, because in our country fascism has been already present for many hours – in terrorist attacks, blowing up the bridges, cutting the railroad tracks, destroying the oil and gas pipelines, in the face of the silence of those who had the obligation to protect them. They were committed. History will judge them.

Surely Radio Magallanes will be silenced, and the calm metal instrument of my voice will no longer reach you. It does not matter. You will continue hearing it. I will always be next to you. At least my memory will be that of a man of dignity who was loyal to [inaudible] the workers.

The people must defend themselves, but they must not sacrifice themselves. The people must not let themselves be destroyed or riddled with bullets, but they cannot be humiliated either.

Workers of my country, I have faith in Chile and its destiny. Other men will overcome this dark and bitter moment when treason seeks to prevail. Go forward knowing that, sooner rather than later, the great avenues will open again where free men will walk to build a better society.

Long live Chile! Long live the people! Long live the workers!

These are my last words, and I am certain that my sacrifice will not be in vain, I am certain that, at the very least, it will be a moral lesson that will punish felony, cowardice, and treason.

THE HEROIC DEFENCE OF LA MONEDA

Shortly after the president finished his speech, the defenders of La Moneda saw the first tanks making their approach and take up positions around the Plaza de la Constitución aiming their guns on the presidential palace. Inside, the President was told that attack was imminent; immediately he left to organize the resistance inside the building. At that moment, the first shots were heard.

What followed was an unequal battle. The number of soldiers surrounding La

Moneda was about 4,000. Army and Air Force helicopters were shooting at the pro-government snipers in the nearby buildings. Inside the palace there were little more than a hundred people, the majority of them civil servants and among them a few women. The twenty or so trained defenders were members of the GAP, the President armed guard, and their heaviest armament consisted of three bazookas and five 30 calibre machine guns.

The heavy guns of the tanks and soldiers began firing at the palace, destroying walls, windows and causing heavy damage to the front of the building. Allende ordered his men to retreat to the interior of the palace.

At around 10:40 there was a ceasefire, and the *carabineros* remaining inside La Moneda left. The president had persuaded his daughters that they should leave, and negotiated safe exit for them. His daughter Isabel recounts these final moments with their father, and how she and Beatriz, came to the decision that it was better to go, and how, without a word, they had embraced him for a final time.

At 11.52 a.m. two Chilean Air Force Hawker-Hunters began the bombardment of the presidential palace – that still had the Chilean flag at the top of its main mast – firing twenty four rockets, all of which hit its target. It was a twenty minutes attack that turned La Moneda into an inferno. Soon the palace was on fire and large parts of its roof and walls collapsed; the air was thick with smoke and dust; the noise was frightening and there was flooding on the first floor. Yet, miraculously, the president, his advisers and friends, so far, had survived the onslaught.

Army helicopters had dropped tear gas bombs and the air had become truly polluted and unbreathable. There were not enough gas masks, so Dr Allende advised his friends to lie-down to inhale cleaner air. The situation for the defenders was desperate.

After the aerial bombardment, the ground troops renewed their attack. The relentless firing was deafening, as explosions pulverized the remains of the building and fed the flames. And thus, the one-sided battle continued for a further hour and the attacking forces, using the heavy guns on the tanks that surrounded La Moneda, continued their assault. The President and his bodyguards repelled the land assault with rifles and bazookas.

At 1.15 p.m., faced with inevitable defeat, and two of his personal guards – Osvaldo Ramos, 22, and Antonio Aguirre, 29, seriously wounded – Dr Allende ordered his friends and GAP guards to surrender, adding that that they should not sacrifice themselves and he would be the last one to leave. They were amongst thirty-eight men and women, including his secretary, who bravely stayed with the President until the end.

At about 2 p.m., the president's advisors, fifteen members of GAP, and three loyal men from *investigaciones* (plain clothes police) emerged from the palace with a white flag. Immediately they were ruthlessly gun-butted and pushed to the ground in front of a tank. Until that point, eight die- hard sharpshooters in neighbouring buildings, defending the President and La Moneda, were still firing at the soldiers. They stopped only when a tank commander shouted at them threatening that the tank would roll over their comrades unless they stopped shooting at the troops.

Based on the account given by Dr Guijón, one of his personal physicians, the President committed suicide at about 1.45 p.m. Two hours before his death, one of his closest friends, the journalist Jorge Olivares, had committed suicide in the besieged palace. According to witnesses, Dr Allende was deeply affected by his comrade's death. Dr Guijón remained with the dead President until army officers arrived. One soldier covered the body with a blanket and two hours afterwards the military took his remains to the army's Military Hospital. The following day he was buried at the Santa Inés Cemetery in Viña del Mar with only his wife Hortensia and a handful of mourners in attendance. [In September 1990, when democracy returned to Chile, Dr Allende would be given a State Burial.]

At 6 p.m., the group lying face down on the pavement were taken to the Tacna Regiment and with the exception of the three plain clothes policemen, the rest – nine advisors and fifteen personal guards – were all killed within 48 hours. Antonio Aguirre and Osvaldo Ramos, the two wounded members of the GAP were taken to the emergency room of the *Posta Central,* where they received surgical treatment for their serious bullet wounds. However, within days and whilst still recovering, they were removed from the hospital by military patrols and never seen again.

A SPARK OF RESISTANCE

The day of the coup, at about 9 a.m., a group of about 85 workers and some fifty armed operatives, most from the socialist party, but also a few from the Movement of the Revolutionary Left (MIR) and the Communist party converged at INDUMET, a factory in the industrial area of Santiago. Their leader was Arnoldo Camú, who had been in charge of a group of socialist militants trained to fight. Before they had time to plan a response, the factory was surrounded by about one hundred carabineros supported by Mowat armoured vehicles and a gun battle took place with casualties on both sides. Reinforcements for the carabineros arrived and the armoured vehicles burst through the gates of the factory. The government supporters were forced out, but managed to retreat towards the factory SUMAR only to be intercepted by further battalions of *carabineros* at *poblacion La Ligua*, where further gun fights took place, again with casualties on both sides. Camú's plan to advance towards La Moneda to rescue the president never had a chance. Eventually, by 5 p.m., the skirmishes were over and he and 15 remaining fighters left the area. Camú, a lawyer by profession, was captured in Santiago on September 23, tortured and killed soon after.

REIGN OF TERROR

After the *coup* and during the days and weeks that followed, throughout the country, thousands were rounded up and held in *comisarías* (Police Stations), military bases, Regiments, prisons, confiscated private dwellings and Soccer stadia. Hundreds were killed without mercy including many foreigners, among them Europeans, South Americans and three USA citizens: two of them being Frank Teruggi and Charles Horman, who had been investigating and writing about political activities by United States military intelligence agents in Chile.

These killings occurred within hours of the arrests, often by a bullet in the head and the bodies simply dumped in the street, public places, morgues or rivers. Many times the victims were murdered in groups, such as the massacre at *Cerro Chena,* of eleven workers of the San Bernardo Railway Machine factory, three students, three farm workers and one security officer (a total of eighteen) on 6 October 1973, all killed by soldiers of the Infantry Regiment of San Bernardo. They were asked to run up the *cerro* (hill) and cruelly shot in the back. Prior to their deaths they were brutally tortured. This level of inhumane behaviour from the soldiers is incomprehensible. These were no executions in the sense that they had not followed a judicial process and a sentence. They were simply barbaric and cold blooded murders of innocent people. This frenzy of assassinations took place in every city, town, and village and in the countryside.

Over the weeks that followed the balance of power among the generals shifted to General Pinochet, who commanded the largest force: the Army.

In order to instil terror amongst the people and, importantly, its own officers and soldiers in regional regiments, Pinochet created a ten-man army unit which came to be known as the *Caravan of Death,* under the control of General Sergio Arellano. The squad, travelled from garrison to garrison, the length of Chile, in a Puma helicopter, and its members personally murdered 97 detainees between 30 September and 22 October 1973. The victims endured unspeakable torture, including gauging of their eyes and mutilation, before they were shot to death and piled into mass graves. The murderous squad landed in many cities such as Valdivia and Temuco in the south; Linares, Cauquénes and Talca in central Chile; and La Serena, Copiapó, Antofagasta and Calama in the north, fulfilling Pinochet's deadly mission.

In November 1973 Pinochet created the DINA *(Dirección de Inteligencia Nacional)* composed of hundreds of especially cruel and vicious members of the Army, Navy, Air force, *Carabineros* (Paramilitary Police) and *Investigaciones* (Plain-clothes Police) under the command of murderous army colonel Manuel Contreras, who became the most powerful and feared man after Pinochet. DINA's task was to hunt down, capture, torture and kill women and men associated with the Socialist and Communist parties, MIR, MAPU (Movement of Action Popular Unitary), Radical Party or any other left wing revolutionary group. The DINA ran dozens of torture and assassination centres; two of the most notorious of which were Villa *Grimaldi* and one in *Simon Bolivar* Street, in Santiago. It has now been revealed that, except for one, all the hundreds of political prisoners tortured at the Simon Bolivar centre were executed. Their mutilated bodies were bundled in potato sacks and made heavier by wiring a segment of steel railway line to the packaged victim, hitherto described by the killers as *paquetes* (parcels) to be taken by army helicopter to the open sea for disposal or ditched at a disused mine shaft at *Cuesta Barriga (Barriga's Hill)*, north east of Santiago.

The DINA was dissolved in 1977 as a result of pressure on Pinochet by the USA government. A yearlong investigation by the Federal Bureau of Investigation, following the death of Dr Allende's Defence Minister, Osvaldo Letelier and his American secretary, Ronni Moffit, in Washington, had revealed that General Contreras, the head of DINA, was involved, and requested his extradition. Pinochet replaced DINA with a new body, the Centro *Nacional de Inteligencia* (CNI), which was equally brutal. However, the systematic resorting to disappearances slowed down, but other human rights violations, including assassinations and torture continued, particularly from 1983 onwards when a resistance movement arose from within the oppressed people of Chile. It began with students' national protests and barricades in the poorer districts of Santiago and other cities. The birth of the Frente Revolucionario Manuel Rodriguez (FRMR), and the women's non-violent movements from 1985 until 1990, were a constant thorn in the dictatorship's side and kept the hopes of eventual freedom alive and were instrumental in the eventual fall of Pinochet.

During the aftermath of the coup and the years that followed, the intelligence services of the Navy, Army, Air Force and Paramilitary Police actively participated in the capture, torture, interrogation and killing of political prisoners. In less than four months, between September 11 and December 31, 1973, at least 1200 Chileans were killed by agents of these intelligence services, the Caravan of Death and DINA.

Although initially opposed by General Leigh, by December 1974 Pinochet named himself President of Chile. Thus he assumed total control and became one of the more ruthless despots in South- America's history, ready to continue ordering the assassination of thousands including his fellow officer, General Carlos Prats, in 1974, in Buenos Aires.

***

The universities in Chile have always been a melting pot of activity and in particular the University of Concepción. I was in my third year of medical studies when Allende was elected. I was raised in a middle class family and I have always been drawn towards helping the poor and destitute. As a medical student, I became involved in voluntary work in the deprived areas of the city of Concepción and gradually developed a social conscience and tried to find an explanation for the extreme poverty I encountered. This precipitated my political development as a leftist, free thinking student. My hero was, and still is, Ernesto Guevara de la Cerna, known as *'Ché'*, an Argentinian doctor, revolutionary and internationalist, who sacrificed his life for the cause he believed in. As a young man he travelled throughout South America and this period of his life he describes in a diary, popularised in the film the *Motorcycle Diaries.* What he witnessed cemented his humanitarian concern for his fellow man. Like all human beings *Ché* had flaws. But he was true to himself and his beliefs to the end. On 9th October 1967, he was killed as he lay wounded on the floor of the school in the village of *la Higuera*, in Bolivia. The sergeant who executed the wounded *Ché* later went into hiding, turned to alcohol and lost his eyesight. In 2007, his sight was restored by a team of Cuban eye surgeons doing humanitarian work in Bolivia.

Initially I joined a left wing university student group, an offspring of a small revolutionary party known as MIR (*Movement of the Revolutionary Left*), founded in 1966 at my University. Around 1970 I became a MIR political activist; however, I never received guerrilla training. Others who did were known as 'operativos', and were the 'armed' wing of MIR. In fact, at the time of the *coup,* my knowledge of weapons was virtually none and still is. (Having read documents, I know now that the MIR had fewer than one hundred *operativos* in Santiago but they were not all armed.)

MIR was reaching out to the poorest, most deprived areas of society – miners, labourers, peasants, fishermen, the homeless and the dispossessed – and it was growing. For two and a half years I spent a great deal of my spare time working as an activist in the coal mining and fishing town of Coronel, near Concepción. It is estimated that at its peak MIR had around 3,000 members in the whole country. Among them there were secondary and university students.

Over the years, I participated in protest marches which on many occasions became violent confrontations with the paramilitary police. With other fellow students, I was arrested several times during these rallies and most probably a 'file' of my activities had built up.

In 1971, a sociology student, Jorge–'*El Trosko*'– Fuentes was elected president of the University Students' Union and I became the General Secretary, a public position that brought me further to the attention of Salvador Allende's enemies. I pay tribute to Jorge, who in May 1975 was detained in Paraguay by the secret police and tortured for four months by agents of *Operación Cóndor*. He was secretly brought back to Chile. His savage, inhuman mistreatment continued in *Cuatro Alamos* and later *Villa Grimaldi,* detention centres controlled by DINA, where he was last seen alive in January 1976. Like hundreds of members of MIR, Socialist, Communist, MAPU and other left wing parties, he suffered the most horrendous torture before he was assassinated.

Operación Cóndor was created by Pinochet in 1975, as a secret programme among South American dictators including Argentina, Paraguay, Uruguay, and Brazil, Bolivia and Chile, to coordinate their secret police, aiming to capture and eliminate political opponents. Its agents were instructed to operate anywhere in the world. One assassination method was the detonation of car bombs which they used in the killing of Minister Orlando Letelier in Washington, USA. Another method was shooting, as in the case of the attempted murder of Bernardo Leighton, a Christian Democrat and ex-minister, in Rome, when he and his wife were seriously wounded, but survived. As recent declassified CIA documents confirmed, these operations against high profile Chilean politicians, were carried out on the direct orders of Pinochet.

***

After graduating *Licenciado en Medicina,* from the University of Concepción, I received a further degree in April 1973 – that of a *Médico Cirujano,* from the University of Chile, the oldest in the country and located in Santiago, the capital. A few weeks later, I took up my first post in Cañete, a small town in southern Chile. The hospital had around fifty beds and with a slightly senior colleague, Dr Miranda, we provided twenty-four hour cover seven days a week in all four major specialities: Paediatrics, Obstetrics, General Medicine and Surgery.

My plan was that after four years I would have earned the right to apply for a place at a Regional Teaching Hospital to specialise in whatever I chose. There was tough competition for these places controlled by the 'Ministerio de Salud',

28

the Health Department of Chile.

As it turned out, the *coup d'état* changed everything. That fateful morning, upon turning on the radio I heard the frightening announcement that a military junta had taken power and ordered people to stay at home. The television channels and radio stations were taken over and martial music was continuously played, interrupted only by the junta's statements. A curfew was declared. I never heard the President's last radio speech because it was transmitted by Radio Magallanes only, in Santiago.

I knew that I would be arrested because of my well-known political views. Only two days before the *coup* I had been an impassioned speaker in support of Allende in the Plaza de Armas, the town square in Cañete. Furthermore, I had co-authored an incriminating letter which had been published in the left wing journal *Punto Final*, six weeks before the *coup*.

The Chilean Army is modelled on Teutonic military traditions; even the helmets worn by soldiers are a copy from the German model. Their efficiency, ruthlessness and capability made any attempt on my part to resist the *coup* futile. A comrade and I hid in the woods initially but soon decided that we would be safer in Concepción. Roads were unsafe and thus over three nights we walked the 75 miles of railway track between Cañete and Concepción. During the day we stayed concealed in the woods and luckily we avoided military patrols. We managed to enter the city undetected and went to my parents' home where we stayed for one day and afterwards went our separate ways. I have forgotten my friend name and I never saw him again. I hope he survived what was to come.

***

I went into hiding for about three weeks, in different houses of relatives and friends of my parents. Being caught in a surprise raid by agents of the army or *carabineros* meant arrest, torture and almost certain death. When these nightly, vicious and terrifying house searches were carried out, the military invariably denied all knowledge of them and hundreds of kidnapped persons were tortured, murdered and buried in secret mass graves. They became known as '*los desaparecidos*' – the disappeared. I kept moving on trying not to be detected by informants who were everywhere. I was isolated and without a safe house. My options were limited: continue to hide; try to escape the country; or surrender. Frankly, my situation was hopeless. I was afraid and I did not want to be caught in the street or in a raid and become a *desaparecido*. I was advised that my best chance of survival was to go to a police station in daylight with an army officer who was a trusted friend of an aunt, who would witness my surrender. And I did so. Looking back, the survival instinct prevailed and that decision probably saved my life.

Many comrades from left political parties, remained at large, bravely regrouping, trying desperately to avoid capture. Others left the country and secretly returned a few years later still believing in the *via armada* (armed struggle).From the MIR alone five hundred and eighty five in total were killed, most immediately after the coup but the deaths continued over the months and years that followed. Amongst all the victims of the Military Junta there were – loggers, peasants and small farmers (many of them Mapuche), – miners, labourers, trade-unionists, fishermen, public employees, teachers, electricians, plumbers, students, street vendors, lawyers, engineers, secretaries, journalists, university professors, and others from all manner of trades and professions. They will never be forgotten. They will live forever young in the minds of those who they left behind and of their *compañeros* (comrades).

After a night of sadistic beatings I was taken to the Regional Football Stadium which was serving as a jail, and a day later transported by boat to the Naval Base in the infamous Quiriquina Island. There, I joined some five hundred political prisoners guarded by armed marines. They kept us in a large gym, sleeping on the floor with blankets for cover. Interrogations and torture took place at night and we went to sleep in fear of being woken and taken away. Many prisoners were never seen again.

***

Every morning, in an empty swimming pool, marines holding high-pressure hoses showered us with seawater. We had bars of coarse soap, but no matter how hard we tried, it would not lather. One night, about one month into my imprisonment, the torturers came. I was blindfolded and taken to an interrogation room. Someone entered and they saluted him as an officer. He accused me of being part of a plan to run clandestine field hospitals, supposedly to treat wounded guerrillas fighting the military. I knew nothing of it and kept saying so. For about an hour, I was beaten and tormented with death threats. Afterwards I was taken outside to an underground shaft that led – via a trap door – to a small cell. It was pitch black and so silent that I lost all track of time. Before leaving, my captors warned that they may never return.

When they eventually came back, around a day later, they bandaged my eyes and took me away for further interrogation and torture. They were angry because I could not answer their questions. Eventually, I was led outside, still blindfolded but I sensed it was night. They force-marched me to the end of a pier, all the time using foul language and making threats on my life. Salvador Allende was their preferred figure of hate and scorn. I could smell the sea and hear the waves as they tied a rope around my neck. They made me feel a large lump of concrete to which they attached the rope and shouted that unless I confessed I would be thrown into the sea and no one would know. I pleaded for my life saying that I could not confess to what I did not know. I have never since experienced such fear and terror. Eventually, after perhaps ten minutes, which felt like hours, they relented.

Later, back at the gym I was told that I had been gone for two days. I was released about two months later. I will be forever grateful to my aunt, Mrs Teresa Segura, for her help and for doing her best to ensure that I came out of the Quiriquina Island alive. Whilst researching for this book I have read dozens of testimonies of Chilean victims of torture and I know that my experience pales into insignificance compared to theirs.

During the aftermath of the *coup d'*état, dozens of doctors from towns and cities all over Chile were arrested, tortured and twenty four of them murdered. Here I will mention some of them, paying a tribute to all.

Dr Eduardo Paredes, 34, Director of Chile Films; Dr Enrique Paris, 40, Professor of Psychiatry; Dr Georges Klein, 27, a French citizen and Government Adviser; and Dr Hector Pincheira, 28, Government Adviser. These four doctors were all arrested as they left La Moneda, the presidential palace the day of the coup. As I explained earlier, they were taken to the Tacna Regiment and were last seen alive on 13th September.

Dr Jorge Avila, 27, detained, in Santiago, by carabineros on 17th September and murdered by shots in the head and chest the following day.

Dr Eduardo Gonzalez, 31, who together with his wife, Natacha Carrion, also a doctor, were detained by carabineros at the hospital in Cunco, a small town, on 14th September. He was brutally beaten and later that day both were handed over to Air Force personnel and taken by helicopter to a Base on the city of Temuco where after he was savagely tortured he was never again seen. Natacha, pregnant at the time, gave birth in prison where she remained until August 1975, when she was forced into exile.

Amongst the doctors that fell, three were graduates from my Medical School:

Dr Arturo Hillerns, 29, arrested in Temuco, southern Chile, tortured and murdered on 15th September 1973 by carabineros;

Dr Bautista Van Schouwen, who was captured in Santiago, tortured and assassinated by members of the DINA on 13th December 1973, a fact denied by the military and, for many years therefore he remained a desaparecido – a missing one;

Dr Miguel Enríquez, who was never arrested but was also hunted down by the DINA and died in a gun battle in Santiago, on 5th October 1974 whilst protecting his pregnant wife, Carmen Castillo, in what can be described as the courageous last stand of a hero against military forces that included a small tank, a helicopter and dozens of DINA agents and soldiers. He received ten bullet wounds including one in the head. Miraculously his wife – initially thought dead – survived but regrettably her baby did not. Miguel and Bautista, five years my seniors, were founder members of the MIR and members of the Central Committee of the Party. I met both a few times and I remember them as charismatic, very intelligent and the finest of men.

Miguel, the legendary revolutionary leader, was the son of my anatomy professor, Dr Edgardo Enríquez, who at the time of the coup was the Secretary of State for Education and a year earlier had been Vice-Chancellor of the University of Concepción, a position that in Chile is known as 'El Rector de la Universidad'.

After the *coup*, Prof. Enriquez was immediately arrested by agents of the military junta and later imprisoned in a concentration camp in Dawson Island, in the Magellan Strait, where he suffered physical and psychological torture. Eventually, in May 1975, with a day's notice, he was escorted to a plane by armed soldiers and sent into exile. I was fortunate to meet my noble *maestro* when I visited Mexico City, years later. He had lost two of his sons, Miguel and Edgardo [killed by agents of Operación Cóndor], a grandson and a son in law, Bautista Von Schouwen, to the hands of Pinochet lackeys and his pain must have been immense, but he bore it all with great dignity and courage.

As a result of the merciless purge of health workers including doctors many hospitals were left without medical staff and this was a problem for the Junta and the managers who had taken charge of the health administration. This explains why they ordered me to resume my career immediately in another town, Mulchén. I had to report to the police daily and they forbade me to leave the town without their permission.

One day in April 1974 a *carabinero* corporal, and the grateful father of a small girl whom I had treated, informed me that a new *Capitán de Carabineros* (Paramilitary Police's Captain) had taken charge. The captain knew that I had already been imprisoned but he had let it be known that my arrest for further interrogation was imminent. I will be forever grateful to this man, who at great risk tipped me off regarding the intention of his superior officer. The following day I fled to Concepción and joined my family. I knew that, within a matter of days, I would be wanted by the DINA, the implacable National Intelligence Agency. I had to leave Chile. My wife had no hesitation in coming with our children and me, although none of us had passports. The solution was to flee to Argentina, because in those years Chileans could enter Argentina with identity cards, which we hurriedly obtained for our babies. (We had ours because by law in Chile, all adults must have an identity card.)

Three days later, we boarded a night train to Santiago. It was one of the saddest days of our lives. I remember vividly the look of hopelessness on our parents faces. In Santiago, we went to the home of Don Ramón Barceló, then in his fifties and a trusted friend of my father. He was also in fear of imminent detention and decided to leave Chile with us. We left on an early morning bus, hoping to reach Mendoza, a journey that took us high up, into the Cordillera de los Andes. First we headed north towards the town of Los Andes, always climbing, then the ever-winding road took us even higher and east towards the border. The bus was full, and as I looked around, I knew that we were not the only ones fleeing Chile. Fear made everybody silent. I remember the collective anxiety as the bus approached the military control post at the Chilean side of the frontier and the relief after we crossed into Argentina.

***

Thus, we left our country behind. I cannot remember how long the journey along the International Road between Santiago and Mendoza took, but it must have been eight or so hours. The next time we would return to Chile would be flying over the Andes, like returning South American swans, bringing one little cygnet. It would be almost two decades later.

Chapter Three

MENDOZA – BUENOS AIRES TO ENGLAND

*'The practice of granting asylum to people fleeing persecution in foreign lands is one of the earliest hallmarks of civilization. References to it have been found in texts written 3,500 years ago, during the blossoming of the great early empires in the Middle East such as the Hittites, Babylonians, Assyrians and ancient Egyptians.' – **UNHCR United Nations High Commission for Refugees***

In Mendoza, we found a budget hotel and we rested. Our plan was to get to Buenos Aires and go to the United Nations High Commission for Refugees (UNHCR). We were 740 miles away and we chose to go by train, a journey that took twenty-four hours. We boarded in General San Martín station, named after Argentina's liberator from Spanish rule.

The first part of the railway track was a serpentine descent to the city of San Martín and later San Luis, before crossing interminable flat plains that the Quechuas called *pampas*. For hundreds of miles we gazed – for the first time – at a grassy prairie stretching away as far as the eye could see. We had read of them in books and we talked about one – *Don Segundo Sombra* – portraying the hard life of the *gauchos*, the pampas cowboys, through the eyes of Don Segundo's shadow, a young man coming of age. Night fell and our children, tired, slept restlessly.

To this day, this is the longest train journey I have ever made. We arrived at the 'El Retiro' station in Buenos Aires the following morning. Looking back my wife endured the ordeal of our escape from Chile with great fortitude and the togetherness between us never flinched. It must have been extremely hard for her to look after a baby and a toddler in harrowing circumstances, but she was marvellous.

We found rooms at a small hotel in the centre of the city and later we went to the offices of the UNHCR. The place was busy with Chileans and following a detailed interview, we registered.

A few days afterwards the High Commission sent us to a camp run by a Dutch charity in the suburb of Moreno. They gave us space in a warehouse, separated by curtains from other families. We lived with about one hundred other refugees from all kinds of backgrounds: teachers, carpenters, accountants, doctors, students, peasants, nurses and the like. We shared chores: cleaning, washing dishes and cooking. The camp was in the countryside and the living conditions were basic in the extreme, but our funds were limited and we had no option. It was autumn and the weather was rather cold but, luckily, our children's health did not suffer. An old abandoned tractor was their favourite play area. From time to time, we travelled by train from Moreno to Buenos Aires to pursue our cases. After about a month, we found a house that, with Don Ramón's help, we rented. It was better accommodation as we waited for our Travel Documents. We had applied for asylum to various countries, one of them the UK. Two months later, we were desperate to leave because we had run out of money and there were rumours of an imminent military *coup* in Argentina – we did not feel safe. DINA agents were operating in Buenos Aires and many comrades were apprehended in this city over the coming months and years including, in April 1976, Edgardo Enríquez, Miguel's brother, who was taken back to Chile, to *Villa Grimaldi*, DINA's infamous torture centre in Santiago, from where he 'disappeared.'

On 30th September 1974 the exiled Commander in Chief of the Chilean army, General Carlos Prats and his wife Sofia Cuthbert were assassinated in Buenos Aires when a bomb on his car was radio- activated by Michael Townley, an American working for the DINA. General Prats had succeeded General Schneider and like him, he had been a constitutionalist and loyal to President Allende. Three weeks before the *coup* he had been forced to resign to his post as Commander in Chief of the Army by the Counsel of Generals. A few days after the *coup,* he had gone into exile. However, even for him, there was no safety and he was killed by direct orders of Pinochet, one year later.

***

The late Harold Wilson, then British Prime Minister, was very sympathetic to Chilean refugees. A few days after an interview in the UK Embassy in Buenos Aires we were told that we had been granted asylum. We flew from Argentina's capital with about fifty other Chileans, on board a Sabena Belgian plane. We landed in the UK on 11th July 1974, a date that is embedded in my brain like a second date of birth. I was twenty-six years old. We entered England at Heathrow, with 'Travel Documents under the Geneva Convention 1951,' a kind of passport with a warning saying that the holder was forbidden to return to the country of origin.

Our dream during that period was to eventually return to our country of birth, like swans returning to their lake. However, the tyrant stayed and we could not fly back. We owe a great debt of gratitude to the British people and their government which granted us asylum in our time of need.

It had been arranged that a charity known as the Ockenden Venture would take care of us. We went to Camberley, in Surrey, to a big mock Tudor house owned by the charity. Located in Prior Road, in a leafy part of the town, it had about twenty large bedrooms and they gave us one with three beds. It overlooked a garden the size of a small football pitch. We were welcomed by two Tibetan refugees, man and wife, who were kind and gentle. Within forty-eight hours, we went to the Police Station where they took our fingerprints, photographs and issued us with identity cards. I remember they were green in colour and the word 'alien' described our status. The police told us to report every week and to carry the identity booklets with us at all times.

***

We did not speak English before coming to the UK and therefore, we appreciated the daily language lessons we received when we sat around a table after a nutritious and healthy breakfast. Not surprisingly, there were important cultural differences and we had a lot to learn. For instance, we Chileans thought that brown sugar was inferior to white sugar and cheaper – when in fact it is the opposite. When asked why we were being given brown sugar, the young Ockenden Venture manager patiently corrected us, adding that the same could be said for bread!

Our initial impressions were of admiration for the affluence surrounding us. Camberley was beautiful and we travelled to the town centre by a bus that we boarded outside the house. It was not until we went further afield that we appreciated that not everywhere was like Camberley and saw how multicultural Britain was, with both poor and prosperous areas in all towns and cities.

We were living off state benefits and we wanted to learn English as quickly as possible and return to normality. At the refugee house we were settling in happily, enjoying the company of other families with children, but we continued to speak Spanish with our compatriots, and this was a drawback. The solution came a few months later when we became friends with the Throwers, a socially conscious English family who lived in Bracknell. They suggested that we move in with them to make faster progress learning Shakespeare's language. Thus for two months we became their guests. Their home was modern with four bedrooms. He was an engineer and commuted daily to Reading; she was a relief teacher.

They rose at 6.00 a.m. and by 7.30 a.m. their three daughters were ready to go school. During the evenings we talked and our command of English improved rapidly. Now we deeply regret not having kept in touch with this family – their generosity of spirit – their humanitarianism was truly exceptional.

With their help, I wrote to the Department of Health at Elephant and Castle in London, submitting an application for a place in any recognised hospital to do a Clinical Attachment, which in those days was the way to assess a foreign graduate's medical knowledge and proficiency in written and oral English.

The problem was that there was a two-year wait because of the large number of overseas doctors applying for a place. I received a depressing reply saying that I had to wait my turn. The letter said that the fact that I was a refugee with a family – living off the state instead of working – made no difference.

I wrote back saying that applicants from India, Pakistan and other places were waiting in their own countries whereas I, on the other hand, was already here. After another refusal, I went to London to see if a face-to-face plea would make a difference, but it was a wasted journey.

***

I was becoming desperate. I had heard that in Ascot, close to Bracknell, there was a hospital called Heatherwood. One day my wife and I decided to walk there with our children, to ask if there was any chance of me doing my Clinical Attachment. It was a long walk and must have taken us a couple of hours, but we were determined to get there.

There was no appointment, nothing pre-arranged. Fortuitously we arrived at the outpatients section and in my very poor English I explained our situation to a sister. She must have seen the despair in my eyes because, after listening, she said that she would speak to the consultant.

Looking back, that first encounter with that compassionate nurse who took pity on us shaped my profound respect and admiration for British nurses.

I will be forever grateful to Nick Roles, an exceptionally caring orthopaedic surgeon, who after hearing my plea, with a single phone call to the Hospital Secretary – in those days the top manager – arranged that from the following Monday I could start my Clinical Attachment at Heatherwood. We walked back to Bracknell with lighter feet feeling happy. There was hope. It was as if a great weight had been lifted from us.

In the next chapter, you will find a description of my early career as a doctor in the UK and my trials and tribulations. What you have to remember is that by force of circumstances, we had been transplanted, so to speak, into a different country and culture. We missed our families and Chile and we had no friends or relatives.

***

We were alien swans, which had to abandon their poisoned pond, and fly across mountains, interminable pampas and an ocean, to land on an island at the other side of the world, which offered cleaner waters. Now we had a chance to build our own nest.

Chapter Four

LANGUAGE BARRIER
– EARLY YEARS

'Language exerts hidden power, like a moon on the tides.'
*– **Alcaeus of Mytilene, Greek lyric poet, 6th century BC***

The Clinical Attachment lasted six weeks and finished just before Christmas 1974. I remember doing rounds with Nick Roles and listening intently trying desperately to understand what had been said. There I was, in Ascot, England, thousands of miles away from my country, trying to be a doctor again. On those days I often thought of my country, and the fate of those that stayed. Initially I kept in touch with other Chileans in exile and travelled to London, where meetings took place. We knew by then that the repression was brutal and many had been killed or disappeared. I remember once alighting at the Seven Sisters' metro station, on my way to the offices of Amnesty International, an organization that works tirelessly for the release of political prisoners from all over the world.

Soon after the start of my Clinical Attachment, I discovered a collection of audio-visual lectures in the small medical library of the hospital. Alone, I spent many evening listening to those tapes and watching the slides, activity that taught me English and medicine. The nurses were understanding and helpful; after the rounds they would patiently explain what I had missed, and thus I made good progress.

The orthopaedic wards were pre-fabricated buildings and separated from the main hospital, where the theatres were located. The patients' journey was on a trolley with a perspex cover in case of rain. It was my introduction to the way British people adapted and coped during and after the terrifying experience of World War II, three decades earlier.

Nick ticked me 'satisfactory' in all sections of the Clinical Attachment form. It was the best Christmas present we could have wished for. I could now apply for a temporary registration with the General Medical Council, if I found a job.

In those years, the structure of a medical career in the UK was different. From the bottom up, there were: House Officers, Senior House Officers, Registrars, and Senior Registrars and finally at the top of the pyramid, Consultants.

My mentor made enquiries and found me a job as a surgical House Officer at a neighbouring hospital. I was beginning my career in the UK at the base of the pyramid. Little did I know that it would take me sixteen years to reach the top.

***

Frimley Park Hospital was the antithesis of Heatherwood and a model of modernity. After six months as a House Officer in General Surgery I worked for one year in the Accident and Emergency Department. We lived in a hospital's house for married doctors, which together with accommodation for single doctors was available at all hospitals.

Our lives had changed for the better. We kept in touch with our families by letters and occasional phone calls. I was earning now and I set up a monthly International Money Transfer for my parents, about five per cent of my earnings. I kept this going until, to my profound and enduring sorrow, they passed away. Even now, as I write these lines my eyes well up when I think of 'mis viejos' (my old man and my old mum) as we affectionately say in Chile. I will forever regret their enforced absence from my life.

***

By mid-1975, I had decided to pursue a career in orthopaedics. As I have already said one of the reasons why I chose this branch of surgery was the promise to my brother Jorge and now, looking back, I can add another: the influence of Nick Roles, a true gentleman, whose kindness I will never forget.

In the UK there are Royal Colleges of Surgeons in London, Glasgow and Edinburgh. There is a fourth in Dublin, Ireland. In those years, the four colleges ran examinations leading to the postgraduate qualification known as the FRCS (Fellowship of the Royal College of Surgeons). This qualification is now known as the 'old surgical fellowship' because since the 1990s things have changed.

In the 'seventies, the way to progress in one's surgical career was first to pass the tough *Primary* and then the even tougher *Final FRCS* examination. Inevitably, the subject of these qualifications would come into almost every conversation among junior doctors. Aspiring surgeons were divided by their peers and nurses into those who had passed the whole examination and those who had not. The former were entitled to be called 'Mister' instead of 'Doctor' and felt proud of it. Being a 'Mister' was – and still is – an honour. This custom originated during the times when operations were performed by barber-surgeons who were not doctors, but misters. Henceforth, surgeons in Britain and Ireland use the letters 'Mr' before their names, rather than 'Dr'.

***

It was in Frimley Park Hospital, whilst I was studying for the Primary FRCS examination that I first met Dr Banerjee, an Indian doctor, who knew a great deal of anatomy, and was able to advise me on the exam. Years later I re-encountered him at Tameside Hospital where he was working as a consultant radiologist and, immediately, we recognised each other and reminisced about old times.

The Primary involved written, oral and practical 'parts' – examinations in three subjects: Anatomy, Pathology and Physiology. It was a marathon over the course of a week. The pass rate was very low. A candidate failing one part of any of the three subjects would have to re-sit all the three subjects again.

The written part involved multiple choice questions as well as essays. The practical anatomy examination included a candidate being quizzed in front of a dissected body – with the examiner asking him or her to identify with a pointer features of the anatomical structure.

I took the Primary in the summer of 1976 in Edinburgh but failed the multiple choice questions in physiology and so the whole examination. It was only after I went to Mexico six years later that I finally got over my disappointment.

From Frimley we moved to Derby. I had obtained a post in Casualty that was attractive because it was tied to a day release position as an Anatomy Demonstrator at Nottingham Medical School.

**

I loved going to Nottingham because of its beautiful university campus that also has a lake inhabited by many water birds, including white mute swans. Once a week, on my way to the Medical School, I walked by the lake hoping to see a brother black necked swan, but it was not to be.

**

After one year of regularly teaching anatomy, I obtained my first orthopaedic post and I learned the principles of Orthopaedic Surgery from Geoff Newton, who later would become the President of the British Orthopaedic Association. I stayed a further year as the first Senior House Officer of Professor Frank Burke, who taught me the principles of Hand Surgery. In Derby, I met Efrén Herrera, a Mexican neurosurgeon. It was the beginning of a long friendship. In later years Efrén, who lives in Puebla, north of Mexico City, would visit us every time he returned to England. We in turn visited him and Marjorie, his English wife, when we went to Mexico.

Whilst at Derby I applied for my first registrar job at the Mayday Hospital in Croydon, London. I was short-listed and the day of the interview, I thought that I had blown my chances! I was very late and running upstairs to the interview, I crashed into Ron Shedden, one of the consultants on the panel, who was coming down. Regaining his balance, he asked: *'Are you Milton Peña?'* Breathlessly, I nodded, mumbling an excuse for my lateness and for almost causing him to fall. He replied: *'It is OK, we are waiting for you.'*

Ron had a special interest in hand surgery and during the interview I gave a good account of what I had learned whilst working with Frank, who had novel techniques, having arrived in Derby directly from Louisville, USA, an internationally renowned Hand Unit. I joined the other candidates and as we waited for the decision of the panel, conversation inevitably drifted into who had passed the Final FRCS. Some of them had it, others the Primary. I had none and I thought I had no chance of getting the job. I felt like leaving.

In the medical world in the UK, the custom is that after a job interview the result is given immediately after the panel deliberation. The applicants are asked to wait and eventually the successful candidate is invited to meet the panel. Thus, I was astonished when a door opened and a smartly dressed lady came out and scanning the room locked eyes with me and said *'Dr Peña could you please come in and meet the panel.'* At my first attempt and yet without any post-graduate qualifications I had obtained my first registrar job!

In years to come, I would not be so lucky and I had many unsuccessful interviews. One of them was in Barrow in Furness, in Cumbria. I remember I decided to go by train from London to Carlisle, and then by another coastal train south, to Barrow. It was scenic but the journey back was sad, I had been rejected and to me, the return, appeared to take twice as long.

As I said, in those years NHS hospitals offered married accommodation and we lived in a semi-detached house, at 59 Queens Avenue, Thornton Heath, within walking distance of the Mayday hospital. We were in the capital of England and during weekends we went everywhere including regular trips to Kew Gardens, which we all adored; to Crystal Palace – to row in the pond and see the dinosaurs – which our children loved to sketch. Mitcham Park and Wimbledon Commons were also close by and we got to know them well. However, it was London, with all its attractions that we never grew bored of. We were happy.

Ramón Barceló, my dad's friend, who had given us refuge at his home in Santiago and been our trusted companion during our escape from Chile until we reached England, was living in London. We met him a few times and he always made us laugh and telling us stories of dad and him as young men. Our children called him *abuelo* (grandad) Ramón. We will be forever grateful to him for his friendship.

***

At Mayday I had good teachers but after two years I needed to move on. An opportunity presented when Ron Shedden recommended me to the leading orthopaedic surgeon at a teaching hospital. It was a post-up the ladder, but I needed to be interviewed. He warned me that the surgeon, named George Bonney, was very eccentric and that during interviews he had the habit of rolling his eyes upwards to the extent that his interlocutor could only see the white part of the globes. And this is exactly what happened! After searching speciality questions George appointed me Locum Senior Registrar in Orthopaedic Surgery at St Mary's Hospital Medical School for a one year term. After the interview proper we talked about Chile and my escape to Great Britain. To my pleasant surprise he told me that he was an admirer of Simón Bolívar, the Venezuelan patriot who dreamt of unifying all the South American countries into one large single nation-state, after liberation from the Spanish. Bolívar's vision was never realised, but he succeeded in driving the Spanish from Venezuela, Colombia, Ecuador, Peru and Bolivia – a country that is named after him.

***

On ward round days at an exact time, George would arrive in a large car to the door of the Churchill Wing in Praed Street. There, the Senior Registrars, Registrars, Senior House Officers, assorted students and Sister Taggart – a unique nurse who ran the department like clockwork – would be waiting for his arrival. After greeting him, the whole entourage would walk to the orthopaedic wards for rounds. He was a great clinician and taught us to observe beyond the bones and the joints and to look at the eyes and the complexion of every patient. He was an exceptionally gifted surgeon and loved to teach.

St Mary's was a tertiary referral centre for nerve injuries and in particular *brachial plexus* trauma. I worked for George's disciple Rolf Birch, who later became professor of Orthopaedic Surgery. Rolf was completely dedicated to his job and from him I learned precisely that – dedication. We spent hours in the operating theatre, re-attaching damaged nerves under the microscope. Once again I was very fortunate to be learning from masters of surgery.

***

I used to cycle to St Mary's from Thornton Heath and soon I got to know London well. You see a different city when you cycle and small details stay with you forever. I remember for instance a man with a beret pushing a bicycle loaded with onions at the handles, frame and seat. I passed him, just before Westminster Bridge, almost every day. After crossing the bridge, I cycled around Winston Churchill's statue in front of the Houses of Parliament and Big Ben and then straight to Buckingham Palace using safe lanes inside St James' Park. Constitution Hill would come next towards old St George's Hospital and after negotiating the always busy crossing at Hyde Park Corner, I would enter Hyde Park and pedal inside towards Speakers' Corner. Eventually, after exiting the park and pedalling along a few back roads I would arrive at the hospital entrance at the Churchill Wing, the out-patient department of old St Mary's.

***

Sometimes I would cycle to the Serpentine Lake, in Hyde Park, hoping, in vain, to find black necked swans among the water birds. There were ducks of all kinds, geese, majestic white swans, cormorants and many other birds, but I never saw a brother.

***

I loved that time when I cycled to work – in spite of my two accidents! One occurred when the driver of a parked black cab opened a door without realising I was approaching. I hit the door, banging my body as I fell, I was not hurt badly and nothing was seriously damaged except the bike's front wheel and handle. I felt sorry for the cab driver who probably would have lost time and money if I reported the incident. He offered to pay for the damage and he took me to the hospital. He arranged for my bike to be mended and returned it later, the same day, sorted. The other accident occurred when a car emerged from a side street not having seen me. I hit it at speed and somersaulted over the bonnet, landing at the other side. Again, no major injury but the bike was a write-off. I bought a new racing bicycle afterwards, made by a firm called *SOLO*. It was light blue. I still have it and use it.

If you happen to be an Edinburgh's 'fellow' surgeon of my generation, the next chapter may bring back memories. In the years since, much has changed: the examinations are held in most large cities with less need to travel; furthermore, failing part of an examination does not mean total failure which, in my opinion, is much fairer.

Chapter Five

EDINBURGH ROYAL COLLEGE OF SURGEONS

'Challenges are what make life interesting: overcoming them is what makes life meaningful.' – **Ralph Waldo Emerson.** *1803–1882 American essayist, lecturer and poet who led the transcendentalist – self-reliance – movement in the mid-19th century.*

It was late 1982. We had been in England for eight years. Chile was still ruled by a despot who cleverly, two years earlier had amended the Chilean Constitution. This allowed him another eight years in power, at the end of which a referendum would take place, to reject or accept a single candidate from the original military junta, for another eight years.

I had been thinking of moving to Mexico because there was the possibility of a job at the University Hospital of Puebla. My friend the neurosurgeon Efrén Herrera, invited me over and I accepted. Everybody called him *'maestro'*, which is the ultimate mark of respect. The historical and beautiful city of Puebla is ninety-seven miles north-west of Mexico City. Everything about Mexico – Puebla, the university, the hospital and the people – reminded me of Chile, but there was no job security and the career prospects were vague. However, the long trip would still change my life – Efrén, who years earlier had passed the Edinburgh Final, encouraged me to do the same.

Firstly, I needed to sit the Primary. Whilst at St Mary's Hospital I enrolled in the then famous Professor Slome's course. It was very useful. St Mary's Medical School has excellent Anatomy and Physiology Departments and I made good use of them. I went to Edinburgh for a second time and passed the examination.

I always travelled to my exam destinations by train. On the way there, it was easy to spot the candidates in the various carriages – alone or in groups – quiet or talking about previous questions or revising. During the return journeys, those who had passed smiled with happiness and those who had failed stared at the night through the window, sad and deep in thought. I have experienced both feelings. That night, whilst travelling back, I felt like I was walking on air, and wrote a note saying how happy I was and that I intended to sit the Final in a year's time. I have found that writing always has a calming, soothing effect on me, in times of joy or sadness.

Around this time, we bought our first home: it was in Shirley, Surrey, and located in a beautiful area, very green and literally one hundred yards from 'Orchard Way' a lovely primary school for our children to attend. My mind, however, was set on passing the Final Examination. I was an experienced orthopaedic surgeon having worked as a Senior Registrar – one-step from Consultant – but the exam in those years, was a general surgical test in the broadest sense of the word. I decided that I needed more experience in General Surgery, even if it meant temporarily going down the ladder.

**

I took a job in the St Helier's Surgical Rotation, in Greater London, which included periods of six months as a Senior House Officer in urology, at St Helier; paediatric general surgery at Queen Mary's in Carshalton and orthopaedics at Epsom Hospital.

To this day, the experience in urology with John Boyd, as far as teaching is concerned, ranks among the very best. He was a wonderful mentor and a superb surgeon. My long clinical test during the Final involved a patient with a kidney tumour, and John's teaching proved priceless.

My paediatric general surgery job at Queen Mary's was also excellent for my education. My teachers were Mr Epstein and Mr Forrester. We managed very complex and life threatening conditions in new born babies. For instance *oesophageal atresia* – a congenital blockage of the gullet which is also wrongly joined to the wind pipe. The new-born regurgitates its entire first and every subsequent feed and saliva pours almost continuously from its mouth. Surgical correction within forty eight hours is the only hope of survival. Another example is *diaphragmatic hernia,* where the stomach and bowel are in the chest as a result of a hole in the muscle separating the chest and tummy. Less complex cases were those of *pyloric stenosis* which should be immediately suspected when new born baby's vomit is so forceful that it flies across the room like a bullet.

Situated in spacious grounds, Queen Mary's cared for a large number of youngsters with *cerebral palsy* and *spina bifida.* They had their own ward and I remember joining them at their parties. I learned a great deal from them and, ever since, I have had a special affection for fellow human beings with these and similar disabilities. This may explain why two of my patients had an open access (no appointment needed) to my clinics: Alan Ford and Reginald Lane. I am proud to have been there for them for twenty four years, until my retirement.

***

After completing this rotation, I felt ready to apply for the Final Fellowship examination. I wrote to the College and I received confirmation of my application. I was to be candidate number 397. As for the Primary, I was advised to attend a preparatory course and in those years, one of the best was at the Whipps Cross hospital, organised by Mr Petroni. The course was helpful, especially the mock oral examination at the end. Each attendee was required – in front of the whole class of about 100 – to face three 'examiners' just as in the real thing. It was nerve racking because everybody was watching. It was videoed and we could rate our performance.

The letter with the schedule and venues for the exams was as follow:

The written examination: at the University Examinations Hall, Roxburgh Place, Edinburgh.

09.30 – 12.30 Thursday 24th May 1984. Principles and Practice of Surgery.

09.30 – 12.30 Friday 25th May 1984. Operative Surgery and Surgical Pathology.

The oral examination: at The Royal College of Surgeons, Nicolson Street, Edinburgh on Tuesday 29th May 1984.

Surgery at 13.40 to 14.10 (30 min) Symposium Hall, Hill Square, Edinburgh.

Operative Surgery and Surgical Pathology at 15.00 to 15.30 (30 min) Main Building.

The letter had a warning: '*Candidates whose performance in the Written and Oral is such that they cannot compensate by the Clinical will be considered to have failed the whole examination and therefore will not be allowed to proceed to the clinicals. There will be no refund.*' (Note by the Author: the word 'Clinical' refer to the part of the process when the candidate's performance with real patients is assessed.)

***

It was my third trip to this fascinating city that has a special place in my heart. As on previous occasions, I had booked a room at the '*Allness Bed and Breakfast,*' on 27 Pilrig Street. Mrs Allness was attentive and reminded me very much of my mum. The evening before the first written exam I did what I had done when I succeeded with the Primary – that was to climb to the top of Arthur's Seat and afterwards watch a late film. It curbed any temptation to revise until late. I went to see *Tootsie*, in which Dustin Hoffman, with such great acting, not only made me forget totally about the exam for two hours, but also took away all my apprehension afterwards. I felt relaxed and slept like a log.

I woke-up refreshed. Thursday had arrived. Mrs Allness' breakfast was wholesome, including a generous portion of Scottish porridge. Later she saw me off at the door wishing me good luck. I walked my way to the Examinations Hall, close to the College.

That day, the three questions on Principles and Practice of Surgery were:

1. Discuss the Diagnosis and management of post-operative deep vein thrombosis.
2. Give an account of the uses of blood and blood products in surgical

practice. Describe the hazards of blood transfusion

3.   Discuss the causes and treatment of post-operative Ileus

Upon seeing the list I relaxed but there were pages of writing to do and to make it legible I had devised a method holding a small ruler on my left hand and scrolling over it. I followed it and after three hours I felt cautiously optimistic with my answers and sure that whoever marked them would be able to read them!

The following day the three questions on Operative Surgery and Surgical Pathology were:

1.   Discuss the aetiology, pathology and management of acute cholecystitis
2.   Discuss the causes of pathological fracture of the shaft of the femur and discuss its treatment.
3.   Discuss the pathological changes which may follow the lodgement of an embolus. Give a detailed account of the operation you would perform in a patient with an embolus in the common femoral artery.

Once again I felt that I knew enough to write satisfactory essays and followed my calligraphic method. All I needed to do now was to wait until Tuesday for the Oral Examinations.

***

That weekend I made a day trip to Stirling, in central Scotland, by the river Forth. I wanted to see the 12th century castle that dominates the city and Robert the Bruce's statue guarding the yard. I was not disappointed; in addition, the view was magnificent with the monument of William Wallace – another Scottish national hero – in the distance. Stirling was pretty and historical.

In the afternoon, I found myself walking the University Campus, which someone had recommended worthy of visiting. The buildings are set in charming grounds and it reminded me of my own university in Concepción. The sky was blue and the students sat and lay casually on the grass, young, happy and carefree.

Suddenly, I came to Loch Airthrey, a picturesque artificial lake, with many ducks, geese and swans by the shore. As l searched for my brothers among the water birds, my mind and eyes played a trick – the illusion was almost complete – but as I got nearer, it was not to be, no black necked swans had reached this pond either.

***

Tuesday finally arrived and I made my way to the College. Naturally I felt nervous but I reminded myself that I had prepared well over the previous year not only reading the necessary books but also the relevant journals to keep my knowledge up-to date. Equally important I had had good mentors and hands-on experience.

The oral examinations are face-to-face. They are a test not only of knowledge but also of maturity and character. Surgery – like all branches of medicine – is not an exact science and in many cases a matter of opinion and judgement. Candidates with weak views can buckle when challenged and are likely to fail. After my orals, I thought I had done well and my gut feeling was confirmed that evening when I learned that I could proceed to the final hurdle, the dreaded *'Clinicals'*. I was in with a chance.

***

I returned to London on the last train. It had been a long and draining day and aided by the sound and rhythmic movement of the carriage, I was soon asleep.

I dreamt that I was with several hundred students travelling from Concepción to the port of Valparaiso, aiming to join undergraduates from all over Chile, on a protest march. It had been a specially hired overnight train, full of youngsters sharing the same ideals and hopes – that our actions would make a difference.

I woke up with a deep feeling of nostalgia for that period of my life. Fortunately, it was fleeting and soon the memories of the dream faded.

***

I went back to Edinburgh on Sunday 3rd June and reported to the College at 8.00 a.m. the following day. Other candidates were already there, looking nervous. Shortly afterwards a bus took a group of us to our allocated hospital: The Royal Infirmary in Perth. During the Clinical, I was required to deal with real pre-selected patients. My 'long case' presented as a patient with a *hypernephroma*, a form of cancer of the kidney. I had thirty minutes to diagnose his ailment by taking a medical history and performing a hands-on examination. Afterwards, I spent another half an hour with the examiner who asked me to demonstrate my findings and answer questions on the diagnosis, treatment and management of the patient's condition. I knew that if I got it wrong I would fail.

Afterwards came the 'short cases' where individuals with external abnormalities are placed in a room and the candidate is required to tell the assessor what he or she thinks is wrong with each. After a frugal lunch at the hospital's restaurant, we returned to Edinburgh to wait for the results, expected at around 5.00 p.m.

***

The tradition then was that the examination's clerk reads out loudly the individual numbers of the successful candidates. The College hall was buzzing as we waited. Results were late. There were about two hundred people waiting and generating so much tension and anxiety that if converted to electricity it would have lit up the complete building. Suddenly, a door opened, the clerk emerged and the hall went deadly quiet. In a broad Scottish accent, he announced that he would *only* read the number of the successful candidates, in ascending order.

My number was 397. The clerk began to shout out random numbers. I could see around me disappointed candidates quietly leaving. Conversely, cries of happiness erupted after others heard their numbers. Some embraced and some jumped in the air for joy. As the clerk reached the 300th my heart rate had increased to 160 beats per minute and threatened to escape my chest – but I was young then. Suddenly I heard him shout: – *'three hundred and ninety seven!'* – I cannot remember my reaction, but it must have been one of relief and ecstasy. I had done it! I had become a Mister at last.

Following tradition, I joined the successful candidates in an inner hall to drink a glass of Sherry with the President and the examiners. Afterwards I phoned my family and they were over the moon. The train journey back to London was the happiest of them all.

***

The Council confirmed my election to the Fellowship and I was entitled to use the designation FRCS after my name, indicating that I was a Fellow of the oldest Royal College in the world, founded in 1502, provided I paid a yearly fee. My family came to the Ceremony of Presentation of Diplomas. More than five hundred candidates sat the Final that spring of 1984. The list shows that only 67 were successful and that the new fellows came from Universities of India, Pakistan, Egypt, Iraq, Ghana, Malaya, UK and many other countries. University of Chile was next to my name.

We spent a few days in Edinburgh: we toured the Castle and Holyrood Palace; walked Princess Street and the Royal Mile; visited the Botanic Gardens; marvelled at the famous Forth Bridge, gazed at the sea and the Port and of course, walked up to Arthur's Seat. From this vantage point, I showed my wife and our children this magnificent city that had given me a key in the form of four historical letters, capable of unlocking many doors. I was thirty-six years old and still had a dream: to become a consultant in Orthopaedic Surgery.

***

As we flew down, we passed over a small pond where many seagulls played merrily in the water. A few turned their heads up to look at the four happy swans with ebony necks. Thus, we soared high and southwards above the Scottish lowlands, following the Pennine hills, far above the English Lakes, the Forest of Bowland, the Midlands and from there guided by the courses of rivers Cherwell and Thames, we flew towards London before finally descending to our nest in Surrey, always whistling.

Chapter Six

BECOMING AN ORTHOPAEDIC SURGEON

*In Greek mythology **Mentor** was the teacher and protector of Telemachus, Odysseus's son, while he was fighting at Troy.*

I had gained the FRCS but to succeed I had temporarily left my speciality. I now needed to return to orthopaedic surgery at a registrar level but this was not at all easy. It was at this time that my unsuccessful trip to Barrow-in-Furness occurred; in those days there was always keen competition for Registrar jobs. However, after a successful interview, I secured a one year registrar post at Bedford General, where I was fortunate to be taught by Andrew Pollen, a caring paediatric orthopaedic surgeon. The journey by car from Shirley in Surrey to Bedford was long and involved crossing London from South to North and I had to start at 5.30 a.m. which I did twice a week. I followed the same route I took when cycling to St Mary's Hospital but after reaching Marble Arch I would take Edgware Road which heads straight north to the M1. After a further hour's driving I would leave the motorway and complete my journey to Bedford. It was a good job and all the consultants were keen to teach. After one year they wanted me to stay but, because of the distance, I did not renew my contract.

In December 1985 I was appointed Registrar at Medway Hospital, in Gillingham, Kent. I worked with John Fleetcroft a pleasant, spiritual and friendly surgeon. To get there from Shirley I cycled daily to Bromley South Station, put my bike in the train and then pedalled up the hill from Gillingham station to the hospital. Part of the job involved going once a week by hospital taxi, to the Isle of Sheppey, in the Thames estuary, to do an outpatients clinic in the morning and an operating session in the afternoon. I enjoyed these journeys because the land, coast and sea reminded me of similar scenery in Chile.

The problem with jobs such as at Bedford and Medway was that they were a dead end in so far as my professional progress was concerned. I needed a post approved for consultant training. The competition for these positions was fierce, particularly in the south of England. Thus I moved north and I found myself working in Wrightington Hospital near Wigan with Kevin Hardinge, a renowned hip surgeon, an excellent teacher and a true master of his art.

Kevin Hardinge was my mentor and secured me an interview for a Lecturer's post with the Professor of Orthopaedic Surgery at Manchester University, teaching orthopaedics to medical students, and working at Hope Hospital in Salford and Pendlebury Children's Hospital, for a one year term.

Professor Charles Galasko was an early riser and his working day began at 6.00 a.m. I went to his office around 7.00 a.m. one morning in the winter of 1989. He offered me the job and afterwards I thought of what Kevin had said weeks earlier – '*Milton, if you are successful, then you will be in the place where the rats are running, competing with each other.*' This post, however, counted towards my eventual registration as a specialist in Trauma and Orthopaedics with the General Medical Council. I worked consistently hard during that year and I prepared my lectures diligently.

***

In Chile, things were changing for the better. In 1988, General Pinochet, nominated himself to be the single candidate to the Presidency on a plebiscite that his amended Constitution stipulated.

Chileans had to vote YES if they wanted the ruthless dictator for another eight years, or NO if they wanted him out. The NO Campaign beat the YES Campaign at their own game by hiring marketing advisers who recommended a media campaign based on images of an optimistic and happy Chile if freedom and democracy were restored. Their slogan was '*la alegria que viene*' (joy is coming). The marketing experts advised against images of the atrocities, torture and death which, although truthful, would not win the Referendum. The *Pinochetistas* had more media resources and funding and ran a campaign relaying the fear of a return to the days of the Unidad Popular. However 54 per cent of more than seven million Chileans voted NO and Pinochet lost the referendum. He and his supporters were fuming. Reluctantly, he stepped down as Head of State but remained Commander in Chief of the Army and still wielded enormous power.

During the days that followed Pinochet's defeat there were a series of spontaneous rallies to celebrate hopes of freedom and democracy. The police acted brutally against members of the press, particularly foreign, in a futile effort to suppress the reporting on the way that the majority of the Chilean people had demonstrated their happiness.

We followed these events from England and were cautiously optimistic that soon a democratic election could take place.

Tragically, on 4th September 1989, Jecar Nehgme, aged 28, a leader of MIR, was assassinated by three CNI agents who shot him as he walked to his home in Santiago. He represented the new generation of students and young Chileans who for a decade had been heroically fighting the Dictatorship. His funeral was attended by thousands upon thousands of mourners carrying the banners of freedom. His father, also named Jecar, a Professor of Public Health, and a socialist had been murdered by agents of the Dictatorship, in October 1973, in Temuco, a city in southern Chile. Like the legacies of Salvador Allende, Miguel Enríquez, José Tohá and hundreds of others, the legacies of the Nehgmes – father and son – will live forever.

In December 1989 Patricio Aylwin, of the Christian Democratic Party, was elected President with a majority of 55 per cent, with the backing of a coalition of parties that had voted NO, which included the Socialist Party, the Party for Democracy, the Radical Party, and the Humanist Party, and were collectively known as *La Concertación*.

∗∗∗

At that time I was living with my family at 'Ribbleton House' a large five bedroom detached house in Crow Lane West in Newton-le-Willows where we lived for ten years. It was a wonderful mansion built in 1907 for a senior manager of the local coal mine, which had closed many years earlier. I had, by chance, discovered it as I leisurely cycled the area one afternoon, noticing the 'for sale' sign. The owner, Mrs Jones, the widow of a circuit judge, in her eighties, showed us the ground floor and left us alone to look at the rest. It needed rewiring and some alterations but we saw the potential and after we agreed on a price we bought it and made it our own. We adored that house and it was witness to a very happy period in our lives. We held many sociable parties at Ribbleton House. I hosted my mentors Kevin and Charles and in turn they invited us to their respective homes.

Newton-le-Willows is a medieval market town surrounded by flat agricultural land and there were wheat fields behind our back garden. Over the years we were privileged to see the fields periodically transformed slowly from green to yellow. Later in the summer, after the harvest machines had gone I would take Pablito and Steph (more on them later) to the field to play with the fresh hay and build straw houses for them.

Pennington Flash, a large water reservoir, was four miles away and was the habitat of many wild water birds including seagulls, ducks, geese and swans. It had an adjacent large park for walkers and a children's play area.

We visited it from time to time taking bread for the birds, but, alas, we never saw black necked swans.

The summer of 1990 was unforgettable because my parents and my parents-in-law came as a group to visit from Chile for two months. Inevitably we talked about Chile, and they explained that the real power was still in the hands of the military, but gradually democracy was being restored. A Commission for Peace and Reconciliation had been set up. Many of the torturers had immunity and others had left the country.

My mum and dad and my parents in law were fascinated with Ribbleton House which was so spacious that they felt perfectly at ease during their stay. We took them on tours everywhere: London, Liverpool, Manchester, Chester, Oxford, Cambridge, Edinburgh, Loch Ness and many other places. I rented a comfortable minivan to take all eight of us to France aiming to stay in Paris for three days. I love driving and I am an unequivocal Francophile and Paris

– which I know very well – was as magnificent as ever.On their return to Chile they stopped in Madrid for a few days before flying back to Santiago.

***

The first Iraq war found me working as a lecturer at Hope Hospital. The Government feared multiple terrorist attacks and asked surgeons across the country to prepare for them. We took the warnings very seriously and we – the lecturers, senior registrars and Charles – met a few times to plan an organised medical response. Luckily the government's fears did not materialise at that time, though, worryingly, we are today once more on the alert against similar threats to our security.

Whilst working for Charles Galasko I wrote a paper which was published in the journal *Spine*. It was entitled *Delay in diagnosis of intradural spinal tumours.* (These are growths inside the *dura matter,* the thin but tough layer that covers the spinal cord and the brain). I learned a great deal whilst researching for this article. Charles was a meticulous surgeon and an excellent teacher. One of the many lessons, I learned from him was to be systematic when searching for an answer to a diagnostic dilemma. Sadly, he was the last professor to hold the Chair of Orthopaedic Surgery at Manchester University in a full academic capacity and employed by the University. With the abolition of the Chair the Lecturers and Senior Lecturer posts in orthopaedics also ceased to exist.

One day in January 1991, whilst getting dressed in the surgeons' changing room at the old Children's Hospital in Pendlebury, Charles remarked that I was ready to apply for a consultant post. Encouragingly, he offered to be one of my referees. I was elated and I thanked him. My other mentor, Kevin Hardinge, another giant of orthopaedic surgery at the time, also agreed to be my referee. There were three hospitals in the North-West advertising for an orthopaedic consultant: Bury, Tameside and the Rochdale Infirmary, and I was shortlisted for each of them. The interview at Rochdale came first – in March 1991 – and I was offered the post, which I happily accepted. My goal had now been achieved. I had become a consultant at last. I was forty-two years old.

***

My wife and I had been considering for some time to extend our family, our two older boys were by this time away at university and we were alone. Pablito was born on a spring day in May 1992, at St Mary's maternity hospital in Manchester. We were very happy. He certainly put a spring in my step and he was undoubtedly spoiled by his two older brothers.

***

A new cygnet had been added to the family of black necked swans.

Chapter Seven

THE RETURN TO CHILE

Nostalgia: Sentimental yearning for a period of the past. From the Greek words 'nostos' – return home – and 'algos' – pain.

I spent six contented and formative years at the Rochdale Infirmary. Because of my long and extensive education and training in orthopaedic surgery, I was able to manage a great variety of conditions, involving almost all aspects of my specialism. During this time I was still living at Ribbleton House in Newton-le-Willows, near to the race course at Haydock. If there was no need to rush, I would take the A 580, which follows the old Roman road between Liverpool and Manchester, until I reached Worsley and moved onto the M 60 (M 62) motorway towards Rochdale. It took me sixty minutes to get to work, but I did not mind – it was nothing like the journey from Shirley to Bedford when I had to cross the whole of London. Occasionally, responding to an 'on call' request to assist, I would take the M62 from Warrington directly to Rochdale.

Fifty per cent of my job plan involved adults and fifty per cent children. After my appointment, I set out to develop a paediatric orthopaedic service, which was much needed in the area. With Peter Burridge, a friendly anaesthetist who shared my interest and with other colleagues, we formed a team, and within two years, we had it up and running.

***

In November 1992, after eighteen years in exile, we returned to Chile for the first time. Pablito, our new baby son, was six months old and although my birth country is far away – some 7,200 miles to Santiago– he travelled well. We landed mid-morning; our families and many friends and relatives were waiting for us. It was an emotional reunion and after clearing customs, we headed, in a convoy of cars, for Villa Alemana where my parents-in-law lived. As we left Santiago behind, it was a glorious day and travelling along, I appreciated the many changes: wider roads, more buildings, but above all I noticed that people looked relaxed and happy, in stark contrast with 1974. Armed paramilitary police, *Carabineros,* were still patrolling the streets in great numbers. I could still, after all those years, experience a feeling of apprehension, when near them. I noted that their attitude, their bearing, was still menacing. Altogether, we spent three weeks there which went by far too quickly. We ambled through the streets of Valparaiso, the port city, and boarded the funicular up the hills to gaze at the sea and the ships in the distance. We visited Viña del Mar, the tourist resort, showing our children all the sites.

Too soon, it was time to head south to Concepción to see my family. My relatives were all waiting at my parents' house next to Dad's timber yard. It was an unforgettable day full of emotion and loving embraces. A few days later I visited Auntie Teresa to thank her for her *vital* help when I was a prisoner in the *Quiriquina* Island. Looking back, she had been like a second mother to me, from those years when I was away from home, finishing my secondary education, in Concepción. I met with Uncle Jorge, the socialist doctor and my guardian during my pre university years, who had been a political prisoner, tortured and eventually released and who had gone into exile, initially to Oxford, England and later Mexico City. I paid a visit to Dr Yañez, who had cured my little brother of his bone infection. I dined with several colleagues of my class, who over the years, had taken care of my parents' ailments and I thanked all of them but in particular expressed my gratitude to Alfredo Pugh and Alexis Lamas. Eighteen years is a lifetime and, sadly, my classmates, except for Alfredo, felt like strangers.

Thereafter, I went back to the campus of my university. It was a bright, sunny day and there were many students about. I stood under the *Medical School Arch* that is the central entry to the campus, leading via a wide pedestrian avenue, to the *Campanile* and the *Forum.*

Without a warning, my mind suddenly took me back twenty years and for a magical moment, I travelled back in time to the summer of 1972. It was a real and astonishing experience, but at the same time fleeting and so incredible, that it is difficult to put into words: the cloudless blue sky; the paved ground where I stood; the magnificent arch above me; and the big trees lining the avenue, were all the same. What had changed were the faces of the students walking by – the youthful smiles that I was longing to see – the long forgotten laughs that I desired to hear and feared would never again be. The realisation of that fact swiftly brought me back to the present.

I walked to the lagoon to see my kin – the black necked swans. There were several couples and little cygnets too, riding on the back of their mothers and fathers. I approached a male swan at the edge and softly told him of my flight so long ago. I told him of the mountains, the pampas, and the new oceans and of a country, far away, where most swans are all white and bigger, and belong to a human Queen.

'*Sorry, friend,*' he replied, '*but I am too young to know of your forced flight.*' And immediately he asked: '*What does the human Queen do?*'

'*Protect all swans, whatever their colour,*' I answered.

He looked at me with incredibly sad eyes and said, '*We need a Queen here, to protect us against the water pollution that is killing us.*'And without waiting for my reply he slowly swam away.

***

It was a wonderful summer and everybody loved Pablito. We toured the scenic south of Chile in a car that our generous friend Fernando Novoa, from the city of Talca, had lent us. We showed the children the lakes, the rivers and waterfalls. We went to the sea and swam in the cold waters of the Pacific; travelled through majestic forests; marvelled at the gracefulness of a bamboo called *colihue*; admired the beauty of the *copihues* – the national flower; gazed at the mountains and endless volcanoes of the cordillera. We got as far as Puerto Montt before going back to Talca to return the car and spent a day with Fernando and his family.

***

Back in England, our new baby brought us enormous pleasure, as too did the visits of our two sons who were now studying in London and Cambridge. By early 1993, we had decided to have a brother or sister for Pablito and we were fortunate that Steph came into this world in November. She was a treasure and her arrival marked a very special moment in our lives: we had a daughter. Twenty years earlier, I was prisoner on an island in my country. Now we were safe and secure in England and the next few years were filled with the joy of bringing up our babies, without fear and in a lovely home.

In 1995 I was nominated by a patient for a Rochdale Council award for services to children, which I proudly received at the Town's Hall. This beautiful building resembles a small Westminster. Peter Burridge, the anaesthetist, attended. He had become a good friend and he and his wife and two daughters came to our home and we went to his, in Bamford, several times. He was a serious cyclist and very fit. Sadly, whilst doing a charity cycle ride from John O'Groats to Lands' End, he felt unwell, collapsed and died. Unbeknown to him he had one of those rare heart conditions that can lead to sudden death in young adults. I have since learned that a number of sportsmen and women have suffered a similar fate and subsequently a campaign was launched for the screening of all competitive athletes to prevent further unnecessary deaths. Presently, school screening has only been conducted routinely in Italy – for twenty years – and according to British cardiologists it has saved lives. At the very least, I would recommend that anybody who is planning to run a marathon or similar exploit to Peter's should discuss this subject with their doctor and have an ECG before commencing training. After all, what can be more tragic or regrettable than losing a loved one in the prime of life only to learn later that it could have been avoided?

***

Whilst in Rochdale I sponsored two Chilean doctors from Santiago to work as Fellows and they were a great success. They brought their wives and children and our lives were enriched by their company.

The first to arrive was Sacha Bittelman, a Hip and Knee Fellow who stayed for two years. He was an excellent surgeon with good training and experience in Chile and he carried out a large number of hip and knee replacements under my supervision. A few weeks after settling into his job, he asked why hospital care at Rochdale was split between two sites. He could not understand the rationale of having an Accident Department at the Infirmary and the surgical, medical, obstetrics, paediatric and Intensive care wards over at Birch Hill Hospital – two miles away. I explained to him that it made no sense to me either and that since my appointment I had been campaigning to have all the services at one site. With the backing of my consultant colleagues, I had formed a Hospital Action Group which attracted local public support. We held meetings, which were attended by the Dean of the Manchester Medical School and the Chair of the Regional Health Authority. We also made a video which showed the inappropriate and unsafe journey of a real patient with multiple injuries arriving at the Accident Department at the Infirmary, receiving emergency treatment, including intubation – a tube down the airways to deliver oxygen – and then being taken by ambulance to the Intensive Care Unit at Birch Hill. I remember showing this overtly critical video in the elegant Board Room of the Infirmary and the expression of disbelief on the faces of the assembled dignitaries.

The second sponsored doctor was Samuel Concha, a Spinal Fellow, and like Sacha a graduate from the University of Chile and a trained orthopaedic surgeon. He stayed a couple of years before returning to Chile.

At this time I also sponsored Esteban, a young Mexican doctor and the son of my neurosurgeon friend from Puebla. Of course, he spoke perfect English, his mother, Marjorie, being English, and he was very popular in the Department; everybody liked Esteban.

***

In 1996, Management decided to close the paediatric ward at the Infirmary. The children with fractures or orthopaedic ailments needing hospitalisation would in future all be managed at Birch Hill hospital. It would mean that after coming to the Accident Department they would be moved by ambulance to the other site. It was madness. It was a money-saving exercise and my arguments against the closure failed to make a difference. I therefore decided to leave. There was a post becoming vacant at Tameside Hospital in nearby Ashton-under-Lyne and I applied for it. There was competition but I was short-listed, interviewed and offered the job, which I duly accepted. I believe that what made the difference was that I was an experienced consultant able to care for patients of all ages. With sadness, I tendered my resignation and I left Rochdale in March 1997.

***

It is noteworthy that during this period, whilst visiting England – and no longer in power – General Pinochet was indicted by Baltazar Garzon, a Spanish judge, for conspiracy in the murder of Spanish citizens in Chile by agents of the junta, conspiracy to commit torture and the disappearance of hundreds of men and women, among other charges. Thus, on October 8, 1998, London Magistrate Ronald Bartle committed the ex-dictator for extradition to Spain. Bartle's ruling was particularly significant for its treatment of the conspiracy charge and of the allegations of 1,198 'disappearances' carried out by Pinochet's regime.

The arrest of the monster caused jubilation in Chile and amongst the community of Chileans in exile across the world. In London, the Chilean Solidarity Campaign worked tirelessly for his extradition. France, Belgium and Germany joined Spain in requesting the same. Jeremy Corbyn, the current Labour Party Leader, added his voice to the requests for handing over the ex-dictator to Spain. Mr Corbyn had travelled through South America and visited Chile in 1969 – journeying the length of the country – and had witnessed the wave of optimism that preceded Allende's election. After the coup, he steadfastly supported the Chileans in exile and it was fitting that he delivered to the British Government the 30,000 public signatures requesting Pinochet's extradition.

The ex-tyrant, who, after resigning from his Commander in Chief post in 1998, had metamorphosed into a senator for life, claimed to have diplomatic immunity. He had the support of ex-prime minister Margaret Thatcher who, during her year's in office, had readily emulated Pinochet's economists' free-market policies, from pensions to education and health reforms, to the sale of state own companies. Lord Lamont, the Conservative Ex Treasury Secretary, also declared himself a champion of the murderer, even travelling to Chile where he was received with open arms by Pinochet's supporters. Jeremy Corbyn was asked to go to Chile to counter Lamont's support for the General, and he obliged, once again showing his unflinching commitment to those requesting that the General faced his accusers in a Law Court.

In England numerous legal rulings took place, some in favour of and others against the extradition. Hopes were renewed when the Law Lords dismissed an earlier ruling by the High Court that as a former Head of State, the general was immune from prosecution. Lords Steyn and Nicholls and the deciding tacit judgement by Lord Hoffman created legal history. Eventually, however, it was left to Jack Straw, then the Home secretary, to have the final say. Against the express request of many organisations, relatives of victims from Chile and countries around the world, lawyers representing several governments, and individuals such as Jeremy Corbyn, Mr Straw allowed the accused General to return to Chile. We now know with absolute certainty that Pinochet personally ordered the execution of many, and conspired in the torture, execution and disappearance of more than three thousand. Mr Straw made his decision, on the basis that the despot was too old and infirm to stand trial. However, the General's infirmity was a sham, and the moment he stepped onto Chilean soil, in March 2000, he miraculously got up from his wheelchair and walked away from the plane.

Nevertheless, his arrest and detention for 503 days in England badly dented his image of invulnerability, and soon he would be facing renewed writs from relatives of his victims, because the courts in Chile no longer considered him immune from prosecution.

Chapter Eight

TAMESIDE HOSPITAL

'The National Health Service was not an experiment, nor was it a mythical utopia, for over fifty years it has provided high quality care to most patients most of the time. It has been the envy of and copied by many other countries, but now it has been made into a laboratory for market-based prescription.' – **Allyson M Pollock**, *Professor of Public Health, Queen Mary, University of London. From her book: NHS plc. The Privatisation of Our Health Care.*

My interview for the consultant post at Tameside had taken place in the hospital's Board Room in Fountain House, a solid single-storey stone building which has since been demolished. At that time I did not know that it had one-time formed part of a Union Workhouse and was an integral feature of the history of my new hospital.

The hospital's location can be traced back to that workhouse which was built in 1849 adjacent to the south end of Fountain Street. It accommodated 500 inmates. The buildings were constructed of local stone from the nearby Barrack quarries. The workhouse overlooked what is now called the Boating Lake.

Life inside a workhouse was harsh and unforgiving. Men, women, children, the infirm and the able bodies were segregated. The food was mainly gruel, a form of watery porridge served three times a day. Charles Dickens describes the grim conditions endured by inmates in his celebrated novel, 'Oliver Twist'. For much of the next century, Union Workhouses comprised some of the most austere buildings in their localities and, judging from a 1905 photograph, the Ashton Workhouse was no exception.

The Ashton District Infirmary was founded in 1861 by Samuel Oldham and Henry Darnton. It provided a place for 'the relief and cure of the sick and the poor living within three and a half miles of Ashton Town Hall'. In 1948, with the creation of the National Health Service by Aneurin Bevan, the Infirmary and Workhouse merged to form the Ashton-under-Lyne General Hospital. In the 1970s, the Darnton Building, by Darnton Road, which had been part of the old Infirmary, housed the Children's surgical wards and theatres, as well as the Casualty and X-ray Departments. The Stamford Building, constructed in the 1900s out of Accrington brick, accommodated the adult surgical wards, the gynaecology ward and surgical theatres. Thereafter, following the establishment of Tameside Metropolitan Borough Council in 1974, the hospital was re-named Tameside Hospital.

***

The subsequent demolition of the Stamford Building and Fountain House was, for me, and I am sure many others, a sad period. From the lofty position of my office on the third floor of the Charlesworth Building, I watched the Stamford Building being razed to the ground little by little. In the words of UK Exploration Forum: *'It was ultimately the sad demise of a thousand stories, laughter and crying, blood and tears, brought into rubble by the arm of the developer.'* Replaced by the large Stamford car park, however, it is a huge consolation to me that the Pennine hills surrounding Ashton and nearby Stalybridge can now be seen in all their majestic beauty.

In a similar manner, from the windows in front of the orthopaedic theatres in what was then the original Hartshead Building, I saw Fountain House and its stone outbuildings, disappearing into oblivion. They were the last vestige of the Union Workhouse. More recently, the Darnton Building and its adjacent land were sold and, following demolition, a large Nursing Home was built on the site, leaving the Silver Springs Building, where the Headquarters of the hospital – a Foundation Trust since 2008 – are presently located, as one of the few surviving remnants of the old Ashton District Infirmary.

***

The Health Investment in Tameside Project, known as HIT, which replaced the Stamford Building, Fountain House, the old laboratory and the old Post

Graduate centre, involved a combination of funding.

The initial work employed *public capital* – in other words it was paid for without incurring future debt – and was carried out between 2007 and 2008, providing an entirely new building with offices and laboratories for pathology, microbiology, haematology and biochemistry; a partly refurbished and partly new education and training centre; and a multi-storey car park.

The main hospital build, however, named Hartshead South, was financed under a *Private Finance Initiative (PFI)* scheme. A group of private investors raised £77.2 million in the open market and paid Balfour Beatty, a construction firm, to build it. This is now leased to the Foundation Trust which is under contract to pay an Annual Service Charge, inclusive of maintenance, from October 2010 to August 2041. All told, by 2041 the Trust will have paid more than £300 million in charges.

The scandal of the true cost of hospitals (and schools) built under PFI schemes has been a matter of intense debate since 1997 when the first PFI building projects were launched by the newly elected Labour government. They were introduced despite widespread criticism in terms of its cost, efficiency and effects on services. By the year 2000 the intellectual case for PFI had been widely discredited. It is not surprising that many Trusts have found it impossible to keep up paying these annual charges, often referred to as 'Unitary Payments' (UP).

Early in May 2010, in my capacity as Chairman of the Senior Medical Staff Committee at Tameside hospital, I met with a partner of PricewaterhouseCoopers LLP (PwC), the major international accountancy company, contracted by the Trust to give advice – at a cost of almost £0.6 million – on how to solve its financial crisis. I was there representing my colleagues and had prepared a list of twenty-five questions, fifteen of which were for PwC.

Question 12 read: *PwC are the Trust's annual auditors accountable in this respect to the National Audit Office. Did PwC anticipate the serious financial problems of THFT?*

Question 14 was: *Has PwC given consideration to a potential conflict of interest when they have now been asked to come and advise THFT how to save £8 million to bridge the gap of £20 million?*

Question 17 asked: *Is PwC prepared to pay compensation to patients or the families of patients if directly or indirectly – proven in a Court of Law – have been affected by measures proposed by them?*

Upon reading the full list of questions, the partner was unprepared to comment, maintaining that it was his understanding that our meeting was designed to be of only an informal nature. However, when pressed whether the advice provided to the Trust would be available as a written document, he revealed that this would not be the case. After a short while the meeting, which was not entirely unconstructive, drew to a close, following which I emailed the Chairman of the Board, the Reverend Tim Presswood, asking for his response to the other ten questions concerning the PFI. Rev. Presswood replied on 2nd June 2010 answering in full. He revealed that the annual PFI charge to the Hospital – the Unitary Payment (UP) – would amount to £5.6 million in 2010-11, of which Tameside Hospital Foundation Trust (THFT) would be responsible for £3.7 million and that this would increase to £9.6 million in 2011-12 with THFT contributing £7.9 million. His response to the following question, I found particularly noteworthy:

In view of the present financial situation of the Trust, and bearing in mind the well-known cases of Foundation Trusts that have fallen into difficulties with repayments over the last few years, did the Financial Director and the Chief Executive Officer of the Trust and the Board collectively, properly consider the availability of funding throughout the whole duration of the PFI contract?

In answer, the Chairman maintained that:

The PFI scheme was the subject of a full business case which considered the full payments associated with the scheme. At the time we took the decision, it was the right decision. Your question is flawed, as it is asking if we had known then what we know now. The statement made in introducing your question is effectively resetting the parameter of the decision taken, citing information that was not available at the time.

It is a fact that warnings regarding the affordability of PFI contracts have been around for at least fifteen years, but were ignored. I leave it to the reader to draw his or her own conclusions to the Trust's responses. Now we have a 'state of the art' new building called Hartshead South but it will cost millions from the hospital budget every year for the next twenty-six years.

I believe that since 1948, the funding of Tameside Hospital has been significantly less than hospitals in more prosperous areas and its finances were precarious long before annual payments to PFI investors.

The historical underfunding has meant a lower ratio of nurses and doctors per one hundred beds and less capital funding for essential equipment year after year. This has been made worse by the annual efficiency savings (also referred to as Cost Improvement Programmes or CIPs) which have led to a relentless closure of beds. Presently, a CIP of 8% of annual budget is required, about £9.7 million every year at Tameside Hospital. After the Keogh review, in 2014, a government injection of £14.3 million was required to help to balance the books. Foundation trust regulator, Monitor, pronounced the hospital 'clinically and financially unsustainable' in September 2014 and revealed plans to spend up to £2 million sending an international consultancy firm to the hospital to help fix the problems and find a long term solution for the patients. (See Epilogue)

***

My practice as an orthopaedic surgeon managing patients of all ages continued until my retirement on 19th October 2014. Occasionally, I had to examine new-born babies because of concerns about their hips or other joints, or – very rarely – in the event of a fracture. Over the years, I treated many children from Rochdale because there is no longer a service there. Fortunately, young children with bone infections such as my brother Jorge had are now uncommon but they still occur and must be managed and treated as emergencies.

What positive experiences from Tameside Hospital do I take with me into retirement?

Firstly, the appreciation shown by my patients and their parents and relatives in respect of my professional work and their understanding of my occasional shortcomings when complications occurred and things did not go exactly according to plan. Secondly, the verbal and written support given to me by many hospital employees over the years, which was a tremendous encouragement. Thirdly, the backings for my campaigning work from innumerable members of the public in the form of personal letters and letters to the press, some of which I describe in this book. Fourthly, the exceptional devotion to duty and hard work of staff in the Fracture Clinic, the Trauma Unit, the Elective Ward and the Operating Theatres, notwithstanding relentless cuts in resources. These were my clinical areas, but the same applied to the A & E and all other wards and units. On many occasions I carried out spots checks to examine compliance with nursing staffing levels on wards during the night or in the early morning hours and I saw their dedication. Fifthly, the improvements driven by colleagues and the myriad examples of good practice which were second to none – the work of CT and MRI services springs immediately to mind. And finally the friendliness and good humour of those indispensable members of the team sometimes referred as the 'invisible people' – porters, cleaners, canteen workers, receptionists, administrative personnel, volunteers and many more; I listed them all in my farewell speech.

***

In the next chapters, I will recount my thoughts and experiences at Tameside Hospital, during the twelve year period prior to my retirement, during which time my professional commitment to patient care brought me increasingly into conflict with the hospital management. I firmly believe that the higher the level of public awareness, the more it empowers users of the health services to challenge poor and unsafe practice. Some of the consequences of Cost Improvement Programmes – bed closures and reductions in the number of nurses, secretaries and doctors in order to 'balance the books' – can be seen in the relevant diaries and narrative that follows.

Part 2

Chapter Nine

DIARIES 2002 TO 2004

'Our lives begin to end the day we become silent about things that matter.'
– Martin Luther King Jr.

INTRODUCTION

Although I had six years of experience as a consultant when I moved to Tameside, in many ways, it was as if I had to start all over again. One 'positive' was that all services were on a single site; another was the friendliness of the people with whom I came into contact.

Within a couple of years in post, I had introduced some new practices: notably, the 'walking to theatre' of patients able to do so, rather than using a trolley. This was routine at Rochdale and after a pilot period Tameside adopted it. At that time the elective orthopaedic ward, the trauma wards, the children's orthopaedic ward and the theatres were all in close proximity, on the first floor of the Hartshead South Building. It was an ideal layout. Little did I know that in years to come it would all fall apart as a result of ward closures.

After a few years I began to realise that in many shifts the nurses were over-stretched and over-wrought because, quite simply, there were not enough of them. On occasions I saw experienced nurses in tears as a consequence of the pressure and their inability to provide even the most basic care due to understaffing.

***

In January 2002, I wrote to Mr Dylak, the Nursing Director and, thereafter, I began to raise formal concerns regarding the nurse shortages in the orthopaedic wards. As a result, nurses devised a pro-forma to complete when shifts were under-staffed.

In October 2002, I was nominated by my colleagues to be the next Lead of the Division and I wrote to Mrs Green, the Chief Executive, highlighting that my first priority, if selected, would be to prepare a plan to improve the nursing establishment. A subsequent external *nursing staffing review* commissioned by the hospital and finalised in July 2003, unequivocally confirmed that my worries were well founded, but it was kept under wraps until 2004 and the full report was never even discussed by the Board. Unaware of its findings, in October 2003, I sent a detailed report to the Commission for Health Improvement, the regulator for hospitals in England at that time. It was based on fifty pro-formas completed by nurses and I requested an investigation. It was acknowledged but regrettably there was no investigation and my effort was in vain. A year later there was no improvement.

***

As if living in a parallel universe, in their Introduction to the hospital Trust's Annual Report 2003/2004 the Chairman and the CEO of the Trust described the 'tremendous achievements of the last 12 months which culminated in the hospital receiving three stars (the highest level) in the NHS Performance Ratings.' The Report, quite properly, described the improvements that had been implemented in several areas of the hospital but failed to mention the prevailing situation on any of the wards. In my view, it lacked candour, openness, and transparency. On the matter of nurse staffing levels, the fifty-six page report contained one solitary paragraph alluding to the *external review* without reporting its findings or affording it the critical importance it deserved. Moreover in relation to the high mortality rates that the hospital was experiencing, the Annual Report sought to dismiss them as 'misleading' – simply the result of the way in which the data is recorded and as consequence of high levels of deprivation in large sections of the local population –

ignoring the fact that standardization of the figures had already factored this in. No correlation was made between the inadequate nurse staffing levels on the wards, the insufficient number of junior doctors and the high number of deaths and it is noteworthy that in the glossy Annual Report the word *'compassion' was nowhere to be found.*

CAVEAT*

During those years, Wards 2 and 4 were Trauma wards and had twenty-eight beds each. Ward 3 was an Elective Orthopaedic ward, also twenty-eight bedded but only twenty-one were for inpatients. The remaining seven were for day-care patients. This arrangement ceased to exist in 2008 because of bed closures under the euphemism: *'surgical redesign.'*

*In the diaries, sometimes I refer to Wards 2, 3 and 4 – collectively – as the 'orthopaedic' wards.

DIARIES 2002

17th January 2002
Today, as I did my rounds in Ward 3, a senior nurse informed me that last night there were only two qualified nurses and not a single auxiliary nurse on duty. The ward was full with thirteen surgical, eight medical and seven orthopaedic patients.

I have noticed over the last few months that frequently nurses have been asked to care for fourteen patients each. I share her concerns that these ratios are unsafe and to make matters worse nurses are looking after medical and surgical patients, which is not their area of expertise.

19th January 2002
Wrote to Philip Dylak, the Nursing Director (ND), yesterday, regarding unacceptable levels of nurse staffing on the orthopaedic wards. I suggested the creation of a bank of nurses and I requested a meeting to discuss my concerns.

20th February 2002
I have not yet received a reply from the ND. Senior nurses in the three orthopaedic wards tell me that many shifts continue to be seriously under-staffed. In the mornings the situation is critical as the wards are extremely busy because doctors, from different teams, all come at once to do ward rounds and there are not sufficient nurses to accompany them. This causes many problems affecting patient care.

2nd May 2002
Received a letter marked Private and Confidential from the ND explaining that the Trust will continue to make every effort to secure a full nursing establishment in each clinical area. On the wards, nurses of all grades tell me that this is not happening.

25th August 2002

I read a copy of a letter from Staff Nurse CA from Ward 2 addressed to a matron, stating that adequate nursing care was not given to the majority of the patients in the late shift in her ward on the 17th August due to nurse under-staffing. Shocking!

1st October 2002

The Senior Charge Nurse of Ward 2 wrote to the Divisional Nursing Officer (DNO) following a ward meeting on Friday 27th Sept, regarding staffing levels. He highlighted the fact that on numerous occasions only two nurses were on duty for the early shift, posing a serious risk to standards of care. John is an excellent nurse, very experienced, a no-nonsense man. He has told me that patients are often unattended and at grave peril.

15th October 2002

Yesterday, at the Divisional Meeting of the Orthopaedic Department, the current Lead Consultant, Mr Ebizie and my colleagues nominated me to be the next Lead. I thanked them, accepted and proposed that I would write to the CEO with my vision for the Division. At this meeting, I once again formally raised my concerns regarding the low number of nurses on many shifts. The matron in attendance announced that the Trust had commissioned an *external nurse staffing review* and that the report is expected next year. The delay is unacceptable. In my letter to the CEO, Mrs Green, I will highlight all these important issues.

17th October 2002

I have written a three pages letter to Mrs Green re: Lead Consultant role. It is an important letter because it makes it absolutely clear that I plan to focus on putting the best interest of the patients first. I say that my first priority is to improve the quality of nursing care in the orthopaedic wards and in due course submit a plan aiming to increase the numbers of qualified nurses in wards 2,3 and 4. My second priority is to plan for an expansion of the Division by appointing more consultants. (See Appendix 1)

11th November 2002

I chaired the Divisional Meeting today as an acting Lead Consultant waiting for an interview for the position with the CEO. I informed the meeting that I have written to Mrs Green stating my priorities if post confirmed. I indicated that I have highlighted the problem of nurse under-staffing at a Coroner's inquest that I attended recently. The issue of inadequate numbers of junior doctors was also raised by my colleagues.

26th November 2002

I was formally interviewed by Mrs Green today for the post of Lead Consultant of the Orthopaedic Division. I had already written to the CEO to this effect. I explained to her that my focus was the patients' welfare and that resources should be found. I have been offered the post for a trial period of six months.

10th December 2002

Today I have become the Lead Consultant. My main priority is the quality of care to our patients in all clinical areas.

DIARIES 2003

20th January 2003

Morale among nursing staff is very low on all the three wards. They tell me that during many shifts patients are placed at serious risk due to under-staffing. Seven nurses accompanied me to the Nursing Director's office in the Darnton Building today. He had arranged to meet me to discuss my concerns, but I took them along to explain the issues first-hand. He was annoyed and refused to hear them but agreed to a meeting with them soon.

5th February 2003

A senior sister handed me a copy of a four-page handwritten letter to the ND, dated 30th Jan 2003. The letter highlights that she had written before, in 2001, and she had then been intimidated by managers as a result. *She stated that the decline in nursing levels went back to 1998.* The subheadings on the letter summarise her worries:

- Staffing levels.
- Bullying and intimidation of staff that raise concerns.
- Poor communication. As a result of staff shortages sisters cannot attend important meetings.
- Deterioration of standards: observations not done or done late; medications not given on time; pressure areas and wounds not monitored; *patients with epidural catheters not monitored as per guide etc.*

Sister M's letter ends with a warning that nurses are worried for the safety of their patients.

10th February 2003

Twenty-two nurses from all three orthopaedic wards attended the promised meeting with Nursing Director, Mr Dylak, to discuss the issues. I was present, as the new Lead Consultant, because I share their worries. It was agreed that the sisters will devise a Nursing Staffing Level Report (a pro-forma) to be completed when shifts are understaffed. The ND reminded us of the on-going external review.

24th March 2003

I have written to the ND today because looking at the Staffing Levels Reports filed by the nurses since the pro-forma went live a month ago, it is clear that there is a very serious problem. I hope and pray that he will take action immediately!

An example: Staff Nurse DW on her report for the late shift Sunday 9th March 2003 on Ward 3 wrote:

'There should have been three trained staff but there were only two. One of them unfamiliar with ward. Each responsible for fourteen patients.'

She detailed how patient care was affected: head injury observations not recorded regularly; sliding scale insulin not checked for over four hours; pressure relief not provided; clinical observations not recorded all shift; intra venous antibiotics not given on time.

2nd May 2003 Friday

After my elective operating list this morning and a quick lunch I went to the Clinical Governance Subcommittee meeting at 2.00 p.m. today, as the Lead Consultant representing the Orthopaedic Division. It took place in the upstairs Board Room in Fountain House. Attended by Mrs Green, the CEO, Mr Dylak the ND, Mrs L Lowe, the PCT representative, Mrs Rice, the Quality and Risk Manager, five Lead Consultants representing other divisions and chaired by Mr Dunningham, the Medical Director. When the Clinical Governance plan was being discussed for approval before its submission it to the Strategic Health Authority, I questioned why 'nursing' was *not* a Clinical Governance item. Mrs Rice, responded by saying that nursing comes within each Division and there was no need to have nursing matters as a regular and specific item of discussion at the Governance subcommittee, attended by Board members.

When the item, 'Commission for Health Improvement (CHI) and Hospital Star ratings', was thrown open for discussion, I explained to the chairman that

I was thinking of contacting the Commission to report my serious concerns regarding the risk to patients due to nursing understaffing, in particular after hearing that nursing matters will not be a regular item of discussion at the Governance Sub-committee. Hearing this, the chair used rather impolite language when referring to the CHI adding angrily that I should not report my concerns *to* the Commission, but to the relevant manager, to himself or to Mrs Green. I think that the CEO was rather embarrassed by the Chair's language but said nothing. I will continue to report my concerns internally but I will write to the CHI if no improvements take place soon.

24th July 2003 Thursday

Eventful day! This morning the interviews for a vacant consultant orthopaedic post took place and as the Lead Consultant, I was a member of the appointment panel. The other panellists were Mr Griffiths, the Director of Clinical Services, Mr Dunningham, the Medical Director, Mr Muddu, Consultant Orthopaedic Surgeon, Mrs Andrew, a Non-Executive Director and Mr R Checketts, a representative of the Royal College of Surgeons of England. There were three candidates and each was interviewed for 45 minutes and answered the same questions. My question related to clinical governance. After they had been interviewed the panellists gave their scores to the HR officer in attendance. One interviewee was outstanding and I was not surprised that he had scored the highest. Once this was announced the Medical Director immediately said that he was unhappy and that this doctor was not appointable. I stated my view that the rules were clear and that I disagreed with the MD opinion. At that point the MD became very angry and shouted: ' *over my dead body you will appoint him.*' His demeanour became intimidating and the panellists felt it.Mr Checketts tried to convince him that the panel choice should be respected. Undeterred the MD insisted and eventually he prevailed. I said that I was displeased and asked for my dissatisfaction to be noted.

This is the second time within the last two months that I have crossed swords with Mr Dunningham and I sense that he does not at all like to be contradicted or have his authority questioned, particularly in meetings attended by directors.

18th August 2003

Two days ago in the sister's office in the theatre the Medical Director told me in an abusive way that I had been sacked for my 'behaviour' at the consultant interview four weeks ago, and left the office before I could reply. I was shocked and bewildered and I phoned Mr Checketts, the only external person from the panel present that day, to ask his views on the matter. He remembered the occasion well and told me that, on the contrary, it was Mr Dunningham who had been out of order, and that he had tolerated his behaviour only for the sake of the unity of the department and to avoid an embarrassing report. He offered his support and I thanked him. Today I received a letter from the MD stating that on the advice of the HR department the Trust has terminated my contract as Lead Consultant. The reason given is my 'unacceptable' behaviour during the interview for a colleague consultant post. It is unfair and I am disappointed; I will consider my response.

23th August 2003

I have decided not to appeal against the decision of the Medical Director regarding his unfair dismissal of me as the Lead Consultant and his subsequent abusive behaviour. I arrived to this conclusion for a variety of reasons, not least that it would be divisive as it would cause embarrassment to the appointed consultant. Furthermore, even the NED in the panel, who after the interview told me that *she 'had heard good things about me'*, is now apparently backing the MD's allegations.On the other hand, not being part of management will allow me to speak and act with more freedom. Nurses and colleagues tell me that they are sorry that I have been sacked. I lasted eight months –two more than Mrs Green's provisional period.

4th September 2003

I sent a letter by e-mail to Mrs Green, the CEO, today, copying in the Finance, Nursing, and Medical Directors and the Chairman of the Board. I requested a meeting to discuss my concerns regarding patient safety.

9th September 2003

The CEO replied stating that the route to raise my concerns is via the deputy CEO/Director of Clinical Services, Mr Griffiths, or the Medical Director, Mr Dunningham. In fact, I have raised these issues at Divisional level, the Clinical Governance Sub-Committee and through numerous letters. I feel like I am going round in circles.

22nd Sept 2003 Monday

I met with the Coroner, at his Stockport Office today, because of my grave concerns about nurse staffing levels on Tameside orthopaedic wards.

He said that he was not surprised and he explained that he had requested the Chief Executive to see him for the same reasons. At the last minute, the CEO had excused herself and sent instead the MD and the ND.

He spoke kindly of the medical and nursing staff. He said: *'The situation is like that of a good football team but with bad managers.'*

I showed him the draft of the letter that I was thinking of sending to the Regulator – the Commission for Health Improvement. He asked for a copy.

After the meeting, my feeling was that he was just as concerned as I was. He specifically mentioned how patients' relatives had told him that their loved ones had not received adequate nursing care in such matters as feeding or turning to prevent pressure ulcers and in general had experienced poor care before dying.

24th Sept 2003 Wednesday

Attended the Annual General Meeting of the hospital. The Chaplain gave a well-prepared talk about the duties of the Trust towards its employees. The CEO pointed out that the Trust was performing as a two star Trust, soon to be a three star Foundation Hospital. There was no mention of the shortcomings in nursing issues or the crisis on the X-ray Department due to the lack of Radiologists. The presentations finished after 7.00 p.m. and only then did the Chairman asked for questions from the floor. (The meeting was due to end at 7.00 p.m.)

A man rose to his feet and began to talk about the treatment received by his 85-year-old mother after she was admitted with a broken hip. I listened intently to his account. It was soon obvious that he was not happy. He said that he could not understand how patients could be properly cared for with so few nurses. He added that over her long hospital stay – four months – he had come to realise that his mum was one among many elderly patients suffering as a direct consequence. He had spoken to other relatives and he was attending the AGM to ask the Board why this was happening. He was angry and the Chairman tried to placate him. Mrs Green intervened and said that his complaint was individual and the meeting was not a place to raise it. It was clear to me that this person had been right to ask for answers publicly.

After introducing myself, I requested that the Nursing Director answer 'Yes' or 'No' to the following questions:

'Do you consider it essential, i.e. vitally important, that after a major operation, frequent checks such as pulse, blood pressure, respirations etc. are carried out by nursing staff as instructed by the surgeon?'

He replied *in the affirmative.*

My next question was, *'Do you agree that if those observations are not carried out the patient's life is at risk?'*

He answered, *'No . . . maybe in a few occasions.'*

I said, *'I disagree. . .'*

At that moment, the Chairman interrupted saying that there was no time to ask any more questions. A young employee of the Trust rose and gave a little speech thanking the Trust for something. It looked to me like a staged ending. Upon leaving, I approached Mr Dylak and asked why he had done nothing to improve nursing care. I told him that patient lives were at risk. He shrugged his shoulders without answering.

25th Sept 2003
Met with Mr Griffiths, the Deputy CEO. He does not understand the implications of having understaffed wards. In addition, it was clear that neither he nor any of the Board directors are prepared to do anything about the suffering of patients mentioned repeatedly in the Nursing Staffing Reports. I gave him the draft of the letter I will send to the Commission asking him to pass it to Mrs Green. I added that I hoped she agrees at last to see me. During the meeting, the deputy CEO took notes. I had asked that my secretary comes along to take proper notes but he had refused.

30th September 2003
Attended the meeting of the Senior Medical Staff Committee today (SMSC), which is the body that represents consultants and senior doctors at the

hospital. I explained to my colleagues that I was writing to the Regulator to raise concerns regarding low medical and nurse staffing levels and the hospital's very high mortality rate, one of the worst in the whole country.

4th October 2003

Mrs Green wrote explaining that her deputy had briefed her and that the Trust was addressing the concerns I had raised by commissioning the Nurse Staffing Review; she would not agree to see me, however. I am frustrated that the CEO has not acted quickly to at least acknowledge some of the points raised in my draft report. How can these executive directors be so detached from what the patients and nurses are experiencing in the wards!

13th October 2003

Today, after working for weeks on the letter/report, I finally sent it to the regulator, the Commission for Health Improvement and copied it to the Coroner. It ended up 17 pages long and the presentation of the facts, I think, is clear. I will hand it to the Chief Executive on Thursday. (See Appendix 2)

16th October 2003 Thursday

Busy day! For the fourth Thursday in a row, I and two registrars saw more than eighty patients in the Fracture Clinic. The X-ray Department is always stretched due to having to process patients from A&E, the wards and various clinics including the Fracture Clinic and this causes delays so that some days my clinic drags on until 1.00 p.m. or beyond. On the wards, patients with fractures are awaiting surgery and therefore those attending the clinic needing operations must wait for a space in the busy operating schedule. The late finish to today's morning list in theatre delayed my afternoon trauma list by one hour with the result that it didn't end until 6.00 p.m. My last task of the day was to organise a transfer to Salford's Hope hospital of a 58 years old patient, with a massive central disc prolapse with *cauda equina*. Arrived home, really tired.

20th October 2003

Mrs Green has written to say that she is disappointed that I sent a report of my concerns to the CHI and that Mr Griffiths, the Deputy CEO, will liaise with the Director of Nursing, Mr Dylak and senior nurse managers to prepare a response. She mentions the external nursing review and the 'allegations'

I made at the Annual General Meeting and that in response the Trust has commissioned an audit of deaths on the orthopaedic wards.

9ᵗʰ November 2003
I received a 14-page response from Mr Griffiths which follows the structure of my report. On the whole, many of his arguments are unconvincing, for instance that the pro-formas were not received in time; that my opinions are subjective; that the patients were not being affected. He does not dispute the numerous responsibilities of a qualified nurse to individual patients that I highlighted on my report to the CHI. Concerning the external nursing staffing review Mr Griffiths acknowledges that it confirms the staffing *deficiency in the orthopaedic wards*. I am still waiting to receive a copy of the report.

12ᵗʰ December 2003
The total capital expenditure for essential medical equipment for the year 2002-2003, for the *whole* Trust, was £827,000. Yearly, each division submits to management a list with the equipment that needs renewing or purchasing. As I explained to Mrs Green in my letter over a year ago, the level of expenditure is wholly inadequate and managers are put in the impossible situation of 'robbing Peter to pay Paul'. Example – if the orthopaedic surgeons have theirs drills renewed the paediatricians will not get the new incubator they require. On the other hand, in the same year the Trust spent £ 0.5m in consultancy fees. Today I wrote to the Director of Finance asking for details of how the consultancy money was spent.

DIARIES 2004

8th January 2004

I have finally received a copy of the long awaited external Nursing Staffing Review by an Agency called Newburgh Technologies Limited and commissioned over a year ago by the Trust. It transpires that the report was finished and presented to the executives on the 10th July 2003. The report is damning, which most likely explains why Mr Dylak, the ND and Mr Griffiths, the deputy CEO have sat on it for six months. The Agency uses what it calls Teamwork Methodology that is based on an answer to the question: How many nurses are required in this ward to achieve a certain level of care?

Teamwork care levels are expressed as a number from one to six, as follows:

Level 1 = Dangerous; Level 2 = Barely safe; Level 3 = Less than adequate; Level 4 = Adequate; Level 5 = Good; Level 6 = Excellent.

The Report says that the achievable Teamwork care level based upon the current nursing establishment in the three orthopaedic wards is as follows:

Ward 2: Level 1 (Dangerous);

Ward 3: Level 2 (Barely Safe);

Ward 4: Level 2.4 (between Barely Safe and less than adequate).

What really saddens me is that I am sure that patients have died because of a lack of action. The Directors have known for six months that in Ward 2 the level of care achievable with the nurses available was *Level 1 (dangerous)* yet they did not act on it immediately and have certainly not communicated the findings to the nurses on the ward or to me.

15th January 2004

I have found time today to reply to the Financial Director after his e-mail on 29th December. He says that the consultancy fees were related to the Health Investment in Tameside (HIT) and Private Finance Initiative (PFI) projects. I asked clarification regarding an item labelled 'other' totalling £2.8m.

27th January 2004

The Nursing Director has written to me admitting that the external review has identified a 'shortfall' in nursing staff that is now being addressed. I must probe deeper and ask why he procrastinated on the findings of the external review, which confirmed unequivocally what the orthopaedic nurses have been telling him and his senior nursing officers for years. I will write to him saying so.

20th February 2004

Mr Dylak has replied saying that the findings of the external report needed to be 'validated' as an excuse to explain the delay. So much for transparency and accountability, so much for compassion and care! He says that the Trust has set Level 4 (Adequate) as the baseline standard for all clinical areas. On the matter of many good nurses leaving because they feel that they are unable to provide safe care, he writes, *'I do not regard turnover as necessarily negative. Indeed, some turnover is quite healthy as it can demonstrate that staffs are developing their professional career.'* Well, that says it all. No small wonder that Tameside continues to have such a bad reputation.

4th March 2004

Shifts continue to have fewer nurses than planned and I am constantly being asked by nurses why nothing has changed. I wrote, therefore, to the Commission for Health Improvement, the regulator, today enquiring why I have not received a meaningful response since I sent the report in October last year.

27th March 2004

The Commission for Health Improvement replied saying that they are waiting to receive a copy of the Trust's Action Plan. I ask myself why the Regulator does not act now. Nurses are disillusioned and some think nobody really cares.

6th May 2004

The Financial Director has finally replied giving a full answer to my questions. He explained the delay saying that he wanted to do the exercise himself to find some useful information to improve this year accounts.

10th May 2004

I received a letter from an organisation called the Healthcare Commission. It has replaced the Commission for Health Improvement. It states that following receipt of the external review report, the Trust's Action Plan, and details of its implementation, it is now satisfied and has decided, therefore, not to undertake the investigation I requested. I feel totally betrayed by the regulators. I feel that I have let the patients and the nurses down. I am very demoralised.

28th July 2004

Staff Nurse BR told me that she was on duty on the late shift in Ward 2 on Friday 23rd and Saturday 24th and on both shifts, she filed Nurse Staffing Reports because they were understaffed. She and a newly qualified nurse on adaptation were the only two qualified nurses caring for fourteen patients each. What concerned her most was that *she had been unable to care and comfort a dying patient,* whilst struggling – and failing – let tend to the basic needs of her other elderly patients.

7th October 2004

Mr Corscadden, the Chairman of the Board has written to congratulate me for my 100% attendance last year, and to say that it has helped the Trust to achieve three star status. I wonder if he has any idea of what really happens in the wards as a result of shortage of staff.

20th November 2004

During my ward round in Ward 4 today, I was handed a Staffing Level Report by nurse SJ, faxed to matron M on 18th. On the late shift (1.00p.m. to 9.00 p.m.) there were only two qualified nurses and two auxiliaries caring for 28 very dependent patients. The shift should have had five nurses although, in my view even five are too few. I said that I will continue to fight for better staffing and urged that reports continue to be filed whenever necessary.

8th December 2004

There are still many shifts where there are not sufficient nurses to safely care for patients. Two days ago on the night shift, on Ward 4, two qualified nurses looked after twenty-eight patients. Courageous ZW, a grade E nurse, filed a report and faxed it to the matron at 03.30 hours in disgust! She wrote in the form, *'several confused patients attempting to get out of bed. Patients waiting a long time for attention.'*

Chapter Ten

DIARIES 2005 – BECOMING A WHISTLE-BLOWER

INTRODUCTION

Why did I blow the whistle to Rebecca Camber of *the Manchester Evening News* (MEN) in 2005 regarding dangerous nursing staffing levels and other aspects of poor care at Tameside Hospital, thus risking my career?

I did it because one day, one of my patients' post-operative observations were not carried out during the *whole* night due to staff shortages. My patient could easily have been found dead. This incident was the catalyst.

The day that the MEN published the story, I was summoned to Trust Headquarters and Mr Woodyer, the new Medical Director that had replaced Mr Dunningham, questioned me aggressively. I was alone and I was intimidated. During the days that followed, I thought that I would be suspended at any time. I knew that I had the support of my patients, family, members of the public, nurses, junior doctors and many consultant colleagues and so did not buckle under the pressure. I needed advice and because I have never been a member of the British Medical Association, I contacted the Medical Protection Society. The Society requested my personal file from the Human Resources Department in order to prepare my defence.

To my amazement, Dr Watson – advisor to the Society - discovered that on 24th October 2003, as an immediate response to my report to the Commission for Health Improvement, the previous Medical Director, Mr Dunningham, had written a letter to the Commission where he stated: *'Mr Peña's motives for writing this document would require the services of a panel of expert psychiatrists.'* In other words the then MD intimated that I was 'of unsound mind'.

Dr Watson also found out that on 10th November 2003, Mrs Green, the Chief Executive had written to Dr Chris Harrison, the Medical Director of the Regional Health Authority saying: *'In a nutshell, Mr Peña's concerns about orthopaedic staffing levels are valid. The Trust was receiving similar concerns from almost every other Division. . .'* the letter goes on to explain that the Board was concerned that I had not raised matters through the proper channels and ends . . .*'I hope that the Trust's response to Mr Peña i.e. Mr Adrian Griffiths letter of reply – and the other two enclosures with this letter are sufficient to assist you responding to the CHI.'* The enclosures were a letter from Mr Dylak (which was never disclosed) and Mr Dunningham's letter, mentioned above, clearly written to discredit me.

DIARIES 2005

5ᵗʰ January 2005

New year and new hopes that the Chairman and his Board, and in particular the ND, will finally become more understanding. One can only live in hope.

30ᵗʰ January 2005

The more senior sister in Ward 2 passed me a copy of a Staffing Level Report she filed on 27th of this month. I am extremely worried that a very senior and experienced nurse has once again felt compelled to raise concerns.

On the form, under the heading: *Which areas of care were most affected?* She wrote:

'Twenty-eight very dependent patients and immobile.

Five admissions/discharges during the shift.

Eight patients requiring feeding.

Unable to carry out basic needs for patients: 1) pressure area care; 2) nutritional needs; 3) continence care; 4) observations; 5) poor communication (no time); 6) unable to carry out four hourly observations. (All bench marking areas for essential care.)

Complaints from relatives regarding patient's nutritional status and having to wait for treatment, dressings and toilet facilities.

Staff unable to take breaks and leaving the ward late.'

At the bottom end of the form she entered: *'Following this I will be putting a letter of concern for patient care and staff safety to matron and Divisional*

Nursing Officer.'

15th February 2005

Reports continue to be written by nurses unhappy that in some shifts they cannot give an adequate level of care. On the late shift on 12th in Ward 2, brave Staff Nurse J.C. reported that there were not enough nurses once again. As a result all aspects of nursing care were affected. On the 13th the same happened and she filed another report. She wrote: *'seventy per cent of patients were confused and some disorientated and wandering. Yet trained nurses were moved to cover other wards. Each nurse had to look after fourteen patients!'*

26th February 2005

Patients admitted to Ward 2 remain at risk. Yesterday there were only two qualified nurses on the early shift, as one was asked to cover another ward. There were two very poorly patients – one had a cardiac arrest whilst the other was rushed to the High Dependency Unit. Patients care was below standard and unsafe as the nurses had to look after the neediest.

14th March 2005

A meeting of the Division took place today in the Orthopaedic Seminar Room. It was well attended including Mr Griffiths, the Director of Elective Services and Sue Wilson, the Divisional Nurse Manager. Mr Obeid, the Lead Clinician was in the chair. The shortage of beds, the delay in providing Physiotherapy for patients sent to other wards and the levels of activity were discussed. I once again raised my concerns that little or nothing had been done regarding under-staffing in the wards.

21st March 2005

I sent a letter to Mrs Green, the CEO, because I remain extremely anxious that post-operative patients with *epidural infusions* (for pain relief) are not being checked according to safe protocol. It is essential that observations are carried out every fifteen minutes for four hours – followed by hourly observations for the next ten hours. The charts show that this is not being done. I enclose with my letter several epidural charts (names blanked) I also sent reports indicating serious understaffing. I reminded her that the issues I raised in my report to the CHI in October 2003 have not been addressed by the Trust. I hope that the enclosed charts will convince her that there is a substantial problem. I send copies to the Chairman, Mr Corscadden, Mr Griffiths, Mr Woodyer, the

Medical Director and my orthopaedic colleagues.

22nd March 2005

When very ill patients go out of the wards for scans or X-rays, they need a nurse escort. This can take up to thirty minutes. During this period the wards become even more understaffed. This was reported by ZW, a staff nurse in Ward 4 last Thursday 17th, when on the early shift she found herself once again in charge of fourteen patients. The practice of moving nurses goes on. Two days ago on the early shift in Ward 2, a qualified nurse was moved to Ward 14. A report was filed and sent to the matron. I wonder what the nurses have to do to make the Nursing Director take notice.

26th March 2005

I feel heartened by correspondence from my colleague BM, the current Lead of the Orthopaedic Division who has responded to my letter of 21st to the CEO; he says: *'I have gone through this and agree with you. Staffing levels are a serious Clinical Governance issue to maintain the quality of care delivered to patients.'*

7th April 2005

Shocked and extremely worried that yesterday I found a patient dangerously hypotensive in Ward 3 with an epidural in situ. Blood pressure had not been checked for eight hours during the night, after a major operation. This person has been put at serious risk. I filled in an incident report, grading it red. I am shaken because I know that this patient could have died in spite of the fact that I have been highlighting these issues for a long time. Yet the directors have not addressed my concerns.

11th April 2005

Mrs Green has written to explain that the Nursing Director met with the nurse managers on 28th February to discuss the standards of nursing care in the wards. However no one informed the sisters or me of this meeting or what resulted from it. The CEO says that a further meeting is planned for 18th of April and we could meet thereafter. It all sounds as if the fact that I almost lost a patient a few days ago is of no pressing importance!

13th April 2005

An email from Mrs Green but it not re-assuring. The same language and same lack of urgency in acting on my concerns. She has indicated that she will meet with me on 11th of May, in other words in one month time. Why not an urgent meeting this week? I can only think that her advisors have no plans to increase the number of nurses for financial reasons, or worse – they believe that there is no problem. I first raised this matter in January 2002 with the ND, that is over three years ago and there has been no tangible improvement. Besides I know that the problem of nursing understaffing extends across the whole hospital. I am seriously considering going public. I have seen articles by a reporter of the *Manchester Evening News (MEN)* on health issues, and I may contact her.

22nd April 2005

Contacted Rebecca Camber of the MEN and arranged to see her at her office this Wednesday. I have given this matter a lot of thought and I am now committed to going through with it. I have discussed it with my family and they support me. I am taking a step into the unknown and they, like me, harbour anxieties about the consequences.

27th April 2005

I met with Ms Camber at the *Manchester Evening News* offices by Deansgate this afternoon. I explained about my serious concerns and that I had raised them both internally and to the regulator during the previous two years. She told me that before publishing she will contact the Trust today or tomorrow to allow them to respond. I said that it was fine with me. I did show her a few pro-formas completed recently by nurses, as examples of understaffed shifts, appropriately anonymised. At the end she asked me again if I was sure of my action and I confirmed that I was, if also a little anxious adding that it needed to be done for the sake of the patients.

3rd May 2005 Tuesday

I have read the article on the front page of the *Manchester Evening News*. The title in big black letters reads SURGEON WARNS OF PATIENT DANGER. Above it another heading: *Lives are at risk in hospital with staffing crisis.* Reading it makes me uneasy. It is a strange feeling that I have never felt before. It is of both fear and pride. Fear for my job but pride for actually doing what, in all conscience, I felt obliged to do. The article quotes the recent forms completed by nurses that I passed to Rebecca. The Editor summarises the situation: *'Surgeon is highlighting NHS failures.'* He adds: *'One wonders how many other doctors and nurses in hospitals up and down Britain are labouring in similar circumstances but have yet to find the courage to go public.'* The Editor's words give me heart.

4th May 2005
Stressful day! I was summoned to the Trust Headquarters to a meeting with the MD, Mr Woodyer and Mr Dylak, Nursing Director. Their questioning was aggressive and intimidating. I said that I had gone public after a patient of mine had been put at risk of death because of lack of observations after an operation. I explained that my concerns had been ignored. It was an awful meeting because the Medical Director came across as disrespectful and incredibly arrogant.

5th May 2005 Thursday
Rebecca called me yesterday to ask how I was. I told her about the unpleasant meeting but most people have been supportive. Today's article by Rebecca states that nurses from the hospital have contacted her. She gives an example of one nurse who has worked at the hospital for ten years but does not want to be identified for fear of getting the sack, who said, *'On bank holiday Monday one qualified nurse was on duty to look after a ward with thirty patients.'*

***

I learned today that the MD acted wrongly when he summoned me to Trust Head offices.

According to Trust Policy in these matters, he should have asked me to take a colleague or a friend. I feel drained and in fear for my job.

8th May 2005
Back at home with a handful of letters and cards of support. One of the cards is from Mrs Y saying: *'I sincerely hope you do not face suspension.'* My loved ones reassure me that I have done the right thing.

10th May 2005
I feel down, and full of doubts. Thankfully, an email from CD and NM, two consultant colleagues today has given me fresh heart. It reads, *'We are consultants in the same Trust and although you are not known to us personally, we are writing to give you our full support with regard to the recent article in*

the Manchester Evening News. It takes many months or years of frustration and some courage to give information as you did, to the paper. We too are extremely frustrated by the management's attitude to our nursing and reception staff shortages and have been battling for months with them. We replied to the Medical Director email last week to say that we support you and the problem should not be denied by the Trust.'

Colleagues tell me that the article in the MEN appeared in the *Daily Mail* and the *Daily Mirror* a few days back. Rebecca warned me that this would happen. Many reporters have called me, including from TV stations. I said that I would not comment any further.

14th May 2005

Encouraging! I have received many personal letters of support and phone calls from several colleagues, including Mr Franks, a surgeon who I met at Salford many years ago. I value them all enormously and I thank the senders. They give me the courage to carry on. One letter from Mrs Janet E Wass is important because she has written to one of the local MPs saying, *'I was present at the Annual General Meeting of the hospital two years ago when this surgeon stood up and publicly drew the attention to this problem. Clearly it has not been resolved and our lives have been put at risk.'* There have also been letters to the local papers, one of them from Ted Connolly, (I.Eng. A.M.I.C.E) in particular, gave me a big lift.

27th May 2005

It has been an awful day! Attended a meeting arranged to begin disciplinary proceedings. This time Michelle Holt, my secretary, was with me. The Medical, Nursing, and Deputy Human Resources Directors were there. Once again, I tried to explain to these people my serious concerns. The MD angrily interrupted – *'the purpose of this meeting is to investigate your actions and not your concerns.'* He asked me if I had received any payment for *disclosing* the information. *'Absolutely not,'* I replied. As before, his attitude was menacing, intimidating and disrespectful. Afterwards they asked me to wait for their decision. A few minutes later Mr Woodyer told me that the Trust will proceed to a formal Disciplinary Hearing and, still threatening, he added that I must not make any further disclosures.

8th June 2005 Wednesday

Yesterday's front page of MEN read *'Whistle-blower in fight for job.'* It sums up what is happening to me. I am to face a disciplinary panel for allegedly not following whistle-blowing policy. It also says that a memo has been sent to all hospital staff to stop them from going to the press. The editorial title says *'So wrong to shoot the messenger.'* Like the previous article, it gives me a boost. The Trust has admitted that my worries are legitimate. So why is it disciplining me?

10th June 2005 Friday

I am glad the week is over. It has been tough. I am at home thinking if I should have handled things differently. I am heartened by the fact that a large number of senior colleagues have come out in my support. One of them is Nick O'Mullane the Chair of the Senior Medical Staff Committee.

The Editor of the MEN last Wednesday once again is spot on. I wonder what Mrs Green and the members of the Board think of these editorials.

16th June 2005

I went to the extraordinary meeting of consultants at *Fountain House* called by Nick O'Mullane to discuss my situation. More than thirty consultants attended including ten physicians, eight surgeons, six anaesthetists, three radiologists, three A&E consultants and the BMA representative. I thanked them for speaking in my favour and for their support. Nick told me that it was the best attendance ever to a consultants' meeting in spite of the time at 6.00 p.m. and the short notice. The media will be informed. My colleagues backing is tremendous and gives me strength.

20th June 2005

Today I have received a letter posted in Dublin from Mrs Deidre Crombie. She says that in 1997 I treated her son Ciaran. She says, *'I have heard about the difficult situation you are under at the moment and I just wanted you to know that you have my support. It is a pity there are not more people like you, in this crazy world, who are willing to speak out for the good of others. My everlasting memory of you is the great care you took of my son, not just the medical side of things, but the after care and the emotional support. I always felt that you were there for us, and that meant a great deal, at that time. Ciaran has never forgotten you. . . stay strong. . .'*

28th June 2005

The latest issue of *Hospital Doctor*, the weekly, freely distributed magazine has two pieces on whistle-blowing. The first in the front page has six photos with the question: *'Why are all these doctors in trouble? Answer: 'For speaking out over poor practice.'* Inside there is a full-page article entitled Whistle-blowers Case File. The reporter begins by explaining what happens to those who are brave enough to blow the whistle on malpractice or poor management. Although the NHS is supposed to be encouraging a climate of openness, it is obvious that its words have not been matched by the action of trust managers.

27th August 2005

Letter from Dr D Watson, medico-legal adviser, saying that the Medical Protection Society will continue to assist me, although the Council has not yet discussed my case and its support is provisional. I have faxed him the letter of backing from my colleague Moez Obeid the current Lead Consultant in the Division of Orthopaedics. Dr Watson advised that Moez should be one of my witnesses. Jayne Clegg, a courageous staff nurse who worked at Tameside until recently has also agreed to testify.

2nd September 2005

Bundle from Ms Sheila Caldecott (SC), who has been supportive since I went to the press. As a result of her enquires Ms Caldecott has found out that in July 2003, the Department of Health issued a pack – called *'So long Silence'* – to all NHS Trusts – ordering them to develop and implement whistle-blowing policies. She has sent it to me and it would appear that the Human Resources Department has done absolutely nothing about it. Ms SC has discussed these issues with the Human Resources Director, with Sir Graham Cato of the General Medical Council and has written to her MP a very well put letter highlighting concerns regarding patient safety. Her support is extraordinary and invaluable.

2nd November 2005
9.40a.m.

I am at the Medical Protection Society offices in Leeds, seeing Dr Watson. It is clear that there are two separate issues to consider: the disciplinary hearing for allegedly not following Trust policies when raising concerns and the defamatory remarks about my state of mind by Mr Dunningham, the Medical Director in post in 2003, who has since retired.

7ᵗʰ November 2005

We had the regular monthly meeting of orthopaedic surgeons today. At the end, I explained about the Hearing on the 9th. All supported me again and I thanked them.

9ᵗʰ November 2005

It has been a strenuous day! Now back at home – recounting it after chilling out with a glass of wine. I needed it. Slept badly last night and got up at 6.30 a.m. Left for Leeds at 8.00 a.m. to pick up Dr Watson. On the way we spoke little about the hearing and more about ourselves. He used to work as an ENT consultant and he is originally from Belfast. He trained at Oxford for six years.

After meeting with staff nurse Clegg and Moez we went to the hearing at 1.00 p.m. Although we had made a request for Mrs Green to attend as a witness, she did not. The Medical Director from Trafford NHS Trust was the external advisor and, together with the Director of Planning and the Human Resources Director of the hospital, formed the adjudicating Panel.

The Trust Medical Director, Mr Woodyer, was the Prosecutor. The Director of Nursing, Mr Dylak, was witness for the prosecution. Dr Watson acted as Defence Counsel.

I thought Dr Watson did a good job constantly quizzing the Trust managers. The Medical Director from Trafford was fair but the MD of the Trust submitted his accusations against me unconvincingly. Nurse Clegg was a credible witness explaining well the common occurrence of seriously understaffed nursing shifts and the consequences for patients and staff. Moez told the panel that he categorically supported my actions. As the hearing progressed, it was clearly established that:

nursing shortages, the main issue, persisted from 2002 to 2005 continuously; the recommendations following the appalling findings of the external review on nurse staffing levels in 2003 had not been acted upon; the Trust was wrong to downgrade the incident – when my patient was put at grave risk – from serious to low. (In fact, it had been a 'near miss' and the Trust should have reported it to the Strategic Regional Health Authority); and that the Trust had failed to communicate the outcomes of the Teamwork Report, displayed a lack of transparency and glossed over serious issues.

I explained to the panel, that my reasons for speaking to the press were my concern that patients' lives were in jeopardy, that neither the CEO nor the Directors seemed to care about the issues and finally my belief that the power of the media and public opinion would change the situation for the better. After the hearing, I took Dr Watson to Stalybridge train station. I thanked him for his invaluable help. He thinks that it is unlikely that I would be suspended.

14th November 2005

I have not been suspended! Received a letter from the Director of Planning summarising the outcome and saying that I have been given a written warning that will remain in place for twelve months, during which time any misconduct could lead to further disciplinary action. The letter is two pages long and the Director goes out of his way to acknowledge the problems in the orthopaedic wards.

28th November 2005

Elizabeth Travers, an investigation officer for the Healthcare Commission has written stating that they are happy that the Trust has resolved the nursing issues in the orthopaedics wards, adding that following the external review, actions have been implemented in line with an action plan which included the following: regular matron ward rounds; staffing levels documented and protocol invoked when they are low; day care beds to be used for that purpose only; etc., etc. Thus the Commission is closing the case.

This is unbelievable! On the wards, the reality is very different.

Chapter Eleven

DIARIES 2006 TO 2008

*'The truth will set you free but it will make you miserable.' – **James Abram Garfield** (1831–1881), 20th President of the USA and a supporter of African-American Civil rights. Like Abraham Lincoln he also was assassinated.*

INTRODUCTION

By far the most important development in 2006 was the birth of a patients' pressure group supported by a local MP. It originated within the community as a direct response to the hospital's failings. The Coroner's public concerns regarding the circumstances surrounding the death of four patients were the catalyst: he had described care at the hospital as 'despicable' and 'chaotic'.

I was not in any way involved in the emergence of this group as I was not aware of it at all and I was not contacted. Below, I give a summary narrative from documents I have reviewed:

On 28th September 2006, Mr David Heyes, MP for Ashton-under-Lyne, wrote to Andy Burnham MP, Minister for Health, a long letter whose subject was: *Tameside Hospital – Coroner's Report*. In parts the letter reads:

'I can tell you that this is not the first time we have heard allegations such as this. Previous comments have come not only directly from members of the public but also from hospital clinicians but never have we heard such a damning indictment from such an authoritative source.'

'The hospital has also an appalling MRSA record. You know my view on this. I believe the privatisation of the hospital's cleaning services has been a major contributory factor...'

'Ironically the hospital has achieved a 3 star ranking and has been considered suitable to be granted foundation status.'

'Previous complaints have been dealt with through the hospital internal procedures.'... 'I hope you will agree that that's just not good enough and... We need an Independent investigation...'

Mr Heyes, however, was in for a disappointment. Rosie Winterton, the Minister with responsibility for the NHS in north-west England, replied on 5th October 2006 saying that NHS North-West was content with the Review Panel proposed by the Trust to address matters.

On 24th October Mr Heyes replied to Ms Winterton in a one and a half page letter saying that the press release outlining the hospital's response was attempting to shift responsibility on to the coroner; that an internal investigation would not restore public confidence; and that the Review Panel team included officials that effectively would be investigating themselves which casts doubt on the objectivity of the entire procedure. The MP ended the letter saying that he would welcome a meeting with the minister to discuss his concerns in more detail.

On 27th October 2006, Mr Heyes met with Mrs Green and Mr Corscadden, the Chairman of the Board and reported that between *eighty to one hundred* individuals had come forward with complaints and that the inaugural meeting of a patient pressure group would be taking place soon. The Trust proposed the creation of a Special Complaints' Panel comprising the Medical Director, the Nursing Director, a member of the Strategic Regional Health Authority, a member of the local Patient and Public Health Involvement forum and a member of Mr Heyes' constituency staff team.

The initial meeting of *Tameside Hospital Action Group* (THAG) took place on Friday 10th November 2006 at Albion Church, Ashton-u-Lyne, and was attended by 80 members of the public with another 20 sending their apologies. Mr Dylak, the ND, was present and tried to answer some of the points raised but feelings were running high and he was unable to finish. Two decisions were reached: to step up the demand for an independent inquiry into the hospital; and to set up a small steering committee to lead THAG and to formulate detailed aims and objectives and to prepare a campaign programme.

In their joint address in the Trust Annual Report for 2006/2007 the Chairman and the CEO wrote: *'in the autumn concerns were raised by the Coroner about some aspects of the standard of care provided. . . The Trust immediately established an Inquiry Panel. . . comprehensive implementation of the action plan will be a key task in 2007/2008.'*

The diaries I kept in 2006 are sparse because throughout the course of that year I was gagged by the Trust following the Disciplinary Hearing and I felt alone and depressed. It is not easy to be openly critical of an employer, particularly if that employer is a powerful organisation that has the resources at its disposal – taxpayers' money – to pay for expensive lawyers and runs a well-oiled propaganda machine with a staff of full-time employees. Moreover, colleagues start to become distant for fear that their support will be noticed by Directors and will damage their career prospects. Intimidation is a potent weapon in the hands of senior management and highly effective in silencing dissent, particularly at open forums and meetings.

***

Late in 2007 I became chair of the Senior Medical Staff Committee (SMSC), which meets every two months to provide a 'forum for debate and discussion for permanent medical staff' and exists 'only to support the best interest of the patients and the consultants in a democratic process.' There was no other candidate and I was nominated by the outgoing Chairman, Nick O'Mullane.

During that year, the Trust was experiencing, severe financial difficulties and to make matters worse, it was faced with the task of saving around £5m in efficiency savings – a compulsory annual requirement of the Health Department amounting in large part to an effective cut in services. It was my view that the Trust needed to explain openly that these cuts were *not* the decision of the Board as such and that if members of the public knew the facts, when they waited for hours on end in A & E or for a bed in the Medical Assessment and Admissions Unit (MAU), or weeks for a scan, and sometimes forever for a secretary to answer the phone, they would be more sympathetic and would not vent their anger at the front line staff – the nurses, secretaries, receptionists, radiographers, porters and so on who invariably found themselves in the firing line. I pleaded with the CEO to engage with the public but the Board was more preoccupied with its increasingly desperate quest to become a Foundation Trust – at almost any price, it seemed.

Sadly, during this period, the strain began to take its toll and my wife – with whom I had flown across half the world – and I grew apart and were later to separate.

DIARIES 2006

24th April 2006

I went to the Medical Protection Society (MPS) office's in Leeds today to discuss my appeal against the gagging. The hearing takes place next Wednesday. This time Dr Watson has agreed that we should have members of the public that support me, to testify.

26th April 2006

The appeal took place today. Met with Mrs Hilda Bridge of Audenshaw, Mrs Linda Drake of Ashton and Mrs Joyce Collins of Shaw' in Oldham, before the hearing, but the Panel refused to allow them to be witnesses and they were disappointed. I thanked them for their support. I am not optimistic that we will be successful.

28th September 2006

The Coroner, to whom I copied my report to the Commission for Health Improvement, in 2003, has criticised 'chaotic' care at Tameside Hospital. He told the *BBC*:

'I have held five inquests this afternoon and in four there has been called into question the care at Tameside Hospital. In most of them it's the nursing care, the basic care of people, things like giving them a drink, making sure their medication is with them. I don't think it is acceptable and I will certainly be bringing it to the attention of the Chief Executive.'

'When I see standards fall below those I think are proper and acceptable I am going to make my views known.'

'It is generally the case that the work done by surgeons and physicians is good work – it is the basic care that is lacking.'

Commenting on the death of one of the patients – a war veteran – a hospital spokesman said . . . *'we would assert that the apparent shortcomings claimed in relation to his care were actually manifestations of his clinical condition rather than defects in his care.'*

18th December 2006
I have read in the local newspaper, the *Tameside Advertiser,* that Mrs Green, the hospital's Chief Executive, has made a complaint to the Office for Judicial Complaints (OJC), which monitors the conduct of all judges, including Coroners. The OJC should finish its inquiry into the complaint by the end of February. Member of Parliament for Ashton-u-Lyne, Davis Heyes commented:' *I feel it's quite disgraceful that the hospital has taken this approach. It fits the theme where, when something goes wrong. It's always someone else's fault.'*

The Trust has taken this action in spite of the fact that last week it released the report of its inquiry panel that concluded that the care of the four patients highlighted by the Coroner, and others, had indeed fallen below standards. Poor attitudes, insufficient training, inadequate communication and non-adherence to clinical protocol are highlighted. On an accompanying statement the Trust said that it is determined that there will be no repetition in the future and devised an Action Plan with 26 recommendations. The crucial matter of appalling nursing levels on many shifts is not mentioned. Instead, matron's rounds and a *'committee'* to monitor nutrition are considered more important.

In my view, the Coroner has seen the deficiencies, the neglect and poor care of dozens and dozens of patients at the hospital over the years. He has a conscience, and he was right to voice his concerns.

DIARIES 2007

12th January 2007

Following the Coroner's criticism of the hospital, more than 120 families have come forward with complaints of sub-standard care. They have formed a hospital action group supported by David Hayes, a local MP.

31st January 2007

The chair of the action group has spoken out after a meeting of Tameside Council Health Scrutiny Panel. He said, *'I really don't believe the hospital understands that we are talking about people's lives here. They have not even considered those people and their feelings, they have not offered any of us counselling.'*

The NHS North West has since commissioned two independent experts to review the complaints and the hospital's internal inquiry and action plan.

9th March 2007

Good news in the *Tameside Advertiser* this week! Following a full investigation by the Office for Judicial Complaints (OJC) – a government watchdog which monitors the conduct of judges – the Coroner has been cleared of any wrongdoing and the OJC has dismissed all elements of the complaint (by Tameside Hospital) on the grounds that the comments made by the corner were entirely within his judicial capacity.

29th March 2007

More criticisms from the Coroner in the news today. Three more cases of appalling care to elderly and vulnerable patients. He is a brave man; he has my admiration and respect.

3rd April 2007

Last week's *Tameside Advertiser* says that a *'Damning independent report has* branded care at Tameside Hospital seriously deficient.' Nursing Professor D F and L T, Director of integrated Governance at North Cheshire Hospitals were asked by NHS North West to carry out the investigation. The coroner's criticisms and my concerns are wholly justified.

30th July 2007

I received a letter from the chair of the Board stating that he was delighted that I had achieved 100% attendance between 1st April 2006 and 31st March 2007. I have been working here since 1997 and never taken a day off. I hope my good health continues.

16th October 2007

Lack of beds remains a serious problem and I have written to the Lead Orthopaedic Consultant today.

5th December 2007

For the last two months I have been the new chairman of the Senior MedicalStaff Committee (SMSC), after being nominated by my predecessor in the role, Nick O'Mullane. I am beginning to realise the enormity of the job. Today I sent my colleagues an email asking for an extraordinary meeting of the SMSC to discuss the 'efficiency savings' for next year that will be around £5m. These annual cuts – because that is what they really are – have caused untold damage and the consequences are felt everywhere –from cutting admin and secretarial support, to radiographers, beds, nurses etc. At the last SMSC, we discussed this and colleagues agreed in principle that the public of Tameside and Glossop should be made aware of the *centrally driven* cuts, most of which are very damaging to our ability to provide good care. The meeting will take place on 16th January at the hospital's Conference Room in Fountain House. In my email, I am asking consultants that cannot attend to voice their opinion by email, simply ticking the box NO – *The public should not be informed*, or YES – *The public should be informed*. I have sent a copy to the CEO.

6th December 2007

Received email from Mrs Green, the CEO arguing against informing the public of the 'savings.' So much for transparency!

DIARIES 2008

5th January 2008

The hospital is once again experiencing serious problems of capacity regarding the admission of emergency and elective patients. This is happening because of the closure of wards, including *seventeen beds* in Ward 4, one of our trauma wards. As a result, all the morning operating lists are delayed and this has a ripple effect on the afternoon lists. There is also a shortage of junior doctors. Yesterday I operated without an assistant. In order to save money the hospital does not appoint locums when junior doctors are on leave.

I discussed these matters with the Lead Consultant yesterday. There is nothing he can do. Thus, I wrote to the CEO to complain about these two issues.

12th January 2008

Mrs Green has written back asking me to raise my concerns via the Lead Consultant although I have done this at Divisional Meetings and in writing on many occasions.

16th January 2008 Wednesday

Today, there was an extraordinary meeting of the SMSC to discuss if the public should be informed of the cuts. About twenty consultants attended and all but two agreed that the public should be told – in the form of a letter to the local newspaper, making it clear that the consultants and senior doctors' action was designed to lend support to the Board. At that stage of proceedings, Mrs Green and the Financial Director entered the room: addressing the meeting she spoke forcefully against informing the public, claiming that it would be bad for the reputation of the Trust and its application for Foundation status and demanding a new vote. In response, I maintained that, to allow a re-vote to take place, she and the director should leave, as their presence would be intimidating. Refusing point blank, she retorted angrily saying, '*This is my hospital and nobody can ask me to leave!*' When I asked my colleagues to raise a hand if they still supported the motion, only two of them stood firm. Satisfied, the CEO smirked, thanked them, and left.

21st January 2008 Monday

My colleague, the orthopaedic Lead Clinician, has written to the CEO regarding the lack of beds and junior doctors. He tells her he has met with Mr Wilkinson, the Human Resources Director (HRD) and Mr Woodyer, the MD and that his patience is running out because we cannot provide safe care to our patients.

25th January 2008 Friday

At last, we have a doctor at registrar level that is prepared to speak up regarding problems caused by junior doctor shortages, mismanagement in A&E, the lack of beds and the implications for training. Talked to him today and it is clear that he is a born leader and he will arrange a meeting with the Lead Consultant to discuss these issues.

19th February 2008 Tuesday

The registrar has given me copies of two letters he has written. In the first, dated 17th February, he writes to formalise concerns he raised at a recent meeting with the Lead Consultant, on behalf of the junior doctors. It is two pages long, highlighting serious issues he has witnessed in A&E including lack of leadership when dealing with patients with multiple injuries and insufficient number of nurses and doctors. He writes, *'All of this leads to my great concern that a critical incident is pending and patient care will be compromised.'* He also highlights the fact that the ward duties for the Senior House Officers are such that they do not have an opportunity to go to the operating theatre to learn surgery. Most of his letter is offering solutions to these issues. Seven orthopaedic junior doctors signed the letter.

The second letter, also dated 17th, is short and to the point, saying that he reserves the right to report to the Regional Programme Director if he feels that, his current appointment is unsatisfactory and will not allow him to progress to year three. As I thought after our first encounter, he is a natural leader and he has guts. I wish more doctors were like him.

14th March 2008

Mrs Green attended the Senior Medical Staff Committee two days ago and we discussed the issue of staffing. Between 2004/05 and 2005/06, the number of nurses has been *reduced by fifty*. Pressure on management forced them to increase numbers again, but overall we are still forty-one nurses down.

1st April 2008

A twelve-month, follow up report by Dame P F and Ms L C, both Registered General Nurses, has been recently published under the Title: Independent Review of services for Elderly people at Tameside General Hospital.

In my view, it is a weak report, with questionable methodology. Still, it points out several important issues particularly regarding staffing.

16th April 2008

Away from pressures of work, Linda Drake, a local resident that supported me in 2005 has introduced me to Julie one of her work colleagues. Like me, Julie likes the outdoors and we are planning to go on a trek soon, which I am looking forward to.

Chapter Twelve

DIARIES LATE 2008 – KILIMANJARO

INTRODUCTION

You may wonder why I mix my passion for the well-being of patients with my enthusiasm for trekking at high altitude. I will tell you. Looking back, after years of reporting and campaigning on issues of care quality and patient safety, the accumulated stress had built up to such a point that I needed the release of something truly physically challenging. Climbing provided me with that challenge and in the process enabled me to gain greater strength and confidence.

Lucien Devies, on his homage to Maurice Herzog the first man to climb an 8,000m peak, Annapurna, in 1950, writes, *'That wonderful world of high mountains, dazzling in their rock and ice, acts as a catalyst, It suggests the infinite, but is not the infinite. The heights only give us what we ourselves bring to them. Climbing is a means of self-expression. Man overcomes himself, affirms himself, and realises himself in the struggle towards the summit, towards the absolute.'* Annapurna is considered to be one of the most difficult of all mountains to climb, even more difficult than Everest, making Herzog's achievement quite extraordinary. He almost died, in fact, and upon his return it took him three years to recover.

***

By 2007, I needed to let off steam. In July that year I went to Chamonix, in the French Alps, on holiday with two friends. One day, on the way down, after a trip up the Aiguille de Midi on the funicular I decided to step off the cable car at Plan de l'Aiguille, at 2317 m, and walk down alone – not a very wise thing to do – but the sky was clear and for most of the time I could see Chamonix below. It was tricky in places but I held my nerve. I loved that experience. It was invigorating and inspired me to take to the outdoors with zeal.

***

My first opportunity to trek at altitude came when I went to Tanzania in Africa, to climb Mount Kilimanjaro raising funds for SCOPE, the British charity for cerebral palsy. You may have seen the small ads in magazines calling it the 'Experience of a life time'. Well, it was! I have supported SCOPE ever since.

To be able to trek such a mountain, however, I first needed to improve my stamina and walk regularly; this helped me to become stronger. When I was abroad and far away from home, I focused on the task ahead and rarely talked about or thought of my work.

I have been extremely lucky to stand on the summit of three of the seven highest continental mountains without, in the process, either me or any of my companions coming to any harm. After each climb, I have returned with more belief in myself. I needed to be tough, bodily and spiritually, because inevitably, my actions at the hospital led to a minority of senior managers and consultants launching personal attacks against me.

***

Another coping mechanism I employed to deal with stress was to learn French which, I did by enrolling at the French Academy, in Manchester in 2008, where I attended lessons for three hours a week. I am still learning French and like English, I will never master it. But my rudimentary French has come in handy on a few occasions. I remember boarding a high speed train in Paris with a colleague, an orthopaedic surgeon like myself. We were going to the Medical School in Tours and, as he sat down by the window, he casually put his ticket on the window ledge and watched it disappear into the gap between the glass and the frame. It was impossible to retrieve it and he was very concerned. With an air of reassurance, I said to him: 'No worries, I speak a bit of French and I will explain.' The ticket inspector was very sympathetic of my colleague's misfortune after I – with great effort – mumbled: *'mon ami ici, il a perdu son billet dans la fenêtre.'* We expected a fine but the inspector accepted the explanation. But when he checked my ticket he told me in French that the tickets were dated to be used exactly a week later! He did not make an issue about that blunder either – made by the organisers of our educational trip to France – and with a friendly smile he moved on. I hope that someone from Virgin trains reads this book!

DIARIES LATE 2008

PREPARATION FOR KILI

20th April 2008

I went to Mt Snowdon today for the first time. Up at 6.00a.m. and got to the start of Watkin Path just after 9.00a.m. There was little traffic. The road from Conwy to Betws-y-Coed was charming but in places narrow. After Capel Curig I began to see a range of impressive mountains before descending the A498 to the car park. Initially the trail was through woods and thereafter a farmer's road on open ground with a waterfall to the right. After the old quarry, it became a steep stone path and as the weather came in the sky became misty and grey. After two hours, it began to snow heavily and I could no longer see the mountain top, but I pressed on. At about 900m, the snow was two feet deep and the path had disappeared. I could see cairns to my right, but also to my left and I knew that I was lost. I heard voices and I shouted *'Hey, hello there!'* Two Welsh lads appeared from under the blanket of falling snow. They were surprised that I was alone. They were also heading for the summit and training for a charity trek to Machu-Pichu. I told them that I, too, was training –to climb Kilimanjaro for SCOPE. They were equipped with snow-axes and seemed quite determined. I followed them. We got to the abrupt final part, normally covered by scree, that in good weather conditions you scramble easily. Today it was treacherous and difficult. Visibility was five metres and I decided that it was unsafe to continue. Descending that steep section of about fifty metres was only possible if I sat on my bottom, breaking the speed with my heels and my walking stick. Thereafter I was able to stand up and trek down, arriving to the car park at around 5.00 p.m., tired but in one piece.

10th May 2008

Today I climbed Snowdon for the fourth time since my first attempt on 20th April. I think that day I made the right decision to descend before reaching the summit. Since then I have stood at the top of the tallest peak in England and Wales, on the third and fifth of May. The snow was gone and both days were sunny. Same Watkin path and alone. Average two hours but with light pack.

19th May 2008
Yesterday I summited Scafell Pike, the highest peak in England. Thinking of Kilimanjaro, sometimes it worries me that I am too old and I will not succeed, in spite of the training in the mountains and the gym. Got up at six and drove to the Lakes. Sat nav is a godsend. The roads from Windermere to the Pike were like a maze and the last bit very narrow. It was a sunny day. The walk began at the Inn and on grassy farmland and then the trail ascended gradually at first but became rather steep later. Chose to go on the scree path to the right that requires some scrambling, passed the disused first aid depot and aimed for the summit. The top was different to Snowdon and covered with big boulders as if a giant god piled them there. Made it in 1 hour 35min.

27th May 2008
Today Julie and I went north to the Lake District to trek Helvellyn ridge. She has accompanied me on several walks already and she is great company. As we approached the ridge the weather changed and with it the wind. A ranger coming down warned us that at the top it was 70mph and it was dangerous. I decided to risk it and continued whilst she waited by the pond below. As I approached the top I had to crawl to avoid being blown off the mountain. It had become very cold and I turned back, eventually to find Julie shivering. We came down in one piece and drove south. I am proud of her.

2nd June 2008 Monday
A nurse gave me an article from *The Guardian* making a plea for the welfare of the porters at Kili, who carry our gear up for very little pay by our standards. It also touches on the very poor clothing and shoes they have and the dangers they face. Some have died. This exploitation used to happen to the Sherpa in Nepal and Tibet, but it has now improved. I wonder if SCOPE pays them better. I will ask Cordelia Hughes, the trip organiser, about it.

I am not even half way towards the £3k sponsorship money that I need to raise for SCOPE. I have decided that I will donate the rest.

8th June 2008

Yesterday several friends, hospital colleagues and I made it to the summit of Snowdon via Watkin path. I am so proud of all of them because none had previous trekking experience. It took us 10 hours. The key to our success was to follow the dictum: *'the slowest set the pace.'* It really was an unforgettable day.

21st June 2008

Today I did eight miles on the Pennine Way starting at Crowden and heading to Black Hill. I have done this walk many times. It is nice and arouses pleasant memories. At a magical moment I found myself walking on paving stones perfectly laid down over shallow ponds in the middle of the moors. I was surrounded by white cotton grass moving rhythmically in the wind – like a symphony synchronous with my thoughts, it felt surreal. Initially, the wind was gentle, but on my return, it got vicious and at some point I had to take refuge behind a boulder. Water found its way into my boots on the swamp, as the path criss-crossed over Crowden Great Brook.

29th June 2008

Ten of us went to Grasmere, in the Lake District yesterday. Among my companions were Pablo, my youngest son and several hospital colleagues. We walked up the path bordering a brook, to about 300m and descended to the town. The scenery was magnificent, the weather good. We stopped at the Original Gingerbread shop and bought souvenirs. We had a lovely meal at a restaurant by the river in front of the church and took many photos.

It was my last walk before Kilimanjaro. I will go from 300m to over 5,800m. Hope the training pays off. Tried my new boots today for the first time. Bought them last week, thinking that my old leather ones, which I have had for eight years, will not be up to the job. They felt fine and have a logo that says *Basque*. My mother's maiden name is Vásquez. Seems like a good omen.

THE ROOF OF AFRICA

Kilimanjaro is a snow-covered mountain 5,895m – 19,710 feet – high and the Roof of Africa. Kili, as it is colloquially known, is a unique and most beautiful volcano. It stands alone and proud in the plains of Tanzania and its massive triangular shape is visible from miles afar and therein lies its singularity: it is not hidden, unlike those in the Himalayas or the Andes. Because of its location and its enormous size, climbers pass through four different eco-zones within a few days, depending on how rapidly they acclimatize and ascend. The first is *the rainforest* with a great variety of fauna – including blue monkeys – and flora; the second is *the heath and moorland* between 2,800m and 4,000m with the characteristic Senecio or giant tree; the third is *the alpine desert* area between 4,000m and 5,000m where only three species of grass can survive the extreme dryness and heat of the day and the intense cold at night. Finally, the fourth eco-system is *the ice cap,* which is like the arctic waste, but almost six kilometres higher and where virtually nothing can survive except a remarkable species of lichen.

Many people believe that climbing Kilimanjaro is an easy task. Do not be fooled. It is true that many thousands have reached its summit and that records have been established for people running up to the top, backwards walkers, skiers, boarders etc. but these are truly exceptional people, not only because of their fitness but also their eccentricity.

A few years ago, a successful expedition of celebrities received a great deal of media coverage and made it look easy and perhaps reinforced the belief that climbing this mountain, that the Maasai* call 'Nga je Nagai' meaning the House of good, is a doddle. It is not, and the main reason why many attempts are unsuccessful is altitude sickness. This is caused by ascending too fast and not allowing the body to acclimatise. Many of the souvenirs – hats, T-shirts, cups and the like – have the words 'pole-pole' written on them, which in Swahili means slowly-slowly, and it is a reminder that rushing up is a big mistake.

Climbing Kili is a truly life-affirming experience and even if you climb with a group of complete strangers, gradually a bond builds between trekkers, guides and porters that grows day by day and with each step. The climb is both a sacrifice and a joy if your heart is in it and, more so, if you are doing it for a good cause. However, Kili is huge and very high. In my mind, the best way to get some idea of its height is to go to the foot of a mountain like Snowdon, look up to the sky above it and imagine a mountain almost five and a half times taller! One in four people fail even to reach the crater at 5,600m, let alone the summit.

Giant mountains kill people; Kilimanjaro is no exception and, on average, two die every year.

Nevertheless, although climbing Kili is not easy, it can be achieved, but training, mental strength and determination are the essential pre-requisites. No technical skills are necessary, just the ability to walk 'pole-pole'. Above the age of ten years, age is not a problem: in fact, the youngest summiteer was a nine year-old and the oldest, the splendid Frenchman Valtee Daniel, was aged 87!

However, no description of Kili can be complete without making a plea for the wellbeing of the porters who climb out of necessity, carrying loads of up to 40kg, many of them still poorly clothed and wearing inappropriate shoes. Sometimes in the past, the conditions were so precarious that injuries to them were a common occupational hazard and, at worst, many of them died. Fortunately, the situation has improved thanks to the Kilimanjaro Porters Assistance Project (KPAP) that began in 2003.

* Maasai: people that speak the Maa language. (Also spelled Masai)

4th July 2008
The 10.15 a.m. Virgin train left on time from Manchester Piccadilly to London Euston. Think I've got everything with me! Underground journey to Heathrow was OK (Piccadilly Line). Got there at 2.30 p.m.; soon afterwards the group began to gather, all quite friendly. Finally, two hours late at 9.20 p.m. our plane with five hundred plus passengers, including many school parties, departed.

5th July 2008
We landed at Nairobi airport at 4.00 a.m. (7.00 a.m. local time). After clearing transit visas for Kenya we boarded a coach for our journey to Tanzania. Kenya is poor and the roads are bad, made worse by crazy driving! People dress colourfully and red is everywhere. As we drove through Arusha, a nice and vibrant city, the coach stopped and Moses, Kenyan and the main guide joined us. We crossed the border after getting visas and a big passport stamp and we continued to travel through arid but also beautiful bushland. Everybody is in good spirits and I am getting to know the team. We stopped at some point to look at Kili that even on the distance, looks massive. On the way we saw Maasai warriors, dressed typically in red tartan and carrying a long

spear, walking down the road. The Maasai originated from the lower Nile and migrated South arriving in Northern Kenya and Tanzania in the 17th and 18th centuries. They are famous for their fearsome reputation as warriors and cattle-herders. Finally, we arrived at the Nakara hotel, in Marangu at about 6.00 p.m.

I have been on the move for almost thirty hours since I left home in Salford! We all congregated in the hotel bar to have a drink and relax before dinner and afterwards Moses, who is very tall, introduced to us the team of guides, porters and cooks which will accompany us during the trip. He reminded us that after breakfast tomorrow we will be taken for formal individual registration to the Naremoru gate, the starting point of the Rongai route at 1950m, on the northern side of Kili. We will trek the Marangu route for our descent, thus completing a big loop.

6th July 2008
It is early evening and we are resting in Simba Camp on the Rongai Route at 2,620m. The first day of hiking has been easy going initially through farmers' fields and later rainforest. The altitude has claimed its first victim: Lucy. She will have to return to the Hotel with a guide. We all wish her well.

7th July 2008
The group reached 3,500m after a climb of four hours at a place on the Rongai route called the First Caves. All are feeling well, having a rest before the afternoon climb to Kikelewa Camp at 3,679m. Last night, it was cold in the tent but my sleeping bag was good. Pity I cannot send a text or receive any messages.

8th July 2008
We have steadily climbed to Mawenzi Tarn at 4,330m, spectacularly situated beneath the towering Mawenzi peak. We will camp here and continue to acclimatise.

9th July 2008
After crossing the 'Saddle', a lunar like landscape which stretches between the Mawenzi and Kibo (Uhuro) peaks, we reached the Kibo Hut at 4,750m early in the afternoon. Several in the group are experiencing bad headaches, a sign of mountain sickness. David Smith, the expedition doctor, has been busy,

we all gathered and he gave us another talk. This time he said that we were fast approaching the 'death zone' above 5,000m. He explained that the best treatment for acute altitude sickness was rapid descent. The gurneys with the big wheels that we had seen scattered on the trail were for that. Several in the group said that they would not attempt the ascent to the summit, due to begin at midnight. After forcing down some food at dinner, I am back in the tent that I share with Teddy as we get into our high altitude clothes – we are both going to go for it. Teddy is a few months younger than I and great company. My head is throbbing and I take two paracetamols. It is about 9.30 p.m. I will stop writing and try to sleep for a couple of hours. Head lamp off.

11th July 2008

Yesterday at 7.15 a.m., I reached *Uhuru peak* the highest point of Mt Kilimanjaro, the Roof of Africa, at 5,895m (19,710 feet) above sea level. Words cannot describe the way I feel. I am so happy. At the age of 59, I have achieved something many can only dream of. I have seen Africa, this extraordinary continent, from its highest vantage point.

I did it by sheer determination. At midnight, after we all drank a hot cup of soup and ate a bowl of porridge, we lined up to start the ascent. I decided to go second, after the first guide – Bajati. I struck up a friendship with him. He is my height and my tactic was to follow him step-by-step, keeping my head light down on his heels on the seemingly never ending zig-zag path. Initially I kept looking up, only to see the lights of other climbers very far up the mountain. It was discouraging, so I stopped doing that and looked down instead. I selected from my memory pleasant thoughts such as previous climbs in England. I kept thinking – tonight is just another Snowdon – I have done it many times and I will succeed. Dawn was breaking when we stopped at *Gilman's Point,* a sub-summit located on the crater's rim. It was very cold, around minus ten degrees Celsius. We had a hot drink and after a few minutes, we carried on. The final push was on a very steep section with a lot of stone and scree that soon changed to névé, a form of hard compact snow. Two of the guides, Elias and Bajati, and I were the first ones of the SCOPE group to reach the summit. It was 7.15 a.m. when I touched the well-known sign declaring it the tallest free standing mountain in the world. Soon, afterwards other team members arrived and we embraced and congratulated each other. It was a beautiful day with a clear blue sky and the views over the African continent were magnificent with Mount Meru in the distance. I was elated and in spite

124

of the altitude and the thin air I was not yet exhausted. I stayed on the summit for about fifteen minutes before trekking down with Bajati and as we walked on the *névé* to the edge of the summit I was able to appreciate the spectacular crater of the volcano and the glacier. The descent was fun and in places we literally slid down the scree, stopping to rest and admire the wonderful views of Africa below us. We reached Kibo Camp safely in four hours. After a brief one-hour rest, we descended to Horombo Huts, at 3,700m, where we arrived at about 5.00 p.m. By then, after seventeen hours of hiking, I was drained but overjoyed that I had succeeded.

This morning the porters gave us a rendition of their dancing and sang traditional songs including *'Oh Kilimanjaro'* in Swahili. SCOPE presented the porters with money donations that we have all contributed. I gave my leather boots and watch to Bajati and my special hat to Elias.

We are all refreshed and I teamed up with Bajati. We sang popular tunes on our way down. On the way out of the park, at the Marangu Gate, each member went to the Rangers post to log out and later we all cheered and smiled as Cordelia took the official photos of the Group with the charity's banner.

We had a lovely dinner to celebrate our achievement. Fourteen out of twenty-nine made it to Uhuro. Several others made it to Gilman's Point at 5,685m – a big achievement. We all received a medal; the group raised more than £100,000. Speeches followed and someone said that in spite of the fact that I was the oldest climber, I was first to the top! The training had paid off.

2nd August 2008

Letter from Cordelia Hughes, the Event Fundraiser from SCOPE, who also summited Kili, enclosing the summit certificate and official photos. We will have a reunion in London on 13th September. Thinking about an attempt on Aconcagua, the highest mountain in South America at 6,962m – 22,840 feet.

BACK TO ASHTON-UNDER-LYNE

4th August 2008

I met with a consultant general surgeon today in the theatre. He told me that he has written to management because there are major issues of quality of care and safety to patients in the Surgical Division. I told him that the Orthopaedic Division has the same problems and that I have done my best to highlight these matters to management. This is not the first time that a colleague from the surgical department has told me how bad things are. One of the main reasons why the letters raising concerns achieve very little, is because the divisional leads – appointed by the CEO – approve every management decision to cut resources. They are enacted under headings such us *surgical re-design,* which are like a magician's illusion when he pulls rabbits out of a hat. The surgeon told me that he sent his letter to the Divisional Nurse Manager and copied it to the CEO, the MD, his colleagues and surgical sisters. I asked him to send me a copy of the letter in confidence, as I am the chair of the SMSC. He said that he will do so, but I should not write to management until he gets a response.

8th August 2008 Monday

The letter from the surgeon reached me today. One of the main problems is lack of nursing staff and he is requesting that this must be immediately rectified. He also pointed out that patients are being moved from ward to ward, two or three times a day, due to lack of beds and that bed managers continue to admit patients into inappropriate wards, not taking any notice of the warnings from ward sisters that it is not safe. He requests an immediate audit of the ward admissions. It is a strong letter from the most senior general surgeon, but my experience tells me that directors will take little notice. However, hope springs eternal as they say!

15th August 2008

It has been a sad and tragic day. At my routine Ward Round at 11.30 a. m. I asked about the progress of Mr X, who had a planned major operation yesterday, I was aghast to hear that he had died earlier, at 6.00 a.m. After reviewing the medical and nursing records, I requested an investigation. In my view, his post-operative care was compromised by the fact that a patient with a head injury needing a lot of attention was admitted into the same bay and the deterioration of my patient went unnoticed. His death was preventable and I feel that I have failed him and his family. The lack of experienced doctors at night is also a contributory factor.

20th August 2008

My sixth trek to Snowdon via Watkin path. This time, I went with Pablo, my youngest son, who did brilliantly for his first long trek. We walked mainly silently but from time to time, we talked about all things: his love for the guitar, his studies and teachers, rugby and about my work. I told him of my anguish because I know that my patient did not receive post-operative care to the best standards, that the nurses had been put in an impossible situation and that the cause of death was a systemic failure. I told him of my despair, because I have fought for so long for better care. He listened, and when I had finished he said, *'Dad, do not take it so hard. It was not your fault, but do not give up trying to improve the care to your patients.'* His words gave solace to my distress. We made it to the top in two and a half hours. It was raining and the return, via the ridge, on a path that is narrow and steep in places, was not easy. As we walked under the trees on the last part of the trail, my thoughts turned to the past when it was I who had walked with my father under tall trees. Silently I wished that for Pablo this day would also be unforgettable. It will be for me.

28th August 2008

After talking to my orthopaedic consultant colleagues about the problems we have in our department, I have decided to write a letter to *The Independent* highlighting the fact that we have not enough personnel in comparison to nearby Stepping Hill hospital in Stockport. They all support the idea, but none is prepared to sign it. I am disappointed, but I understand their fears.

9th September 2008

The letter to the Editor of *The Independent* is ready, but the Lead Consultant believes I should let the Trust know. Therefore, I have sent it to the deputy CEO for him to approve. The letter is factual, under the heading – *Inequality of Resources in NHS Trusts.* It says that Tameside Hospital serves a population of 250,000 and has *six* consultant orthopaedic surgeons, *two* specialist Registrars, and *one* Trauma Coordinator nurse. By comparison a neighbouring Trust that serves a population of 350,000, has *sixteen* orthopaedic consultants, *seven* specialist registrars and *three* trauma coordinator nurses. The letter also mentions that the British Orthopaedic Association had recommended *ten* orthopaedic consultants for our hospital. This letter does not in any way attack the Trust, and I am hopeful that the managers will allow me to send it. After all, it merely explains the reality and they have made a pledge to be open and transparent.

14th September 2008

Mr Griffiths, the deputy CEO has written saying that the Trust does not support my letter to *The Independent*. I am flabbergasted and extremely disappointed because it can only help the Trust. It does not make sense to me. The Lead of my Division says that I should not send it. Obviously, the managers have spoken to him to put further pressure on me. I wonder if they have heard of freedom of expression, it is unbelievable!

3rd October 2008

Today I wrote a three-page report for the Coroner, via the Legal Services Officer of the Trust, regarding the death of my patient Mr X. The last paragraph states that I am not happy with the standard of care and that I reported it as an incident and an investigation is on-going.

5th October 2008

I have been training regularly for Aconcagua. Keeping a record of all my treks, the distance and the weight that I carry. Yesterday seven of us: Prash, a registrar, and his wife Pauline, Wiqqas, another registrar and his girlfriend, my secretary Michelle, Julie and I, went from Crowden to the Dovestone Reservoir and back. Done this trek four times over last two months, sometimes alone and sometimes with company i.e. Pablo or Julie. I carry 20 kg in my rucksack made up of heavy stones and it caused me to trip and fall once, but carrying weight is good training for my trip to the Andes. The registrars Wiqqas and Prash are the ages of my older sons and are superb company and their partners and Michelle made it enjoyable for Julie, who has been to many of my training trips. It was a twelve mile round trip and although it was windy at the reservoir, we all enjoyed it.

20th October 2008

The Trust solicitors wrote suggesting that I should omit the final paragraph of my report on Mr X. I suppose they are doing their job. Nevertheless, I am *not* removing it.

22nd October 2008

I replied to the Trust solicitors, giving them nine reasons why I must decline their request to omit the final paragraph of my report to the coroner following the death of patient X.. These are 1) Lack of recorded observations between 12.30 p.m. and 9.00 p.m. after his operation, which had finished at 11.00 a.m.;

2) Lack of observations from 4.00 a.m. the following morning until he was found unresponsive at 5.45 a.m.; 3) The inappropriate transfer of a patient with a severe head injury into the bay where Mr X was recovering from a major operation, owing to the fact that the ward where this patient had been initially admitted had been closed for the weekend; 4) The fact that the nursing records showed that Mr X's care was neglected, because the patient with the head injury became confused and aggressive, requiring lots of individual attention; 5) I am concerned that the investigation into the circumstances of Mr X death did not include a statement from the security guard who was called to restrain the patient with the head injury, who had been agitated for the previous two nights; 6) Failure to act at 4.00 a.m. when Mr X was deteriorating; 7) Failure to catheterise as advised at 02.30 a.m. by the doctor; 8) Failure to administer diuretics, hugely significant omission, given that cause of death was congestive cardiac failure and the post mortem found the patient's lungs full of fluid; 9) I am concerned that the doctor who attended Mr X at 2.30 a.m. said – in his statement – that his visit was cut short by a call to A&E where he was detained for a long time and later assumed that Mr X was better, when in fact he was deteriorating rapidly and died at 06.00 a.m.

20th November 2008 Thursday

Attended the inquest on Mr X at the Coroner's Court in Stockport. It was a sad day for the family and for me. He had put his trust in me and I feel that I have failed him. Read my statement indicating that in my view the care had been sub-standard. The verdict was that of death by natural causes. At the end, I expressed my condolences to the relatives; they said that they did not blame me. It was little consolation. I wonder what the coroner really thought of the care this man received.

2nd December 2008

Went up the footpath at Indian Head yesterday with 25kg on my back. It has become my favourite training spot because it is not very far from the hospital by the Dovestone Reservoir in Saddleworth. My records say that I have climbed it ten times since August, sometimes twice in a day! I have been training regularly for Aconcagua.

10th December 2008 11:10 p.m.

Just arrived back at my flat in Salford. Yesterday and again tonight, I have been by the embankment at the Dovestone Reservoir going up the steep 100 feet gradient. There was a foot of snow and it was an excellent training ground. There was a full moon and no need for lights. Yesterday I did seven trips up and down in 45 min. It was cold but I did not feel it! Today I did ten trips up and down in 90 mins. A cop's patrol car came by and approached me. They were friendly and I told them that I was preparing for a mountain in the Andes – they wished me good luck.

30th December 2008 10:35 p.m.

It is -4 degrees Celsius, back from a three hour trek with 20kg to the far end of the Dovestone Reservoir. Since my last entry, I have been there a further ten times including Christmas Day. On the 16th I trained with my new plastic boots and my crampons. The heavy boots felt a little tight on both sides of my heels and I have tried to make them just a little more spacious by forcing a beer glass inside – it is just the right size – and leaving it a few days. Hopefully it will do the trick.

Chapter Thirteen

DIARIES 2009 – MOUNT ACONCAGUA

Aconcagua is the highest mountain outside Asia and the pinnacle of the Americas. It is 22,840 feet high or 6,962m. It is in the Andes, in Argentina and 20 km from Chile. Mendoza is the nearest city and most climbers start there.

Its name means 'stone sentinel' in the Quechua language. It is a big wedge shaped *cerro*, which rises just east of the main Andean chain, receiving less snow fall than the main range and thus great areas of it are wind battered bare rock and scree. It is situated in the Aconcagua National Park. A climbing permit is needed and this is only given after officials check a comprehensive questionnaire – detailing the climber's experience and health.

Climbing it is a serious undertaking and very much harder than Kili because it is over 1,000m higher, with greater risk of altitude sickness; the weather is notoriously severe with sudden extremely high winds; the terrain is more difficult, with extensive scree, rock debris and giant icicles known as *Penitentes* and climbers have to carry their own loads above base camp, all of which demands an expedition of two to three weeks, or longer if the weather is unfavourable.

Summits success ratios are lower than Kili and there are more deaths per annum even though only around 4,000 attempt to climb it compared to near 15,000 attempting Kili. In terms of overall difficulty and grading on a scale from one to nine, Kili is graded two, Aconcagua five, Denali seven and Everest nine. Described as technically easy, unless it is climbed via the Polish Glacier, Aconcagua, however, can never be under-estimated. Because its height is well within the so-called 'death zone' it can cause lethal altitude sickness. Sub-zero temperatures and devastating winds above 16,400 feet make it a mountain to respect. Climbers must be prepared to climb at altitude carrying at least 20kg and have the mental strength to stay on a cold, windy mountain for days on end in primitive conditions.

DIARIES 2009

INTRODUCTION

During 2009 the shortage of beds, under-staffing amongst nurses and junior doctors continued to affect the hospital. In June it reached a crisis point and I wrote to my colleagues urging them to attend an extraordinary meeting of the SMSC. I also wrote to the Board Directors pointing out that the Trust's response to the Healthcare Commission Investigation into Mid-Staff failures was flawed because it did not acknowledge that we had the very same issues. Having written to the Divisional Nursing Officer in August and to the ND in October that year, and not getting a satisfactory answer I contacted Mrs Sarah Dunnett, an assessor at the Care Quality Commission (CQC) – successor to the Healthcare Commission – and sent her copies of recent correspondence with the Directors.

Late in 2009 I communicated to Mrs Green my intention to campaign for legislation on mandatory nurse and midwife to patient ratios in hospitals in England.

8th January 2009
Back from the gym after a ninety-minute of workout. Been going twice a week when not hiking. Already trekked up to Indian Head, which stands high above Dovestone Reservoir, twice this year for about six hours each day. I have also been exercising on odd days with a heavy pack at Kersal Moor. This preserved land is just across Moor Lane where I live in Salford and ideal for endurance training. It used to have a horse-racing track in the last century.

19th January 2009
Wiqqas, my trainee orthopaedic registrar, googled 'Aconcagua Mountain' and, after seeing its size, could not believe that in a couple of weeks I will

attempt to summit it. He showed me reports on the Internet that there have been five deaths already this season. The latest tragedy involved an Italian female climber and her guide, an Argentinian-American, who was very experienced. There is a disturbing video on *YouTube* of the attempted rescue which I watched. I try not to worry but it is a reminder of the risks I will be facing.

21st January 2009 Wednesday

I am anxious that I am about to leave for Argentina and that whilst I am away my patients may not receive acceptable standards of care, particularly at week-ends and night. I must write to the CEO and the Board, including non-executive directors who must be made aware of the problems we face. I will do so, even though Mrs Green, the CEO, does not approve of direct communication between consultants and non-executive directors, a position which, incidentally, is contrary to one of the recommendations of the report from the Bristol Inquiry into the management of the care of children receiving complex cardiac surgery, at the Bristol Royal Infirmary, published in 2001.

23rd January 2009 Friday

Busy operating schedule today but I gave myself time to write to the CEO, copying in the Chairman and entire board including non-executives, and my orthopaedic colleagues. I highlighted my main concerns: some days there is only one senior house officer for all the wards, instead of four; patients are not reviewed daily, seriously affecting their safety; patients with infections are being admitted to the (elective) ward where patients who have undergone joint replacements are recovering, raising the risk of cross infection; owing to bed shortages, the day ward is being kept open twenty-four hours, without sufficient or adequately trained staff; escalation wards which are poorly staffed, continue to be kept open and serious incidents are occurring, such as the administration of medicines to the wrong patient, and the journey of many patients involves them being moved from ward to ward, thereby seriously compromising their care. I have said in the letter to Mrs Green that I am concerned that when I am away, the care of my patients may be affected due to the prevalence of these issues and I urge the managers to find an urgent solution in discussion at Board level – which I emphasised.

25th January 2009

Aconcagua preparation finished today with two hours at Kersal Moor. My records of training for Aconcagua show that since 20th April 2008 – when I went to Snowdon for the first time – I have done sixty outdoor treks in all kinds of weather, not counting Kilimanjaro, often carrying up to 25kg (about 55 pounds). Worried about altitude – over 3,000 feet higher than Kili at 22,000 plus feet!

Julie came by this evening as she did before I went to Africa and helped me to check my equipment item by item. The list is huge. Everything has to fit in a heavy-duty hold-all. Flying Iberia tomorrow at 7.55 p.m. from Gatwick to Barcelona and from Barcelona to Santiago, arriving there at 9:35 a.m. on 27th January. From there, my plan is to take a bus to Mendoza repeating the journey I made in 1974 when my family and I escaped from Chile.

27th January 2009

Landed in Santiago on time but my entire luggage did not arrive. It includes bag with all my gear for the climb. Officials tell me that it has been left behind in Barcelona. They will do everything possible to get it in the plane arriving tomorrow. My plans of taking a bus today to Mendoza are in tatters.

28th January 2009 Wednesday

Luckily, my luggage arrived and I collected it safely from the carousel. I have bought a ticket to fly to Mendoza. Yesterday I stayed at a hotel in Santiago that had twenty floors and in the afternoon, I climbed all twenty floors twenty times to exercise my joints after the long flight. Later I ate a Chilean dish made of crushed corn and minced beef, onions and condiments. It is baked and it is called *'pastel de choclo.'* Choclo is the South American Spanish word for maize or corn. It was delicious!

29th January 2009

I am in Mendoza after landing with my equipment yesterday. A taxi took me to the hotel 'El Condor' as pre-arranged by INKA, a mountaineering company. The hotel is comfortable and located in a quiet area of Mendoza that reminds me of the city of Talca in Chile.

Yesterday I met Federico the Argentinian guide and my fellow climbers, Larry an American; Andrés an Argentinian from Buenos Aires and Karin a Scandinavian who is attempting the summit for a second time. I guess Larry is mid-forties, he is medium height and strong; Karin is mid-thirties, average height and also looks fit; Federico is early thirties, stocky and muscular; finally, Andrés is tall, slim and the youngest – late twenties.

Today we paid 1,500 Argentinian pesos and completed the compulsory forms, which will allow us to enter the Aconcagua National Park to climb the mountain. We will have a steak dinner tonight and tomorrow we will start our adventure. I am already getting on well with Larry who is a clinical pharmacist in the USA.

30th January 2009, Villa de Penitentes, Friday.

After a good breakfast, we placed our bags in a rented van and drove a short distance to a shop specialising in mountaineering gear in Barcalá Street, aptly called Chamonix, to rent plastic boots and a sleeping bag for Andrés. It was a well-stocked place and prices were reasonable. We were almost out of Mendoza when our guide realised that he had left his sunglasses in the shop and we came back for them via Avenida San Martín, named after the great Argentinian national hero. Spirits were high and we were not in a hurry. We had lunch at a restaurant by the Carretera International in the valley of Uspallata. The scenery reminds me of similar valleys in Chile, at the other side of the Andes. After four hours through fertile lands, we have arrived at *Hotel Villa de Penitentes* at a ski resort. It is summer so there is no snow but it remains open for climbers. We sorted out our equipment into two piles: the clothes and equipment packed in the big duffel-bags to be taken up the mountain by mules to *Plaza Argentina* at 4,000m, was weighed and each carefully marked; the other, is the gear we will carry in our rucksacks, our sleeping bags, walking poles etc.

Tomorrow we will commence the trek at *Punta de Vacas* (Cow's Point) at 2,400m and follow the Vacas Valley route. On this trail, it will take us three days to reach base camp at *Plaza Argentina* over 25 km away.

Andrés is feeling better, he was sick several times during the journey today. Food poisoning, most probably.

31st January 2009

We have reached *Pampa de Leñas* (Plain with Firewood) after a four hour trek. We started at midday, after a short bus ride from the hotel at Penitentes. Last night we had an excellent dinner, our last proper meal for the next three weeks. The hotel had many pictures of *Cerro Aconcagua* as it is called here – it looked big. Today we have not seen it yet because it is hidden by the mountains flanking the valley. Beautiful day and the trek was gentle. We ascended 500m and spirits are high. Andrés has a great camera and has taken many photos. I have taken a few. I am sharing a tent with Andrés. Karin and Larry sleep in the other and we had a few jokes about it. The tents are spacious enough and not difficult to set up. We secure the ropes with stones that are plentiful – rather than pins – which is a first for me.

1st February 2009

We are now at *Casa de Piedra* (House of Stone), a small hut next to a huge boulder used as a ranger post. We have been treated to an *asado*, an Argentinian barbecue, prepared by *arrieros* who are taking the mules up with our bags. I said that I was Chilean and I enjoyed chatting in Spanish with them. They work hard during the climbing season. We drank what I though was a decent Argie red.

The night came and Andrés gave us our first lesson on the stars of the Southern Hemisphere. He is a keen amateur astronomer. The starry sky, like in Africa, was unbelievably beautiful. Federico, our guide tells us that we are now at 3,200m (10,500 ft.). Tomorrow we cross the Vacas River and we will climb to *Plaza Argentina* at 4,200m Because of the altitude gain, the 12 km trek will be tougher.

2nd February 2009

I am writing whilst we are resting half-way up *Plaza*. Foolishly, I sat down into what I thought was inviting green grass, it turned out to have sharp little spines. I swore loudly in rough Mancunian and my companions laughed. Andrés, Karin and Larry crossed *Rio Vacas* (Cows' River) by horseback. I chose to wade it with Federico. There came a point when all of us had to take our boots off. It was waist deep and the water was freezing. Weather remains good. We had our first sight of Aconcagua in the distance. It is massive.

3rd February 2009

Yesterday, after a six hours trek, we arrived at *Plaza Argentina*. We went directly to INKA'S mess tent for drinks and some food. We found an American climber there, breathing heavily, looking ashen and clearly affected by altitude sickness. He had gone as far as 5,000m and had to turn back. He had seen the camp doctor who had advised him to go down. He left lots of stuff in the mess; including an energy-rehydration powder called 'Gatorade' that Larry says is good. We plan to spend two days here for acclimatisation.

It is cold here at night and I am now certain that my sleeping bag is not up to scratch. Skinny compared to Andrés's that is thick with feathers. I looked at the labels: mine says, Up to minus four; his says, Up to minus twenty-eight! I will have to sleep fully dressed from now on.

We are all acclimatising well according to our guide. Last night at the mess tent Federico measured our blood oxygen saturations with a small device known as a pulse oximeter and recorded them. Mine was 86 per cent and my companions all scored similar readings. At sea level, a healthy individual's arterial blood is 98 to 100 per cent saturated with oxygen, whereas at 6,000m a reading of 80 per cent means good acclimatisation.

From now on, we will be measured daily. We discussed the controversial subject of Diamox, a medicine used to prevent altitude sickness. Larry, Andrés and Karin are taking it. I am not, based on my Kilimanjaro success without it.

There is a medical hut at this camp and we all went for a check-up. I met Javier, a young Argentinian doctor employed by the National Park. He was pleasant, late twenties, lives in Mendoza and is trying to specialise in orthopaedics. My blood pressure was slightly high and Javier recommended that I reduce my salt intake.

The rescue helicopter came early yesterday morning and took a climber down. It was also loaded with what appears to be waste. Its colour is bright yellow. We all came out of our tents to look at it. It flew away like a giant noisy locust.

I often think of what lies ahead. The task looks daunting and I begin to entertain thoughts that I may not succeed. I get a boost looking at the list of the training I did, which I carry with me. It also brings pleasant memories of home and I re-live the walks I have done with Julie and my friends.

I think very little of the hospital and its problems. My companions and I have decided not to talk about our jobs and it is a good decision. Larry is a keen cyclist and mountain biker and has thighs to prove it. He has done a lot of trekking in the US and, after Aconcagua, he wants to climb Mt McKinley in the Denali National Park in Alaska.

This is Andrés first mountain. He misses his wife and little daughter Gala like crazy. In the tent, we speak in Spanish though his English is quite good. He is an accountant and works for the family firm. We get on well and he is good company. Every night he shows us the sky and the passing satellites that orbit the earth, which he knows so well.

Karin is rather serious and reserved, but is gradually becoming more friendly. She has been to Everest base camp, the Alps and to this mountain before. She climbed to about 6,500m before her party had to retreat because of a violent storm and she hopes that it does not happen again. She is an engineer and uses all her holidays to go trekking.

Tomorrow we are going to Camp 1 that is at 5,000m (16,405 ft.) For the first time we will be heavily loaded with *cache* which we will carry up the mountain. We will leave it there and come down. The idea is that we will react to the higher altitude by producing more red cells and haemoglobin and thus acclimatise.

Yesterday we all went for a walk around the camp and saw mules coming up the trail with yet more gear for climbers sharing our dream: to climb the roof of the Southern Hemisphere.

4th February 2009

Happy the day is over. We took *cache* to Camp 1 and are now back at *Plaza Argentina*. It took us six hours to get there and two hours to return. It was tricky in places because the scree – loose rock – that covers the glacier is very slippery in places and it kept sliding down as we tried to move up. Saw the *Penitentes* for the first time. They are tall lumps of solid ice. Their name derives from the fact that some of them resemble a penitent, a person in penance, slightly crouched forward. There were thousands and we gave them a wide berth because walking through them would have been crazy even with crampons. Higher up the track was clear but in places covered by hard snow. Eventually we reached Camp 1 and were happy to unload our large rucksacks filled with *cache*. Tomorrow we will return to Camp 1 with the rest of our gear.

5th February 2009, Camp 1. 5,000m

Camp 1, resting. No more luxurious mess tent until we are in *Plaza de Mulas* in about one week, after the summit attempt. We are in good spirits and oxygen readings are fine for all. Tomorrow we move higher to a place named Camp *'Cólera'* (Anger) because of a fight between two rival guides in the past. We will be loaded and it will be hard, particularly the first hour when our bodies are stiff and cold. We will gain about 1,000m (3,275 feet) and it will take us around nine hours.

9th February 2009, Camp Cólera. 6,000m

We have been at Camp Cólera now for three days acclimatising and waiting for the weather to improve. Today the sky is clear and the view from here is simply magnificent. I can see the Andes north, south and west towards Chile. We are the only ones at this camp, as most climbers prefer to be at Camp Berlin 200m lower.

The last two nights we have had winds the likes of which I have never experienced before. I feared that the tent would be blown away in spite of the heavy rocks securing the ropes. The noise and the rattle generated were unbelievable and kept Andrés and I awake. The altitude makes us breathe very fast and we are constantly in danger of becoming dehydrated. Therefore, we drink an average of five litres of fluid a day. I use my pee bottle at night and it is full by 6.00a.m.

Andres has had two moments of panic when he awakes gasping for air. I calmed him down and explained that it is normal at 20,000 feet.

Since we left *Plaza Argentina*, I have worn my special boots called 'plastic' boots. They are black, made by a company called Scarpa. They weigh 1kg each and they have a rigid two inch sole. The outside is indeed made of thick plastic-like material similar to a ski boot. They are two sizes larger than my normal shoes, because they have to accommodate an insulated second boot that goes over my socks that are extra thick. In the morning, the boots are frozen and it takes several minutes to put each one on properly and secure the laces with cold stiff fingers!

We all squeeze into Federico's tent and he tells us that the weather forecast for tomorrow is good and we will go for the summit. We must leave at 4.00 a.m.

so we must rise at 3.00 a.m. to get ready.

11ᵗʰ February 2009

It was not meant to be! Yesterday we got up as planned and started just after 4.00 a.m. We had head torches and we zigzagged our way up steep loose scree in the dark. I was second, following the guide. At daybreak we arrived at a steep gully which took us to a small rather dilapidated hut, triangular in shape called 'Refugio Independencia' a rather grandiose name for what is claimed to be the highest refuge in the world. We took a break there and I ate two high calorie chocolate bars. After five minutes, we moved on the 'Portezuelo del Viento' (Windy Ridge). At this point, the weather suddenly changed and it began to snow heavily with fierce accompanying winds. We continued traversing from the ridge towards a long gully known as the 'Canaleta' that is filled with boulders of all sizes, talus and scree and goes all the way to the summit.

According to Federico we managed to get to about 6,600m – indicated by a landmark known as 'El Dedo,' the Finger – before strong winds and the heavy snow created a whiteout which made it too dangerous to progress further.

We had a brief discussion and Federico ruled that we had to return. He did not want a repeat of the tragedy – a month earlier – when a female Italian climber and her guide had died during a sudden storm. It was about 10.00 a.m. and we would have otherwise succeeded in our attempt. We were so close to the summit! We are all deeply disappointed.

To make matters worse our guide is suffering severe toothache that painkillers no longer can control. He wants to descend to *Plaza de Mulas* camp where there is medical attention. We all understand. I feel sorry for all of us, especially Karin.

13ᵗʰ February 2009

I am writing in the mess tent at *Plaza de Mulas*, a large crowded base camp on the other side of the mountain. It is full of tents, huts, logos, flags and banners of different commercial expeditions, not only from Argentina but from all around the world. INKA has several spacious hangars and huts erected for the season, including a separate kitchen for all its clients. We are sleeping in a communal hut with comfortable bunk beds. There is also a place nearby where we can pay for the privilege of having a primitive shower, the first in two weeks. It is a rustic arrangement but the water is hot. We will change into clean clothes from our bags that the mules have carried from *Plaza Argentina*.

I am going to have a second attempt at the summit. The rest of the group are going back to Mendoza tomorrow. I have asked Federico to arrange for INKA to send another guide as soon as possible. It will cost me $1,000 but I know it is worth it. I look up to the mountain's steep slopes leading to the summit almost 9,000 feet up and prepare myself mentally for the climb: initially, to trek all the way up to Camp *Cólera,* carrying heavy back packs, and from there to try again to reach the top.

14th February 2009

Feels very odd to be alone in the mess. This morning I embraced my friends as they departed for Mendoza where they will be tourists for a couple of days before returning to their homes on the 16th. They will go down to a camp called *Confluencia* by descending the *Quebrada de Horcones*. Late in the afternoon, they will reach the Horcones camp at the end of the trail. Larry has invited me to join him at Mt Shasta in California in the summer and I am looking forward to that.

15th February 2009

Javier Gutiérrez, my new guide, has arrived and we discussed the logistics including food and equipment. We will take one tent and food for three days. The weather is good and we plan to ascend tomorrow directly to *Camp Cólera* and, if the weather is OK, go for the summit the following day. The idea is to travel light and do it fast. I have the advantage of being well fed and rested for three days and I have been to 6,600m already; in effect, a perfect way to acclimatize.

I have met a group of Polish climbers who are also sleeping in the bunkhouse: a father and son in his twenties, and two friends. They have been here for three days and have been trying to acclimatize by going up to 5,000m and coming down. One of them, the father, is in a bad way and has severe acute altitude mountain sickness. A helicopter will take him down tomorrow.

I washed some of my clothes yesterday and left them outside on some rocks to dry, but in spite of it being sunny, they froze stiff as a board. I hung them inside the hut in the hope that they would be defrosted when I returned.

18th February 2009

Summited yesterday at about 2.00 p.m.! It was the hardest thing I have ever done and I am so happy to have succeeded at my second attempt. I could not have done it without the help of Javier. The climb up the *Canaleta* was very challenging and halfway up I was taking ten steps at a time and then resting for a few seconds putting my whole weight on one leg and resting the other, before moving on and doing another ten steps. When I finally reached the summit and saw the famous *cross* I was so relieved. I embraced my guide with tears in my eyes and thanked him. The feeling that I experienced was one of immense joy mixed with pride and disbelief. I had done it! I was actually standing on the highest mountain in the Americas and highest south of the Equator. Unfortunately, there were clouds and visibility was poor. We took photos. I had made a promise to Matthew, a young friend, that I would take Homer to the top, and he is perhaps the first Simpsons' character to climb Aconcagua! After some fifteen minutes, we began our descent. I was very tired and in the *Canaleta*, we roped for my safety. We got to *Camp Cólera* around 7.00 p.m. It had been a very long day – eighteen hours – and for me the effort had been extraordinary and I was exhausted as never before. After some food and drink, I went straight to the tent and slept all night. Three Argentinian climbers who were in the camp also made it. Today we are going down to *Plaza de Mulas*. I feel on top of the world, literally.

20th February 2009

Back at Mendoza. Just finished an invigorating breakfast at the 'El Condor Hotel.' We came down safely from *Plaza de Mulas* yesterday. It was a long day. We started at 8.00 a.m. and got to the rangers' station at Horcones by 6.00 p.m. The trek follows the Horcones River and is a long walk back to the end of the trail. We presented our papers at the ranger's post to be officially signed off the Park. After an hour's wait, the taxi arrived and took us to Mendoza and we got to the hotel around 10.00 p.m. The first thing I did was to phone Julie who was thrilled that I had succeeded.

I am all packed and going back to Santiago at midday. I plan to go to Villa Alemana, a town near Viña del Mar, to visit family to and keep a promise I made a long time ago.

BACK IN TAMESIDE

6th March 2009

It has been a month since I came back from Aconcagua, enough time to realise that with regards to nursing levels absolutely nothing has changed in my absence. A senior sister tells me that all too frequently there are shifts without sufficient staff. The junior doctors' shortage, not only in our division, but across the whole hospital, also remains unresolved.

18th April 2009

I have asked SH, my new secretary to email the Director of Information requesting latest figures available regarding number of qualified nurses per 100 beds at our hospital and the same for doctors, and the latest mortality figures. I will use the information when I contact the managers.

13th May 2009

The Director has responded: we have 48.9 doctors per one hundred beds compared with 80 at the Manchester Royal Infirmary (MRI) and 142 nurses per one hundred beds compared to 237 at the Infirmary. Our Hospital Standardised Mortality Index is 120.1 compared to 103 at the MRI. Our Mortality rate has consistently remained one of the worst in the whole country for ten years!

20th May 2009

Email from a senior nurse saying that in a *twenty-five bed* trauma ward in a particular Birmingham hospital, the ratios of qualified/auxiliary nurses are: - Early shift 5/4; – Late shift 5/2 and Night shift 3/2; which is the same establishment for our *thirty-seven bed* trauma ward at Tameside! This is not a surprise to me.

2nd June 2009 3.00 a.m.

I have read the action plan by the Trust Executive Group to address the main issues arising from the Healthcare Commission report into the severe failings in emergency care provided by Mid Staffordshire NHS Foundation Trust between 2005 and 2008. The plan does not fundamentally tackle the similar issues adversely affecting our hospital. I stayed late to write a four-page letter to Mrs Green, the CEO, Dr Mahmood, the MD and Mr Dylak, the DN, copied to several directors, middle rank managers and all senior doctors. In the last paragraph, I remind the addressees that the Board has a corporate responsibility to maintain adequate standards of patient care. (See Appendix 3)

Too late to go home and I am sleeping in my office tonight where I keep a sleeping bag and a mat. I will shower in the theatre in four hours before doing my rounds.

5th June 2009
CEO has replied saying that the veracity of some of the facts I stated in my letter cannot be denied. It is however so disappointing that she does not appreciate the importance of the issues I have so painstakingly brought to her attention.

10th June 2009
Yesterday I stayed late in my office. At 8.00 p.m. I sent the CEO and the Directors an email begging any one of them to come to Wards 3 and 5 to see for themselves the problems caused by the lack of beds – there were *seventeen patients* waiting in the corridors of Ward 5. It was chaos! Today it was the same situation. I added that I had spoken to the Director of Nursing, who denied all knowledge of the nursing shortages.

11th June 2009
A healthy debate has arisen among the consultants regarding the implications of the Healthcare Commission investigation into Mid-Staffs. Our main problems are the lack of beds, the shortage of nurses and junior doctors and consultants. A consultant geriatrician, LGA, highlights these very issues in an email today.

Tomorrow, I am joining Larry Owens in America and I will have a chance to recharge my batteries.

MT SHASTA

At 14,162 feet, Mount Shasta is a large volcano in Northern California and one of the greatest mountains in North America. It is at the southern end of the Cascade Range. It stands solitary and can be seen from far away, as it rises

11,000 feet above the surrounding lowlands. For British climbers it is three Snowdons one on top of the other and covered in snow. It attracts thousands of climbers each year and provides excellent opportunities for crevasse rescue training, ice and seracs climbing, and for getting general experience in snow and ice before attempting larger mountains such as Mount McKinley in Alaska.

12ᵗʰ June 2009 Friday

Flew to USA via Salt Lake City to Sacramento where I joined Larry. We rented a 4 x 4 Toyota and we headed for Shasta – 220 miles away – on the Interstate 5. We talked about Aconcagua and ourselves. I noticed very fertile land – rice fields – olive plantations – corn fields – beetroot – vines, and orchards of all kinds. As we headed north, far away on my right I spotted a huge volcano that Larry identified as Lessen, one of the many volcanoes of the Cascade Range.

We crossed Shasta Lake – the strangest lake I have ever seen, shaped like a long-legged spider – and, less than an hour later, Mt Shasta came into view: a perfect snow covered volcanic cone. Eventually, after driving for four hours from Sacramento, we got to Shasta village, a beautiful place with wide streets and pretty houses, set against the backdrop of a tall, white mountain. The weather was gorgeous. We went immediately to the small offices of Sierra Wilderness Seminars (SWS) where we met James Brown, who was our main guide and 'McKenzie', a young woman trainee guide; Stephen, an engineer was also in the group. It was Larry's second time on this mountain. Seven years earlier, he had come with his teenage son, but they had not summited. He badly wanted to do it this time. James Brown was likeable, in his late twenties. At his request we called him JB. He was a Biology graduate and a ski instructor who had decided to become a professional mountain guide. McKenzie was in her early twenties, also a college graduate, who had chosen the same path as JB. It was her first attempt to summit Shasta.

After carefully inspecting our gear, JB was satisfied we had everything. We checked our provisions – for five days – we loaded our cars and drove off to begin the 'seminar' in ice and snow.

17ᵗʰ June 2009

Summited Mt. Shasta today in good weather. We were all roped up and climbed it safely. After enjoying a glorious view of the Range, we descended, practicing *glissading* and avoiding crevasses. We broke camp and walked down for three hours to our cars at the end of the road.

Back in Shasta we celebrated by having a big delicious steak lunch with fries, salad – the lot. I introduced my friends to a drink that Chileans call *'malta con huevo'* which is one Guinness, one raw egg and sugar to taste, blended for a few minutes. My American friends loved it and we had two jugs.

21ˢᵗ June 2009 Sunday

Shasta Mt reminds me of the volcanoes in the Southern Chilean Andes, such as Llaima, Villarica, and Osorno. I learned a lot from JB and Mackenzie and it was a fantastic experience. It was great to climb with Larry Owens again. Unforgettable trip.

BACK IN TAMESIDE

22ⁿᵈ June 2009 Monday

Found a copy of a letter on my desk, sent to the Medical Director, by ten consultants from the Medical Division. It has been copied to CEO, DCEO/ DES, HRD, ND and me as Chair of the SMSC. In part it reads, *'You will be aware of the continuing turmoil in the Division of Medicine. In advance to the visit by the Royal College of Physicians, a group of consultants had aired their concerns about the dysfunction in the Division. . . '* The clinicians explain that the Lead post was renewed for one year in 2006 and further renewal has not been discussed since. They want a new Lead in post by October this year. This request is set against the background that at Tameside the appointment of all the Divisional Lead Consultants is the prerogative of CEO Mrs Green and nobody else. In their letter, therefore, these senior physicians are effectively questioning the CEO – for if lead consultants meekly toe the line and generally do not raise concerns about sub-standard care, then they are kept in post 'ad infinitum.' In principle, the 'Lead of division' position should be rotated among consultants every three years and he or she should be free from corporate pressure to conform regardless of the consequences for patients or staff.

26ᵗʰ June 2009

I stayed late in my office today to send an email to my colleagues informing them that I am calling for an Extraordinary Meeting of the HSMSC on 7th July. It will take place at the Seminar Room, Ward 28 of the Charlesworth Building. The only item in the agenda is the 'Shortage of beds, nurses and junior doctors at Tameside Hospital'. Part of the email reads:

'The shortage of beds across the Trust continues and I am informed that patients with complex medical co-morbidities, are being assessed in inappropriate places due to lack of beds.'

'The escalation wards 4 and 41 continue to be poorly staffed by nurses and as a result patients' observations, fluid charts recordings, basic needs and administration of medications are not being done in time or worse not at all.'

'The situation with junior doctors has not changed and in the orthopaedic, surgical and medical divisions there are serious issues that need to be addressed.'

'The Board must recognise that the financial situation is not an excuse for substandard and sometimes unsafe levels of care. The lesson of Mid Staffordshire must be learn and the Trust must apply for extra-funds to finance the measures outlined above' (I had asked that wards 4 and 41, now escalation wards, should be made normal wards again with permanent nursing staff, allocated doctors, receptionists and equipment.)

I ended the email saying: *'I urge you to attend, especially those of you affected by these issues. This is too important to be discussed at the next ordinary SMSC due to lack of time.'*

28th June 2009
It is a Sunday and I have some time to write my diary. The shortage of nurses on some shifts continues and nurses tell me that dependent patients are not getting even basic care. The problem is particularly bad in Ward 4. Ten days ago, I was in America away from it all!

7th July 2009
It has been a busy day that ended with the extraordinary meeting of the senior doctors in the Seminar Room very close to my office. Those present included three consultant surgeons, four consultant anaesthetists, four orthopaedic surgeons, one physician, one radiologist, two obstetricians and

me. Management was represented by Mr Griffiths, the deputy CEO and Dr Mahmood, the MD. Helen, the personal assistant of the MD took the minutes. It was a good attendance and my colleagues were able to explain to the managers the daily problems they encountered. The MD stated that he was aware that there were major problems with emergency admissions and that most patients are usually seen by the most junior doctors. Mr Griffiths related the issues of financial constrains currently affecting the NHS. He explained that there had been an increase in trauma cases which had a knock on effect-on capacity. He admitted that ward 4 had been open as an escalation ward for four months and this was not acceptable. Management was looking at the problem and hopefully will return these wards to permanent and fully staffed clinical areas. Before bringing the meeting to a close I mentioned to Mr Griffiths that the Board is running out of time to improve the situation, that it need to listen and changes need to happen.

15th July 2009

The ordinary meeting of the SMSC took place yesterday at the Board Room, Silver Springs Building at the usual time of 12.45 p.m. with eight consultants physicians in attendance in addition to another seven colleagues of assorted specialities with Mr Griffiths representing the Trust. Helen, the pleasant and quietly efficient PA to the MD, handed me the typed minutes of last week's extraordinary meeting which amounted to four pages of deliberations. Upon reading the minutes I am glad that I called for it because it would appear – judging from what the deputy CEO said yesterday – that the Trust is at last listening. Among the medical consultants was Nick O'Mullane, the most senior of them all. Like me, Nick speaks his mind and criticised the current bed management process in the Medical Division which has many flaws: multiple ward moves and patients staying in the Medical Assessment and Admissions Unit (MAU) too long, to name just two.

2nd August 2009

Back in my flat after doing a Waiting List Initiative (WLI) at Tameside, thus bringing much-needed funds to the Hospital. Today I was handed a copy of a report concerning Ward 4. This ward was officially closed a long time ago as part of the *'surgical redesign'* but has re-opened as an 'escalation' ward with seventeen beds. There is no permanent staff, no receptionist and it is very unsafe. A staff nurse felt compelled to write the report because on her night shift she was the *only qualified nurse* supported by *a single auxiliary* who was unfamiliar with the ward. As a result patients suffered because their care was sub-standard and they had to wait for their painkillers, medications etc. How can this be allowed to continue?

12th August 2009

Serious problems with staffing continue. A courageous staff nurse wrote on her Staffing Level Report: *'During an early shift on the 10 August 2009, I was moved from Ward 2 and took handover for ten patients in Ward 4, of which five were heavily dependent, requiring full care with hygiene needs, elimination needs and dietary intake. The nursing auxiliary was needed to escort a patient to another department leaving two staff for seventeen patients in total. Five patients required feeding at lunchtime. This was difficult to achieve with only two staff members. It was difficult to meet all patient needs during this shift due to staffing levels and patient dependency.'*

20th August 2009

Wrote to the Director of Finances, asking for detailed info regarding how we will achieve a 3.6 per cent savings to our annual budget next year. These so-called *efficiency savings* have caused untold harm to patients year after year.

29th August 2009

Sent to the Divisional nurse manager a detailed email regarding incidents during August when the nursing staffing levels on Ward 4 (now an escalation ward) and Ward 2 have been appalling. The managers continue to leave *one qualified nurse in charge of seventeen patients* on Ward 4. Because of shortages in other areas, nurses from Ward 2 are moved, at the last minute, to surgical or medical wards.

I do not expect much to happen after this email.

4th September 2009

Response from the Finance Director. Apart from saying that £4.7million in savings was required and other generalities about reducing costs and generating extra income, there were no details. The main priority of the Board is to ensure that the books are balanced. It's clear to me that patient care is secondary to finances.

11th September 2009

The Trust's financial situation is dire and Mrs Green has arranged for two meetings with the consultants to give an account of the Board's response to this latest crisis. Several colleagues have asked me to discuss it at the Senior Doctors Committee. I have arranged for *three extraordinary meetings* to take place on Thursday 8th, Tuesday 13th and Thurs 15th.

***

Received an email from Joe Horiskey, owner of Rainier Mountaineering Inc. (RMI), saying that my climbing experience is sufficient to join the May 18th 2010 expedition to Mount McKinley (Denali) providing that I get further training this winter in crevasse rescuing, belaying etc. I will certainly do that. Everything that I have read on this mountain says that of the seven highest continental summits, with the exception of Everest, Denali is the toughest, certainly tougher than Aconcagua because it is very cold and it is close to the North Pole. Furthermore, each individual must carry and pull heavy loads. No Porters or mules there!

13th September 2009

Larry Owens emailed today saying that he is not joining me for Denali climb. He feels he is not ready and needs more training. He will continue to prepare hard and may do it in 2011. He says that Rainier Mountaineering Incorporated, RMI, are the best and the guide *Brent Okita* is good. He has been with a group to Mount Rainier with Brent. Pity, I was looking forward to climbing with him again!

21st September 2009

At Orthopaedic Clinical Governance Meeting today, chaired by the Divisional Nurse manager, I raised the issue of unsafe nursing staffing levels and the fact that I was still awaiting a reply to my email. I also reported that I had written to the Risk manager regarding serious incidents in Ward 4 when patients received the wrong medication (two cases) and one was discharged home with medication belonging to a different patient. These incidents are a reflection of systemic failure in this escalation ward.

23rd September 2009

Read a two page letter from the Divisional Nurse manager, basically saying that she sees no problem and the senior sisters have reassured her that safe care was being delivered. Just as I suspected - nothing will be done. What a farce!

2nd October 2009

Very important letter signed by Dr Mahmood, the Medical Director and Mr Griffiths, the Deputy CEO/Director of Elective Services, in which they acknowledge the doctors' and nurses' frustrations that many patients with acute illnesses or injuries are not being admitted into the right ward. The letter outlines the Trust commitment that from this week-end (3/4th October) a policy called: *'Right patient Right ward'* will be in operation at all times, enabling the best possible standard of care for patients.

I sincerely hope this is successful. This letter was circulated to the Financial Director, senior nursing managers, lead consultants, business managers and all consultants.

19th October 2009

Nurses tell me that care of patients continues to be compromised due to poor staffing levels in many wards. Furthermore, escalation wards remain open and patients are admitted into the wrong wards every day. Having already written to the Divisional Nursing Officer and getting nowhere I wrote to the Nursing Director expressing my concerns.

1st November 2009

Received a reply from Mr Dylak, the ND, where he says that the qualified nurse to patient ratio on the escalation ward is *one nurse to ten patients* and the nursing philosophy of the orthopaedic unit is to actively encourage the nursing team to support each other. This means that he believes that nurses can go to other wards to ask a colleague for help – just like that – even if in that ward they may be busy too! I have been raising these issues with this director for eight years and little has changed.

5th November 2009

The Chairman sends me the same old letter saying that I have achieved 100 per cent attendance. Well, it appears that all the training for climbing mountains is keeping me reasonably fit!

6th November 2009

I sent an email to my colleagues explaining that I have written to the Care Quality Commission (CQC), successor to the now-defunct Healthcare Commission, enclosing copies of recent letters to hospital directors, regarding the lack of beds, shortage of junior doctors and nurses.(See Appendix 4)

20th November 2009

There is no improvement! Many patients end up in poorly staffed escalation wards, where they do not receive appropriate care, particularly at week-ends. The CQC has responded to my email saying that they are gathering information.

Looking forward to a day in Snowdon tomorrow, to get away from it all.

21st November 2009

Back from Snowdon. Completed the Watkin route in four hours today. Carried a thirty kilo back pack and I felt it. Preparation for Denali is going well.

8th December 2009

Last night, I emailed Mrs SD, an assessor at the CQC North West, *requesting a major investigation at Tameside.* I have been on call this week-end and the combined effect of lack of beds, nurses and doctors continues to put patients at grave risk. It ends up being a long email in which I explain all my concerns and ask various questions such as the roles of various other bodies like the Strategic Health Authority, the governors of the Foundation Trust, the PCT, and Monitor, the regulator for foundation trusts, regarding these matters. I also ask if the Chairman and the Chief Executive of the CQC had been made aware of my concerns. I finish by saying that I would be grateful for an answer within 21 days.

16th December 2009

I received a hand written letter left by Jim Booth, a BBC producer – *'Dear Mr Peña: I work for Panorama and I called round for a confidential off-the-record chat about the quality of care at Tameside. This is for a possible programme about Foundation Trusts. I know you spoke out in 2005 about care and you might not want to repeat your concerns, but I am keen to get a sense of what is going on in 2009. Could you possibly call me on my mobile or email me.'*

I will consider this request carefully over the next 48 hours. The fact is that no improvements have been made and my vital concerns remain unresolved.

18th December 2009

Finally I have received a reply from a manager regarding the *serious medications incidents* on the orthopaedic Unit some months ago. The reply does not answer all of my questions and today I have written to him again. These were near misses, and I cannot understand why these incidents are graded *low* simply because no apparent harm has been done to the patients.

Chapter Fourteen

DIARIES 2010 – BBC PANORAMA

INTRODUCTION

Why did I accept the invitation of Jim Booth, then a producer at the BBC, to participate in the *Panorama* programme about Foundation Trusts in 2010?

I did it because little had changed in the intervening years since I earlier went public with my concerns, particularly with regard to improving nurse staffing levels, and because of my firm conviction that as many as two deaths in every hundred at the hospital could have been prevented with better care. Pressure from public opinion and the media can force institutions to change; the scandal over MPs expenses is but one example of this and, by the same token, NHS Trusts can also be compelled to address deficiencies and to improve standards.

***

In the February of 2010, I launched a national campaign for the introduction of legislation on minimum nurse and midwife-to-patient ratios. The MD and a number of Lead Consultants wrote to the media criticising me, arguing that it brought the hospital into disrepute. To this day, six years later, still I cannot understand what motivated these senior consultants to send this ill-judged letter to the press.

In my view, the case for mandatory, in-patient nurse-to-patient staffing ratios has been scientifically and statistically made by numerous studies over the last twenty five years. It well established that better nurse/patient ratios are associated with shorter hospital stays, lower complications, and lower in-patient mortality.

The argument against national minimum nurse staffing levels is that a 'one-size-fits all' approach is inappropriate: trusts, it is said, need the freedom and flexibility to set nursing establishments in accordance with local conditions, ward lay-out and prevalent case mix. It is additionally argued that the set minimum will become normative and thereby militate against lower nurse: patient ratios on wards where the case mix is more demanding.

The argument is erroneous. It is a smoke screen erected to conceal and perpetuate the existing reality in which the discretionary approach affords trusts the 'freedom' and 'flexibility' to operate with inadequate staffing levels or an unsuitable skills mix as witnessed not only at Tameside hospital, but hospitals throughout the country and, most notably at Mid-Staffordshire.

***

At Tameside, the intimidation of employees who dared to raise awkward issues remained prevalent. I mention just one example: at an open forum early in 2010, the Clinical Risk Officer of the Trust tried to voice serious concerns but the CEO interrupted her and prevented her from continuing. Many employees witnessed the incident and I referred to it in my report on the Systemic Failure of Governance by the Board, sent in October to the Secretary of State for Health. (See Appendix 8)

2010 was a year when Tameside Hospital again found itself trying to deal with a succession of crises. The devil, though, is in the detail and I hope that when I explain, the reasons for my actions will become clear.

DIARIES 2010

9th January 2010

New Year, same issues. It is a typical winter's day. I am in the theatre waiting for my next case – a total knee replacement – on a whole day operating list. I have told Jim Booth that I will participate in the BBC *Panorama* programme about Foundation Trusts. I am looking forward to a week in Flaine in the French Alps with my daughter Stephanie, in a month's time.

28th January 2010

I have emailed the Rev. Presswood, the Chairman of the Board, requesting an urgent meeting. I referred to numerous letters I have sent to the CEO and members of the Board for many years. I asked him, *'Where is the compassion and dignity the Trust professes to uphold in its mission statement, when patients wait in chairs in the MAU for twelve hours or more for a bed?'* I will inform him that I have accepted an invitation to participate in a BBC *Panorama* programme. (See Appendix 5)

1st February 2010

This is unbelievable! The Chairman has said that my request for a meeting with him is *highly irregular and improper*, although on this occasion he is prepared to make an exception. It reinforces my impression that the Chairman is not doing what he is supposed to do, i.e. together with the non-executive directors, be the critical, or, at least, challenging voice of the Board and ensure that quality of care and patient safety is not sacrificed at the expense of meeting targets and balancing the books. He does not seem in any rush to meet me. I asked my secretary to inform him that I am away on annual leave from 13th to 20th February.

2nd February 2010

Twenty-six consultants attended the SMSC meeting yesterday. Thirteen sent their apologies. There was a long discussion on the effects of lack of beds across the hospital, which causes patients to be admitted to escalation wards or to be found a bed in a ward that is completely inappropriate for their medical condition. I stated that I had written to the Chairman in November 2009 and again recently, raising these issues. It was a well-attended meeting considering that it takes place at 12.45 p.m. and for a few years now our employer does not provide any refreshments, even water to drink. This policy, obviously to save money, has been in place for about four years and applies to all meetings that doctors attend, including Divisional meetings. As a result many doctors arrive late because they go for lunch, or do not attend at all because of long queues in the canteen. The Trust also abruptly stopped the provision of drinking water in clinical areas, such as theatre, recently. This caused angry protests by the consultants on the intranet, resulting in its eventual reinstatement.

8th February 2010

At 3.00 p.m. Luke, Simon and Steve from BBC *Panorama* came to my flat today, as arranged. Simon interviewed me whilst Steve filmed. The questions were very direct. Hope that my answers were clear and to the point. Time will tell. During filming I felt relaxed and at ease. They left at about 7.00 p.m.

I am now committed to this course of action for the benefit of patients, the community and the nurses. My feelings right now are those of relief that the interview is completed. I must be daring and endure the wait and hope that the Board and senior management will finally resign so that a new era can begin, providing safe care and ensuring no further preventable deaths.

9th February 2010

A colleague consultant orthopaedic surgeon wrote to the Lead Consultant to complain about the lack of beds to admit his elective patients. He copied in the MD, Dr Mahmood, and managers. All the patients of another colleague were cancelled today for the same reason. I stayed late to send an email to the CEO, Mrs Green, and the Medical Director and also copied in the Chairman, although I do not expect much from them by way of response.

10th Feb 2010

Woke *up at 4 a.m. Mind racing – thinking of my involvement in BBC Panorama and its implications for my career.* I rationalise that I will inform the Chairman beforehand and that my reasons for participating are valid. I know that systemic failures are costing lives.

Yesterday the *Manchester Evening News'* front page headline read: '*I won't quit,*' says crisis hospital boss, referring to Tameside. I hope that this public debate will bring about the resignation of the CEO and the Board. Enough is enough. The people of Tameside and Glossop deserve a hospital that provides care to the highest standards on all shifts, day and night, seven days a week – so that the vulnerable do not suffer as a result of shortages of nurses or doctors, or because they are cared for on inappropriate wards.

A senior consultant commented pretty well on point on the hospital intranet today saying:

'*Ultimately quality care provision is not rocket science – providing acceptable medical and nursing staff/patient ratios and correcting for extra capacity while taking care not to "rob Peter to pay Paul" usually does it. Also dedicated speciality wards for patients are the norm because they work.*'

I agree entirely with his opinion. What a tragedy that the Board at this hospital has been languishing in a state of denial for so many years.

12th Feb 2010

5.00 a.m.! Woke up again with my mind in overdrive. Yesterday, I sent an email to my colleagues asking for a Vote of No-Confidence in the Board. The situation has reached a critical point. The email copied to the Chairman of the Board, the CEO and the MD reads:

Subject: Vote of Confidence in the Board of Tameside Hospital Foundation Trust.

Importance: High

Dear colleagues:

'*After a long period of reflection and following discussions with several senior colleagues, I have come to the conclusion that it is now necessary to ask all the senior doctors at this Trust (Consultants, Associate Specialists, Staff Grade doctors and Speciality doctors) to participate in a secret ballot appertaining to clinicians' confidence in the Trust Board.*

The Ballot will take place on Thursday 25th February, between 9.00a.m. and 5.00 p.m. in the Post- Graduate Centre. I will arrange for the presence of impartial observers at the vote and subsequent count.

The ballot will simply say:

I do have confidence in the Board   I do not have confidence in the Board

13th Feb 2010

As I had anticipated, the pro-management consultants have immediately rallied to defend the Board on the Intranet, despite what has been happening at the hospital for such a long time. Rather than respond individually, I have written again to all my colleagues copying in the Chairman, CEO and MD explaining that those supporting the Board now have an opportunity to express their support through the democratic process. I reminded my colleagues that those who had no confidence feel constrained to express their views in open meetings, and I pointed out that many consultants supporting the Board worked in non-clinical areas less affected by systemic failures.

Parts of my email read:

'Can any of you, hand on heart, tells me that Dignity in Care no longer matters?' Think of the Medical Assessment and Admissions Unit in the evenings, with patients waiting for hours for a bed sitting in chairs. Are patients safe in escalation wards? Are nurse/patient ratios always safe?'

The email went on to acknowledge that improvements had been made in some areas and congratulated the consultants involved, but added that, unfortunately, there continued to be a significant minority of patients whose care was sub-optimal and that, regrettably, this had not been addressed by the Board. I urged everybody to attend Mrs Green's especially arranged forum to take place one day before the ballot, where they could hear the arguments from the MD and CEO in defence of the Board. I ended by saying that I would not be campaigning as I will be on annual leave for a week.

***

On a happier note, I got an email from James Tyler, a former Senior House

Officer who is now a Specialist Trainee in the South East Thames rotation, saying that being a Registrar is challenging, but he is coping. It has made me think back when I took my first post as a Registrar at the Mayday hospital in Croydon, a lifetime back. I remember when I did my first hip operation on my own! James attaches a draft of the paper we are writing on a new technique to close the surgical wound after a knee replacement. I have emailed him back to confirm my approval.

19th Feb 2010

Just back from Flaine, a ski resort in the French Alps, where I was on a skiing holidays with Steph, my daughter. What a week! Steph fell as she snowboarded and dislocated her left shoulder on the piste. I was skiing in front when I heard her shouting as she fell. Fortunately, my assessment showed no associated fracture or neural or vascular damage. She was in severe pain and we were high up and isolated. I knew that it would be some time before help arrived. I managed to put it back easily and within seconds the pain stopped. We will not forget this past week. It was a succession of character- building incidents: missing luggage and snow board, wrong bus etc. Still I could not forget the hospital issues and my efforts to improve the quality of care. I am told that on Monday there will be a special meeting called by the clinicians who are opposed to a vote of no confidence in the Board.

22nd February 2010 Monday

The special meeting called by pro-management clinicians – concerned about a possible vote of No Confidence in the Board – took place today. They were surprised to see me. About twenty attended including a handful that support my views and dared to go. The majority made statements defending the Board and, after listening to their arguments, I agreed not to proceed to a formal vote at this moment in time. The situation at the hospital is one where, in reality, 'the Emperor has no clothes' – an opinion I make no effort to conceal.

Today, I received an email from a manager answering the questions I addressed to him in late December last year. His response does not inspire confidence. In my view, many of the serious drug administration errors – giving wrong medication - by nurses occur when they are under remorseless pressure, on shifts that are too demanding for the number of staff on duty. One of the cases involved an insulin drip started on a wrong patient; another patient was given amitriptyline by mistake. Need I say more?

25th Feb 2010

Read the Editorial in *The Independent* newspaper today entitled, 'The real lessons of this NHS disaster,' It derides Health secretary, Andy Burnham's claim that the scandal of appalling patient care exposed at Mid-Staffordshire Hospital Trust was 'ultimately a local failure', pointing out that, *'For one thing Stafford is not the only hospital that has put patients' lives at risk in recent years.'* This is all too true, as is the editorial's further comment that Mid-Stafford is a tragic reflection of the abject failure of the regulatory system. From 2005 to 2008 Stafford was adjudged by the regulators and the Department of Health to be performing well, achieving Foundation Trust status, supposedly the benchmark of excellence. The regulators turned a blind eye to cost cuts, says the editorial . . . which could just as easily have been describing the situation at Tameside hospital or, I suspect, many other hospitals throughout the country.

1st March 2010

So much has happened during the last 10 days. The earthquake and tsunami in Chile. So far 750 victims. Still do not know about my brother and family in Concepción. Hope they are safe.

***

The BBC *Panorama* programme will be aired next Monday. I live in hope that it will finally trigger some answers from the Board. I have read the reports from Alberti, de Thome and Robert Francis QC., regarding Mid-Staffs Foundation Trust which highlight all the same issues that we are experiencing at Tameside. Makes me more determined than ever to continue my campaign for improvement here.

3rd March 2010

I went to Trust headquarters to a meeting with the Chairman, the Rev. Presswood. Mr Dylak, the Director of Nursing, and the Medical Director, Dr Mahmood, were in attendance. I had requested the meeting to inform the Chairman about my participation in the BBC *Panorama* programme. He appeared unconcerned with the daily problems caused by the hospital's lack of capacity. I gave an example of a patient of mine that last night was woken and moved to another ward at three o'clock in the morning. He replied by saying that these untimely movements of patients were part of the modern NHS! He was completely unaware of the Report and recommendations of the

Royal College of Physicians from 2008 which highlighted serious concerns regarding patient care. Neither did he have any meaningful answers to my questions on Clinical Governance and the Trust's lack of transparency. Sadly, I emerged from the meeting convinced beyond any lingering doubt that the Chairman was anything but the strong, independent voice that is supposed to provide one of the essential checks and balances designed to ensure the robust, integrated governance of hospital trusts. On the contrary, it became clear to me that under his leadership the Board's main preoccupation would remain the Trust's finances, to which patient care would continue to be subordinated. I told him quite openly that his answers and arguments at the meeting only served to reaffirm my view that I should have no confidence in him or the Board.

8th March 2010 9: 30 p.m. Monday

Watched BBC *Panorama* about failing hospital Trusts. I was nervous because I did not know quite what to expect. It explained that the current system of hospital regulation is based on self-assessment, on which basis the Care Quality Commission (CQC) rates trusts as 'excellent', 'good', 'fair' or 'weak'. The CQC only actually inspects 20 per cent of trusts each year, rating the performance of the remainder on assessments provided by the trusts themselves. Brian Jarman, Professor of Epidemiology and Public Health at Imperial College, London, stated that he could not believe that hospitals had been self-assessing for years. Of 28 hospitals randomly inspected in 2008/2009 the CQC found that 60 per cent had assessed themselves inaccurately. I stated in the programme that public opinion was needed to improve safety and that Tameside Hospital did not have enough staff or beds to provide the necessary level of care for vulnerable patients; on many wards, the ratio of nurses and doctors to the number of patients was not always adequate. Regarding the much higher than average mortality rates at the hospital, I gave my personal opinion that one to two per cent of deaths were avoidable. Professor Jarman's contention that mortality rates should be considered a potential indicator of poor care – with the caveat that statistical errors can occur – came across well. The tragic testimony to poor care of patients and relatives interviewed in the programme was deeply moving and saddened me enormously.

13th March 2010

Yesterday I met with Mrs Green and Medical Director, Dr Mahmood. Beverley Daniels, personal assistant to the MD took notes. The CEO began by explaining that the aim of the meeting was to determine and agree a constructive way forward following the recent media coverage. Both Mrs Green and the MD questioned why I felt the hospital had benefited from the programme and in particular my appearance on it. I explained that given that the serious issues I had been reporting – both internally as well as to the regulators – remain largely unresolved, the Trust was running the risk of becoming another Mid-Staffs. In my view, the action I had taken was justified. I expressed my frustration that for many years nursing shifts have been under-staffed and the use of inappropriate escalation wards has continued. I raised the matter of funding and reminded Mrs Green of an offer made three years ago by the senior doctors to support the Trust Board in a request for extra funding. The CEO once again rejected the offer saying that the tariff system was yielding adequate funding. I explained that I intended to start a campaign for legislation on mandatory nurse/midwife-to-patient ratios. Mrs Green asked for twelve months to 'turn things around' without any contact with the media. I said that I have waited eight years for change – real change – and it has not happened.

I think that the *Panorama* programme has shaken her but she and her advisors are not prepared to act swiftly. For instance she remained of the opinion that consultants could not communicate issues of serious concern directly to the Non-Executive Directors. The meeting was cordial and continued for ninety minutes. We agreed to a further meeting in two to three weeks' time.

20th March 2010
Drove to the Lake District, to trek Great Lansdale Pike, with Julie. As with many mountains, the trail in places runs close to a brook which provides us with a primeval background of colour and sound. I carried a 30 kg backpack in preparation for Denali. It is a steep climb and we stopped at the tarn for refreshments and a rest. Thereafter, we carried on to the summit. It was heavy going for both of us but, because of the weight I was carrying, I was slow and Julie kept pace. Before leaving we went to the bar of the Great Lansdale Hotel to have a well-deserved drink. Wonderful day!

24th March 2010
A consultant obstetrician sent an email on the hospital intranet asking for my resignation as Chair of the Senior Medical Staff Committee (SMSC). According to him, complaints against the hospital will increase because of my

appearance on Panorama. Within an hour of his email, a senior consultant replied directly, commenting that:

Where we have good doctor/nurse/bed/patient ratios – e.g. ITU, Obstetrics – we get good results; Tameside punches above its weight – e.g. today's Daily Mail article on an obstetric/ITU success.

Where we have poor ratios, results are not so good and Dr Foster [the independent body that compiles comparative mortality rates for trusts in England] has put us on the CQC radar. Two types of environment, same hospital, two outcomes. Unfortunately, the human psyche is prone to give poor results greater weighting. So we have to give them due attention. I wonder how it escaped your notice the inadequate number of beds, doctors, nurse and medical staff we have had at Tameside for a considerable number of years. It is this situation that has severely compromised the delivery of care to our patients and it is right and proper that this be discussed openly and freely otherwise the problem will never be solved. Sadly, owing to the hierarchical and tardy system of management, Tameside has not been effective at delivering changes that benefit our patients, in fact it has had the opposite effect, and hence the bad press. Putting patients first must be the first consideration . . .'

30th March 2010

I am at my office getting ready to chair the SMSC meeting at 12.45 p.m. today. This is our first meeting since the BBC *Panorama* broadcast. I have done my rounds and my patients are doing well. Walking the corridors is a mixed experience. Many colleagues and people stop me and say that what I did was brave; that what I said was correct and needed to be said. Nurses in particular tell me so. Porters approach me to offer their support, and make no mistake – they, as much as anybody, know what happens at our hospital. They fully appreciate how busy and over-stretched nurses are as they move patients from ward to ward in the endless juggling of hospital beds – and, quietly and respectfully, move bodies. Similarly, many paramedics (ambulance men and women) have recognised me and assured me that what I did was correct. However, a minority of staff, including high-ranking managers and doctors in leading positions walk past me as if I were not there; they disapprove of what I did and, it is clear from their faces, they despise me for it.

A letter received today, from a stranger who is writing a book on leadership and saw the programme, gives me heart when he says that there are hundreds and hundreds of people who are with me all the way, even though they may be silent in expressing their views in these difficult times. Thank you, Prof NJ.

31st March 2010

Yesterday, the SMSC meeting was attended by 22 consultants. Various items were discussed including bed capacity with a consultant highlighting the fact that there had been several occasions when junior doctors had felt bullied into moving patients to other wards. Regarding *Panorama*, I made it clear that I presented my personal opinion. Several pro-management consultants were upset. Nick O'Mullane was the only one who came to my defence.

1st April 2010

A second get-together with Mrs Green, at her request. Long meeting which achieved very little. I said that if there is no change I may write to the Secretary of State and the regulator, Monitor and that I would wait for the CQC's forthcoming report, following its recent inspection of the hospital.

I do not believe in the capacity of the present management to change anything in a real and meaningful way. In my view the members of the Board collectively and individually do not recognise with clarity and courage the need to improve.

14th April 2010

An editorial in the *Manchester Evening News,* entitled, 'Patient Care', goes to the heart of the debate to launch my national campaign for legislation on nurse- and midwife-to-patient ratios, acknowledging, in summary, that it would be costly at a time of public sector cuts. Still this is no justification for neglecting patient care. The separate article in the paper on this issue by its health correspondent, Amanda Crook, is fair.

16th April 2010

Marion, a nice lady who works in admin and is a keen rambler and WH a nurse matron, who also likes trekking, and I, have been trying to organise an official Tameside Hospital trip to Mount Snowdon for 8 May, but we cannot do it by coach because the insurance is too much. We will go in our own cars. Marion, who works in planning, joined the hospital only recently; she has seen deficiencies and has been critical of certain bad practices.

22nd April 2010

My campaign for legislation on nurse- and midwife-to-patient ratios is reported in the *Tameside Advertiser* today. I placed a petition on-line. I said that it is not illegal for a hospital to leave one nurse to look after seventeen or more highly dependent patients – which is why hospitals can get away with it.

Also in the *Advertiser* is an open letter to the media from the hospital's Medical Director and the Lead Consultants from A&E, Paediatrics, Radiology, Pathology, Surgery, Medicine, Obstetrics and Gynaecology, together with the Safety Lead, regarding my campaign, saying in part:

'His call for national legislation (on nurse- and midwife-to-patient ratios) has led to further criticism of the hospital and does real harm to the confidence people have in Tameside. It cripples the morale of our staff and is not conducive to taking us forward and restoring public confidence.'

This is unbelievable! Suffice to say that I went to most wards in the hospital and collected over three hundred signatures from nurses and midwives and did not encounter a single nurse or midwife that objected to the campaign; I was overwhelmed by their support.

23rd April 2010

Our other local paper, *Tameside Reporter*, yesterday carried an article mentioning the campaign and noting that David Heyes, the local MP for Ashton-under-Lyne, supports it. I have a great deal of respect for Mr Heyes: he cares about health issues and his record proves it. On the other hand the MD sees the campaign as bad publicity, missing the point completely.

26th April 2010

I met with Marion and WH today to discuss the forthcoming trip to Snowdon. We are doing the Miners' Path. We are expecting about twenty trekkers. Hope the weather is ok. It would be good training for me. I will be carrying my pack with 30 kg, largely made up of two sizeable stones.

30th April 2010

Just back from a big day of trekking at the Great Lansdale Traverse with Dominic and Andrew, two male nurses from the Intensive Care Unit, and their friend Colin and my friend Richard, who works on the Trauma Unit. We did Pike of Stickle, Loft Craig and Harrison Stickles in eight hours. Colin's legs gave out on the way down and Andrew showed his strength by carrying him part of the way.

2nd May 2010

Readers' letters in the latest edition of the *Tameside Advertiser* gave me heart and the courage to continue my campaign for improvement: JG Coulthard writes that it costs nothing to treat patients with dignity, highlighting the need for more compassion; Abdul Ahmad asks the top managers to take more responsibility for the cuts to capacity to save money, resulting in patients waiting for beds most mornings; Ray Hake's missive describes the frequently chaotic and hurried discharge of patients due to the lack of beds; and correspondence from Paul Tucker from Ashton is as clear as mountain water, asserting that there are many excellent staff at Tameside hospital who are demoralised and frightened to speak out and going on to explain the need for national legislation on the ratio of skilled nurses (and midwives) to patients.

Letters of support also from: David Rhodes from Ashton; Edward Walton from Audenshaw; Brian Morrison from Hyde; and Penny Weir from Dukinfield. I thank you all from the bottom of my heart.

12th May 2010

The Iceland volcanic eruptions continue to disturb aviation, and many flights in Europe and from America are cancelled daily. I hope that it does not affect my plans to go to Alaska. I have trained hard for this trip including pulling a heavy tyre along Chew Road up the steep hill from the Dovestone Reservoir to the Chew Reservoir. Later, I progressed to pulling a sledge weighted with sand bags up the same road. I have done it at all hours, even at night using a head torch. I think that I am ready.

16th May 2010

Julie has come to help me to check every item of my climbing gear. We went through the list and we packed them inside my heavy-duty duffel bag. Last minute: big problem – the ashes from a volcano in Iceland have ruined my flight plan. Trail Finders is desperately trying to re-route me. Luckily, I left an extra day spare and so may still get to Anchorage on time.

Chapter Fifteen

MOUNT MCKINLEY (DENALI)

Mount McKinley, in Alaska's Denali National Park, is one of the coldest places on earth and colloquially referred to by most climbers simply as Denali. Some say, only half-jokingly, that climbing Everest is a good preparation for it. At 20,320 feet, 6,194m it is only slightly higher than Kilimanjaro and much lower than Aconcagua but demands greater effort, mental strength and experience.

Denali's latitude, close to the Arctic Circle, makes it harder to climb than mountains of similar height elsewhere. Because the earth is not a perfect sphere, the atmosphere is thinner at the poles. Physiologically, the summit is equivalent to 7,000m near the Equator. Night temperatures of minus 40 degrees Celsius, at camps as low as 4,000m, can occur. The dangers of altitude sickness, broken bones, hypothermia, frostbite, or even death are ever present; it should never be under-estimated. Denali in the aboriginal Athabascan language means the 'Big One' or the 'High One.' It is a very fitting name. There are 30 possible routes up, but 90 per cent of climbers take the West Buttress. Getting to this route requires flying into the Kahiltna Glacier at 7,200 feet where Base Camp is situated. Climbing season and exploring the National Park runs from late April to early July. During those months, rangers live on the mountain in tent camps to help to protect the environment and provide assistance. About 1,200 climbers a year try to get to the summit; success rate is about 52 per cent.

TALKEETNA

The old railroad town of Talkeetna is at the junction of three rivers and in the local Athabascan dialect, the word means, 'Where the rivers join.'

The Alaskan railway starts at the seaside town of Seward going north through Anchorage to Talkeetna and then on to Denali National Park station before finishing in Fairbanks. Talkeetna is a quaint town that has evolved into the place where climbers prepare. In 1993, it was placed on the National Register for Historic Places. It is also a day trip haven for flight-seeing around the scenic views, for jet boat rides and for fishing.

RECOLLECTIONS OF MCKINLEY

After I landed at Anchorage airport, I was anxious to see my equipment bags on the carrousel. I did not want a repeat of my Barcelona to Santiago experience on my way to Aconcagua! Luckily, within a short time, my black duffel bag and red ski boots' bag – which I use to carry my equally heavy mountaineering plastic boots – arrived. I shouldered my bags and moved off to search for my fellow climbers.

Seeing a small group of climbers milling around, I asked if they were with Rainier Mountaineering Inc. (RMI), the American climbing company that had organised the ascent. A friendly person, with Japanese features, but perfect American English, confirmed the fact and welcomed me. He was Brent Okita, the main guide and the man in charge.

After a while, other flights landed carrying more climbers. Eventually, we were all gathered together and we boarded a mini-van that took us to Talkeetna.

I studied the group; all except one – Dennis – were younger than I. Several were even younger than my two older sons. Some were in their mid-forties. They all looked fit and strong. Dennis was bearded and reserved. He looked like a seasoned old climber, as was proved to be the case throughout the trip.

William was a fireman, early thirties, medium height, and very strong. Craig was a KIA car sales clerk, almost seven feet tall, slim and wiry. He shared a tent with Joe, a strong-looking entrepreneur.Kristian was tall and sturdy, late twenties, very self-assured – he had climbed to the summit of Aconcagua. He had the best gear and clothing of us all. His boots were the then, recently developed, technical high-altitude 'Millet' boots. He was the only one in the group with a satellite telephone and he shared a tent with Pearce, who was of similar age and a physician's assistant. I had not heard of this profession before and I enjoyed his company.

Mickey was mid-forties, a businessman, married to a doctor. He was an American of Mexican descent but did not speak Spanish. He was fit and confident of summiting. He shared a tent with Dennis. I shared a tent with Larry – not to be confused with Larry whom I met in Argentina – who was in his late forties, a lawyer for a private corporation, very fit and well prepared.

As we arrived in Talkeetna, before entering the small town, we crossed the railway line and went into a small airport which has several air-taxi firms that take climbers to, the fancily named, Denali International Airport at Kahiltna Base Camp.

We parked the mini-van next to a container at the airfield where we put our gear and a short time later, after stopping at the driver's souvenir shop, we walked to our hotel on the edge of town. It reminded me of frontier towns by the Chilean Andes.

***

The following day after a gigantic breakfast, we went to the Rangers' Cabin to register. We waited in a large sitting room admiring pictures and books on display. On a wall, I noted a map of the mountain and about 100 pins stuck on it, each pin representing a climber already processed to trek the mountain this season. Soon there would be twelve more pins on it – our team.

Eventually we were called to a small classroom and a ranger gave the group a short power point presentation regarding the etiquette in Denali National Park. Special attention was given to sanitation and waste. The Clean Mountain Can (CMC) has been in use since 2001. (A strong plastic barrel serving as a toilet). It has a secure top and can hold about seven litres of human waste. It is compulsory above Basin Camp. We all registered individually, obtained our permits and left on foot to sort out our equipment.

We took temporary possession of a hangar and Brent asked us to display our equipment and food on the floor, so he, Walter, and Carrie, the other guides, could check it. As he read and checked the equipment, item by item, from a long list, he noted that I did not have three essentials: over-boots, feather-and-down trousers and an avalanche receiver. Brent made it clear to me that unless I managed to get all three I would not be boarding the plane. He was deadly serious. My only chance was that I could find them in Talkeetna. I went in search of them with Larry, who himself needed over-boots, and I was lucky that I found a second hand avalanche receiver for $500 as well as the other two missing items. After two hours, I returned to sort out my gear and the provisions that I had hurriedly bought in a supermarket on the way to Talkeetna from Anchorage a day earlier. My fellow trekkers had brought most of their snacks from home, already neatly packed for daily consumption. My food supply was a mess and worst of all, as I discovered later, it was the wrong type because most of it froze and, in consequence, I carried useless weight up the mountain. Tortillas and Pringles were fine, salami and bagels were not. At last, I got myself sorted, and my bag was weighed. Brent showed us the tents and we practised erecting them. We tried our snowshoes and learned how to load our sledges. We also practised with our avalanche receivers.

The weather was overcast the following day and after another big breakfast, we left for the airport – hoping. Eventually, around mid-day, we were given the all-clear to go and we were all relieved. Inwardly, I was a little apprehensive and I am sure I was not alone, but none of us showed it. We took off from the tarmac at almost sea level for a flight over rivers, woods and tundra and then the One Shot Pass. From the air, the scenery was amazing. Eventually we saw Mount McKinley. It was spectacular. The glaciers leading to its summit looked cold and fearsome. The unwelcome thought flashed across my mind that the climb was going to be a difficult one, but I quickly dismissed this negative notion. We took photos, gasped at the mountain, and looked forward to our adventure on it.

After about thirty minutes, we descended to the Kahiltna glacier where the pilot skilfully landed the single engine plane on ice at Base Camp.

We carried our gear away from the plane. The place was crowded with climbers, a few waiting for their taxi-planes, others camping in tents and the rest, like us, beginning the climb.

Brent distributed the communal equipment – food, pots for cooking, tents, fuel containers and CMCs – in equal lots and we loaded one each on to our sledges, together with personal things and duffel bags. I carried a can with ten litres of fuel, a pot and a bag of food.

We divided into two groups, the members of each group roped to each other. The process of roping became routine after a few days. There is a necessity to maintain the right tension on the rope, control the sledge in front, and stop it sliding at the ridges. The weather was good and rather hot. However, the sun weakens the snow bridges over the crevasses and makes them perilous, hence the need to stay roped at all times.

***

Upon leaving camp, the first part of the way is downhill and we descended 175 metres. The descent is known as Heartbreak Hill, because it is hard when returning.

After the downhill, we steadily climbed 350 metres in a semi-circle around Mount Frances and after six hours, we arrived at Ski Hill Camp. The first task was to flatten the snow on the site chosen for camp. After being reminded by our guides of the importance of always holding the tents, because they can be blown away, we set them up. The ropes were secured to the snow by pickets, our axes and walking sticks.

The kitchen-cum-mess was a deep round hole in the ground with a snow seating ridge cut around it and a snow 'table' at the centre from where a pole rose to hold a specially made canopy. We found similar holes, left from earlier groups, in all the camps which we took possession of. We built snow walls around our tents and the mess, so we all got used to cutting the ice blocks with saws and building the walls. It was a team effort. To keep snow clean to make water, the guides marked a pee hole, with a long thin wand and a small flag. The CMC (toilet) was left at a discrete place behind a snow wall. This became a routine at every camp.

We huddled together for warmth in the kitchen hole. We took our mats to sit on and we always looked forward to breakfast and the dinner at night, our chance to have something hot. The evening meals were a time when we got to know each other. The food was prepared by our guides, who took it in turns. Tortillas and burritos were a great favourite, as was spaghetti, fried bacon and mash. We shared our own food as well. My appetite was always good but it was Kristian who ate for two, every day!

The mountain was busy with climbers going up. We were a big fraternity sharing one dream: to stand at the top of Denali. Women and men, young and old, we were all carrying big rucksacks and pulling heavy sledges. I saw the effort and pain reflected in their faces, as I am sure they saw it in mine.

***

Day after day, we walked up the trail in the snow pulling our sledges. I was happy that I had done endurance training in England, pulling a heavy tyre many times up the road from Dovestones to Chew Reservoir and later a sledge packed with sand bags. It allowed me to keep up with my companions.

The higher we ascended, the more we all realised that we were a team and we trusted each other with our lives. Under the expert guidance of Brent, supported by Walter and Carrie, we pushed up without any major setbacks, other than stepping into occasional very small crevasses and a few minor slips with sledges when going from Ski Hill Camp to Kahiltna Pass Camp.

Mental strength is essential to climb a big mountain, and Denali is no exception. We would walk for hours with only snow and ice all around day after day and, inevitably, it becomes monotonous and impossible to calculate distances. As on previous mountains, I kept a 'mental movie' running in my mind, hour after hour. Parallel to it, my senses were alert and focused on the task ahead.

A particularly challenging stage of Denali lies between Basin Camp and High Camp. We did this section twice. Firstly, for cache and for acclimatisation, and two days later, for good. There is a steep 50 degree headwall that we ascended using fixed ropes aided by a device called a Jumar, a mechanical hand-held ascender. This wall is part of a bergschrund, an enormous crevasse that separates the moving glacier from the mountain. I carried a 30 kg sack on my back and I had to summon all my strength to get to the top. I had to, because I had other climbers following me. Every 50 metres I had to unhook myself and then re-hook to the rope at the other side of a picket fixing the rope to the ground, whilst quickly carrying on pulling myself upwards using the ascender. It was hard work and very cold on the glacier up the headwall. I was using the Jumar with my right hand and in my effort to exert a firm grip, I kept my fingers clasped and immobile and my hand froze. I shouted to Walter who was ahead of me. He gave the obvious answer, *'Change the Jumar to your left!'* I did so and continued to the top of the headwall, where I removed my gloves. My right hand was the colour of red wine and painful. I rubbed it for a few minutes and it gradually recovered.

We were on a ridge above Washburn Thumb, above 5,000m when I heard the scream, *'fall-i-ing...'* Mickey, who was in my group, had slipped down the edge and shouted out, followed by successive yells from all of us. I threw myself to the ground burying my axe in the ice. For a few, interminable seconds my fear was all-consuming and I thought this was it – that the fixed rope and axes would not hold and we would fall down the abyss to our deaths. Mercifully, however, they held firm and, after a few minutes, we got to our feet, composed ourselves and continued on our way up. The shout from Mickey had been a trained response, drilled into us. The drill is that the instant you begin to fall you must yell fall and bury your axe and it applies to everyone. It had been a frightening experience.

***

The first summit bid was a success and included Brent and everyone else except Mickey, Pierce and me, because we simply were too tired for it. Carrie, the young guide, was left in charge of us.

Our turn to reach the top, however, came the following day when bravely Brent led us up, except, that is, for Mickey, who heaved and sighed: *'I've run out of gas.'*

As we approached the summit ridge the weather closed in, the wind increased and the temperature dropped. It must have been minus 15 degrees Celsius. There was a group coming down and as we waited on a very narrow ledge for them to pass, one female climber pointed at my nose and said, *'Your nose is frost-bitten.'* I had not been aware of it and I covered it with my neck bandana.

I was so lucky to have had Brent, an exceptional guide who summited twice to give Larry, Carrie and me the chance to get to the top. Summit day was for me the hardest day of my life, harder than Aconcagua. At the top, I felt such an indescribable array of emotions: happiness, pride, fear and apprehension, because I still needed to get down safely. I am not religious, but I felt grateful to the creator for allowing me to experience that unique feeling of achievement.

***

It took two days to get down. We were all limping due to sores on our feet and other minor injuries. From Brent, I learned many things. One of them was that the best way to treat a blister or a pressure sore on the feet is using duct tape. A few days into the climb, William – the fire-fighter – suffered massive heel sores. He showed them to us. I knew that Brent went to his tent every morning to treat them, but I never enquired how, until the day of my summit, when, on the way down to high camp, I too developed blisters on both my feet. I told Brent who, to my surprise, took his duct tape and skilfully applied a piece over the blisters. It was magic! Instant relief! Since then I always carry duct tape with me. It is also invaluable to mend equipment, poles, tents, clothes and a myriad other things. In fact, I accidentally stabbed my down jacket with my axe and I repaired it with tape immediately, whilst perching on a ledge high on Denali.

During our descent, we had our second whiteout, at night, just after Windy Corner. One moment it was clear and the next all went white with snow and wind. We were roped and our two separate groups were about a mile apart. Using our torches, we trekked down at night because it is colder – making the snow bridges over the crevasses more solid with less chance of them breaking under our weight. During the whiteout, we stopped and it cleared after an hour, allowing us to keep going. We had a plane to catch!

Dawn came and we continued to descend. Eventually we got to Ski Hill where we took a break. We re-started but the tiredness was evident in all. We had been walking since midnight and we still needed to ascend Heartbreak Hill. Eventually we reached it. I told myself that it is just like going up to the Chew Reservoir. In reality, it was four times harder, but we all made it. Within three hours we had all landed safely, back in Talkeetna. We had a big celebration meal planned. I was looking forward to a long shower.

The celebration dinner was fabulous. Carrie dressed up and looked like who she really was, a lovely young girl. Every one of us admired her courage and strength. Brent presented us with certificates and we made speeches thanking him and the guides. Afterwards we went to a pub and had a few more beers and in spite of our tiredness, aching limbs and blisters, we still had some energy for dancing. I said my good-byes at midnight and limped to the hotel. For all of us it had been an exceptional and unforgettable experience.

***

I had three days to spare before my flight back to England and I decided to take the train to Fairbanks the following day. As I said at the beginning, I love trains. The journey from Talkeetna to Fairbanks is spectacular and Fairbanks is really the last frontier. I visited a factory called The Great Alaskan Bowl, where they make maple woodcarvings with engravings. I bought three small bowls with Denali engraved on them and I asked them to engrave the dates of my successful summit. One I gave to Julie, the other to Michelle, my secretary, and the other was for me – to display proudly.

Chapter Sixteen

DIARIES LATE 2010 – VOTE OF NO CONFIDENCE

Every vote and every voice has value and should be heard;
Everyone should be able to shape the decisions that affect their lives;
Our institutions should reflect the people they serve;
People should be able to hold those in power to account.

The values of the Electoral Reform Society, founded in 1884 and the oldest organisation concerned with ballots and elections in the world.

INTRODUCTION

In May 2010, I was re-elected chair of the Senior Medical Staff Committee (SMSC) amidst a hurtful and venomous campaign against me from a small number of consultants. One of them – an obstetrician – stood against me as a pro-Board candidate. There were 88 votes and I obtained 61. The ballot was secret and the counting supervised by the British Medical Association industrial relations officer.

Having won the overwhelming support of my colleagues, it was the continuing failure to provide compassionate and safe care to many patients – particularly, but not exclusively, on emergency pathways – and the utter incapacity of management to effectively address the situation, together with the publication of the Francis report into the scandal of Mid Staffordshire Hospital Trust, that left me with no further options other than to request a Vote of No Confidence in the Board.

It was in October 2010, therefore, that I wrote to the Rev. Presswood, the Chairman of the Board, to inform him that arrangements for the vote were underway. He responded by insisting that the right and proper thing to do was to call for a meeting and have a show of hands. This was clearly inappropriate – unethical, in fact – and tantamount to coercing everyone into making an open declaration. There are votes that must always be totally secret – and this was clearly one of them.

It was an extremely serious matter and I wrote to the Electoral Reform Society who initially accepted my request for them to conduct the ballot. However, after consulting – in writing – with the Chairman of the Trust they withdrew their offer.

In retrospect, this U-turn on the part of the Society probably affected the outcome because a number of clinicians did not vote for fear that confidentiality might be compromised or that the way individual votes were cast might be deduced by management from the distribution of the vote and the list of actual and eligible voters.

This unanticipated possibility derived from the fact that all doctors eligible to vote were on a list from which the Director of Human Resources, as a member of the adjudicating panel, ticked the name of everyone that cast a vote. Thus, although the vote was secret the Director knew exactly who had voted and this may explain why out of 121 ballot papers sent to eligible voters by post only 91 were returned, during a two-week period.

The ballot was designed to determine whether there existed, in the first instance, sufficient support for a motion to thereafter proceed to a full Vote of No Confidence in the Board. In the event, the motion was won by one vote – 46 for and 45 against. However, in the circumstances, a decision against proceeding was taken in order to maintain unity and to avoid further polarisation and division.

This, though, was not the end of the matter. The vote had demonstrated the strength of feeling and extent of disquiet amongst senior medical staff but the Chairman, it transpired, failed to report events to the regulatory body for foundation trusts, Monitor, which was a requirement under its Terms of Authorisation. The Trust would subsequently be held to account by the regulator for this infraction.

***

At this juncture, a few words about the way in which payments known as Clinical Excellence Awards influence clinicians behaviour at meetings – if they dare to attend at all – might be useful.

Like all hospitals in the UK, Tameside has a system in place that rewards consultants who have improved services, undertaken research or teaching or who have served on management committees in a given year. That, at least, is the theory underpinning these rewards.

There are around thirty awards per year and each is worth about £3,000.

After I became the Chairman of the Senior Medical Staff Committee in 2007, I brought about openness and transparency in the process of granting these awards. For the first time ever, the names of the successful consultants were published and their applications for the awards were made available.

A specially convened panel meets each year to decide how to distribute the awards based on a points system by means of which the relative merits of contending applications are adjudged. The panel consists of five Directors, always including the CEO and the Director of Human Resources. The other five panel members are consultants who volunteer for the task, have the approval of the consultant body and are not themselves applying that particular year.

Each panel member is a marker and scores the applications individually and secretly. I was a marker one year and, at a meeting of the panel, I witnessed first-hand how the CEO fought tooth and nail to give three awards – £9,000 – to particular consultants that year.

The allocation of these awards is controversial, at best. There has always been a concern among consultants with regards to the manner in which the five Directors mark their applications. I recently sat on an appeal panel because a colleague was unhappy that he had been in receipt of only one award. This doctor believed that some of the Directors had marked him down unfairly. His appeal was unsuccessful.

I am of the belief that many clinicians who, in private, support my concerns around patient safety and the quality of care, fail to register their support openly, in meetings or in writing. This is because they are fearful that to do so would jeopardise their chances of an award with the five Directors of the Trust Board, who score their applications.

Among my staunchest detractors in the SMSC, there are some of the consultants who have been granted the maximum number of awards (nine) within a period of only a few years. For the record, after seventeen years at Tameside I have zero awards. I applied only twice, but without success.

DIARIES LATE 2010

2nd July 2010 Thursday

Saw the *Manchester Evening News* article by Sue Carr and Amanda Crook on my re-election as Chair of the Senior Medical Staff Committee. The election, by secret ballot took place immediately after I returned from climbing Mount McKinley, the hardest climb I have done so far.

The result of the ballot confirms that I have support among my senior colleagues. I will continue to campaign to improve care and safety at TGH.

25th July 2010

A nurse showed me an article in the *Advertiser* last Thursday. It is about a report by the Tameside Local Involvement Network (LINk) calling for improvements in basic care at Tameside hospital, following serious deficiencies raised with the LINk by patients and their relatives detailing vulnerable and elderly patients not being fed, not having access to drinking water, not being bathed or showered and being routinely left lying in urine-soaked beds or festering on soiled mattresses for hours on end. A common thread is the consistent finding of inadequate nurse staffing levels. These are the same issues that some nurses, doctors and I have been reporting since 2002!

31st July 2010

At the last Senior Medical Staff Committee meeting, it was agreed that the Chair should attend the Trust Board meetings as an observer. The meeting also agreed that the SMSC should request to see the job plans of the members of the Trust Board, the deputy directors and managers down to divisional level. It was felt that a more thorough understanding of how the Directors and managers work will allow a better relationship and improvements in standards of care. Thus, today I wrote to Rev. Presswood, the chairman of the Board, accordingly.

10th August 2010

Tameside Hospital is in the *Manchester Evening News* today, once again for all the wrong reasons. The Coroner has criticised the level of care given to a patient who collapsed and later died at the hospital in July 2008. He was 40 years old and was admitted three times within nine days and discharged twice. He was first diagnosed with indigestion, then a chest infection and died two days after he was admitted for the third time.

The Coroner ruled that he received 'sub-optimal care' on a number of occasions and that a 'significant delay' in treating him with drugs to dissolve blood clots could have contributed towards his death.

Expert consultant Dr E told the inquest that he should never have been sent home. He said that thrombolytic drugs should have been administered as soon as possible after he collapsed. It also took eight days for the report of chest X-rays to be sent to A&E, against a national standard of 48 hours.

12th August 2010

The Chairman has replied to my email. He says that it is the role of the Medical Director to attend Board meetings and therefore is saying 'No' to the SMSC request that I should attend as an observer. He also says that managers do not have job plans, which are applicable only to senior medical staff.

14th Sept 2010

I am at a crossroads once again. I wrestle with my thoughts regarding what to do. The Trust Annual Members Meeting is tomorrow and I must decide if I should publicly ask for the resignation of the Board at TGH. I do not have confidence in the CEO and the board and I have said so to her in person and on the hospital intranet. There are many colleagues that share my view that the present Board is no longer capable of running this hospital safely, particularly for patients on acute/emergency pathways.

15th September 2010 Wednesday 10 p.m.

Eventful day to say the least! I am back in my flat writing my diary. I was operating all day and I did not finish until 5.45 p.m. After changing, I hurried to the Annual Members Meeting. It was in a new wing of the hospital, built under the Private Finance Initiative (PFI), but not yet officially open. There were security men everywhere.

At the entrance, I saw Liz Degnan and her sister, Christine from the Campaign for Change at Tameside Hospital, who, together with Rod McCord and Derek Pattison from Tameside Hospital Action Group (THAG), Paul Broadhurst and other campaigners were picketing the meeting and handing out leaflets entitled, Sack the Board. They carried placards posing the question: How many more deaths, Mrs Green? The press were there and I was asked to be photographed with the demonstrators, to which I agreed. We then entered the meeting which was packed and began at 6.00 p.m. It had been well planned and was stage-managed in minute detail. The presentations by the Trust executives were unbalanced and afforded no recognition to the need for change. The new facilities were the talk of the day, not the care of patients. During the limited time allocated to comments and questions from the audience at the end of the meeting, a speaker from THAG challenged Mrs Green about serious failings in patient care, issuing from a recent Care Quality Commission (CQC) report that she had somehow neglected to mention in her presentation! Without demur, I seized the moment and expressed my full and unequivocal support to the campaigners' petition for the Trust Board to resign. I added that I had reported the Trust to the Health Care Commission on three separate occasions, in 2003, 2005 and 2009, requesting an investigation, particularly in respect of low nurse staffing levels, and I had been ignored. My public request for the Board to resign will, I have no doubt, cause a reaction. However, I have to lead by example.

18th September 2010 Saturday

Glad this week is over. The word has spread that I have publicly supported the community action groups calling for the resignation of the Board. Some managers are not happy and I can see it in their faces. If looks could kill, I would have been dead a long time ago. The majority of the nurses tell me that they are happy that someone is stating the obvious and that it is time for change. Privately, many medical colleagues support calling for a vote of no confidence.

23rd September 2010

The Medical Director wrote saying that my conduct at the Annual Members' Meeting has caused the Board serious concern. He has asked me to meet with him and the Human Resources Director tomorrow – I can bring a friend. I have emailed him saying that it is too short notice.

24th September 2010 Friday

Today, I decided it is time to see how many consultants and Staff Grade and Associate Specialist doctors (SAS) support the Board. As the Chair of the Senior Medical Staff Committee, I sent an email to them saying that my view that I have no confidence in the Board has been well known for some time and that at the hospital's recent Annual Members' Meeting, I publicly stated that I supported the public campaign calling for the Board to resign. I am asking those who retain confidence in the Board, i.e. those who disagree with my view, to please say so, sending me and the Chair of the Local Negotiating Committee a confidential email. I ended by saying that I was not launching a debate by email, but that anyone who so wished could discuss the matter with me privately, or at the SMSC meetings.

Must go for a long walk tomorrow to clear my head!

27th September 2010

Chaired the SMSC meeting today, which 35 colleagues attended. I reported that on the 24th I had sent an email asking the consultants and senior doctors to indicate their confidence or otherwise in the Board. Pro-management consultants were vociferous and unhappy. As I expected, consultants who are in sympathy with my views remained silent. My detractors have started an email debate. One consultant has been brave enough to ask for a secret ballot. My request to establish how many support the Board has caused the displeasure of the lead consultants and the Medical Director who must be seen to be loyal to the CEO – no surprises there.

29th September 2010

The obstetrician that was defeated in the election for chair of the SMSC has sent a malicious email by the intranet yesterday saying that the reason that the issue of no confidence in the Board has been raised is because certain people – me included – are angry that the Trust has decided to stop the Waiting List Initiative (introduced to clear the backlog of patients awaiting surgery) which, he alleged, was more lucrative than private practice! This is, of course, preposterous.

This is a man who I hardly know, who has on previous occasions also personally attacked me in emails. It is disheartening because there are many colleagues who are new to the Trust who may well think that what he is saying is accurate.

Today, I discussed the matter with a trusted colleague who advised that I should consider making a formal complaint. This loyal friend has agreed to be with me at the meeting with the Medical Director to discuss my contribution to the Annual Members' Meeting, but he cannot make it on the re-arranged date of 1st October. I have, therefore, asked for it to be rescheduled.

30th September 2010

Email from a consultant general surgeon who agrees with me on calling for a vote of no confidence. He highlights his frustration on many issues including patient safety. This brave surgeon gives me a boost to continue to fight for better care. Several consultant surgeons are prepared to raise concerns openly.

4th October 2010 Monday

AE, a consultant orthopaedic surgeon entered the email traffic last Friday, answering the consultant that attacked me. He stated that he has known me and worked with me for many years and that I am motivated only by what I see as sub-optimal patient care. He disagrees with my approach to resolving matters but maintains that my motives are neither personal nor selfish.

10th October 2010 Thursday

Last night I stayed up until very late watching the rescue of the 33 Chilean miners (one is actually Bolivian), trapped underground for 66 days. Today, it is front-page news in all the papers in the UK and the whole world. *The Times* entitled the story, The Miracle of San Jose. The mine is in the Atacama Desert in the north of Chile, but, as one reporter put it, there were enough tears of joy to turn the desert green as the men came up. They had been trapped 2,000 feet below the surface for seventeen days before, on 22 August, they managed to send out a message saying: 'We are well, here in the refuge, the 33 of us.'

Andrew Billen, a TV critic for *The Times* wrote, '*God's blessing shone on the miners – and on 24-hour rolling TV. The view of the cynics that good news is not news was put to rest.*' Television news crews from all over the world kept the cameras filming even at 3.00 a.m. as the Fénix 2 – the torpedo-shaped metallic rescue capsule – prepared for its first descent. Chile was in the spotlight with the world watching and the engineers carried out a flawless rescue. Chileans are proud people; I am full of admiration for all these men, but there is no doubt that the incident revealed the appalling conditions in which the miners in many mines in Chile work. Much need to be done in this respect.

13th October 2010

On Monday, I sent an email to my colleagues informing them that only two clinicians have said that they support the Board, although eighteen others have emailed disapproving of my request. In fact, it would appear that from about one hundred doctors, the majority were disinclined to make their views known. I, therefore, suggested that I would organise a proper secret ballot. This has caused another six or so consultants to enter the debate, mostly from the Obstetrics, Paediatric or Pathology Departments, in other words doctors who do not deal routinely with frail or elderly patients or who are not clinicians. Interestingly, no physicians, geriatricians or general surgeons have lined up against me.

15th October 2010 Friday

Drained! The meeting with Dr Mahmood, the MD and Mr Wilkinson the HR director took place this afternoon. My friend and colleague was with me and took notes. It lasted about an hour. The managers had copies of the articles and pictures in the local press showing me standing side by side with the campaigners and their placards. I remained calm and reaffirmed that I believe the Board should resign as they do not understand that the Trust cannot improve matters given the level of savings required over the next thirty years. Moreover, the Board is refusing the backing of many consultants whom, I added, would support a request by the Board for more resources. I also made clear my feelings about the refusal of the Board to allow the Chair of the SMSC to attend Board meetings simply as an observer. They are to inform me of their decision. I thanked my friend for his invaluable support.

16th October 2010

I am grateful to Janice Newton from Hadfield, Glossop, for her letter of support for what many nurses, campaigners and I stand for. It was published in the *Tameside Advertiser* last Thursday.

19th October 2010

Yesterday, I sent a letter to the Chairman explaining that a ballot for a vote of no confidence in the Board is to be organised by the SMSC and will be conducted by the Electoral Reform Society, whose agreement I have obtained. I asked that the Trust send an up-to-date list of consultants and SAS doctors working at Tameside, to the Society's head office in London, so that appropriate arrangements could be made. Meanwhile, I continue to write the report that I will send to the Secretary of State for Health. It has taken me several months, includes seventy references and is now thirty pages long. Like all documents that I have written over the years I am typing it myself. It has been re-written many times and I have been assisted by various consultant colleagues. I have never taken a course in Microsoft Word, and so, for me, typing it is a laborious process but I am happy that I have now learned how to 'justify' the text and how to operate a number of other, previously mysterious features!

20th October 2010

Three consultants, who disagree with my actions, have organised a meeting of senior staff for Friday 22nd. They enclose a copy of the SMSC Constitution. This is not an SMSC meeting, but I will attend it.

22nd October 2010

Received a letter marked 'strictly private and confidential' from the Chairman, Rev. Presswood, arguing against the vote and saying that if I proceed with it, it would be unconstitutional. He is saying that a debate at a senior doctors' meeting is needed. The problem is that many doctors will not go or will not speak for fear of their careers or of being marked down on their merit award applications. Most are wary of the directors who attend or that someone will inform management of what they said or did. This was apparent today when I joined the meeting at Werneth House called by the three consultants who have taken exception to my actions. It was attended by about 20 consultants, almost all of them supportive of the way the hospital is being run. A couple of consultants who privately support my views kept quiet.

24th October 2010 Sunday

We went to our favourite second hand bookshop, in Uppermill, today, Julie and I. I spotted 'Annapurna' a classic of a book written by Maurice Herzog, a Frenchman and a legend in climbing history. He was the first man to climb an 8,000 m mountain. I also bought 'Man of Everest', in which Tensing, the Sherpa who climbed Everest with Hillary in 1953, tells his story to a ghost writer named James Ramsey Ullman. I cannot wait to read these two great treasures. I also bought a book on the origins of the English Language. Julie bought two novels. Uppermill is a quaint Pennine village with pretty little cafes and we went to one close by. Afterwards, we went for a walk and as we passed a small pond we saw a large goose standing by a stone wall, so still that initially I thought it was a garden ornament. However, I watched as his keen, wary eyes followed us. He was probably guarding his nest. There were ducks and other fowl, but no black necked swans or even white ones!

26th October 2010

Today, I met, by previous arrangement, with three pro-Board consultants – a radiologist, a physician and a paediatrician – who are strongly opposed to calling a vote of no confidence. Two of them were polite when putting their arguments forward; the other one, however, was abusive and tried to be intimidating, at which point I left. Having made clear my exasperation at the complacency and prevarications of the Board, I explained that I had agreed to meet to discuss the issues amicably but was not prepared to be insulted.

27th October 2010

I sent the report that I have been preparing for the last few months to all the consultants and Staff Grade and Associate Specialist doctors (SAS) today, as an attachment to a two-page letter in which I set out the basis for a Vote of no Confidence in the Board. (See Appendix 6)

1st November 2010 Monday

I stayed late at my office today to compose and send a confidential email to the Chairman responding to his letter of the 20th of last month in which he expressed his opposition to the proposed vote. I reply by saying that I understand his concerns, and that is why – firstly – I am balloting to find out if the Senior Medical Staff Committee has a mandate from the members to – thereafter – call for a vote of no-confidence. The count will take place on Friday 12th and I have invited an Executive and non-Executive director to attend. Unfortunately, the vote will not now be conducted by the Electoral Reform Society since, after receiving a letter from the Chairman of the Trust, the Society withdrew its offer. The voting system will, however, be completely confidential. All the materials used, including envelopes, paper and accompanying voting instructions have been paid for from my own pocket.

8th November 2010

In response to my concerns about the hospital, Mrs Green has written a long letter to all consultants and copied in the Staff Grade and Associate Specialists (SAS). As on previous occasions, the CEO argues that most of the concerns that I raised are 'historical' and those which are not are due to constraints imposed by the wider economy. By confusing inspections (of which the Trust has had four recently) with investigations (of which the Trust has had none), her letter effectively glosses over requests for an investigation not only by myself but also by the coroner and by the local MP. Moving on to the issue of hospital mortality, Mrs Green seeks to explain, without success, why for almost ten years, under her leadership, we have had one of the worst mortality rates in the country. She does at least, however, acknowledge that there is a problem with regards to bed capacity, but without offering any meaningful solution. She implies that because it happens in other trusts it is acceptable at Tameside! Moreover, unprepared to admit that so-called efficiency savings cause poor care, suffering and avoidable deaths, she attempts to justify cutting nursing expenditure to balance the books. Unbelievable statement from our CEO!

12th November 2010
Disappointing result on the vote! Despite thirty consultants voting in favour of holding a Vote of No confidence and although there is a majority of one in favour if the Staff Grade and Associate Specialist doctors (SAS) voted are added, I feel that the mandate is insufficiently conclusive to call it. I will write to the Secretary of State for Health to inform him the result of the vote and will enclose the report explaining my concerns. (Appendices 7 and 8)

26th November 2010
A proposal by the Medical Director to create what he calls an Acute Care Admissions Unit at Tameside is being talked about as a panacea to solve all the problems of the hospital. His idea is to admit all manner of acute surgical and medical admissions into a single ward, like an extended Medical Assessment and Admissions Unit (MAU). The disadvantages of such an experiment are many. There is no space in the present MAU and it will precipitate the disappearance of training for the specialities. The surgical tutor has sent a memo to the MD stating categorically that the trainees in general surgery and orthopaedics will not be involved. Senior sisters tell me that no one has consulted them regarding the nursing establishment for this proposed Unit.

31st December 2010
I have once again achieved 100 per cent attendance and received a standard letter from the Chair. Rev. Presswood thanks me for my dedication, loyalty and commitment. I wonder if he really means it. Looking forward to my skiing holidays with daughter Stephanie, I hope that she likes Livigno, in the Italian Alps. Last year we had a traumatic time in Flaine.

Chapter Seventeen

DIARIES 2011 – THE INVESTIGATION

Let me speak to you honestly, frankly, openheartedly. You are a liar.
*– **Le Duc Tho**, North Vietnam representative at the Paris peace talks, to Henry Kissinger, US National Security Advisor, 1972. In 1973 he received the Nobel Peace Prize but refused to accept it because the other recipient, Kissinger, had violated the truce.*

INTRODUCTION

2011 was another year crammed with significant events both personal and in respect of the Trust. My busy life as a full-time consultant orthopaedic surgeon continued with daily ward rounds and three outpatients' clinics and three operating sessions each week. Additionally, there were a number of professional meetings to attend, such as the 8 a.m. 'trauma' gatherings with the junior doctors after being on call for 24 or 72 hours on a weekend. Also, weekly teaching sessions, and monthly Divisional as well as 'business' meetings, to discuss finances and performance. My role as the Chair of the Senior Medical Staff Committee also kept me on my toes; I did most of the work it entailed out of hours and often at night, in my office.

I needed to maintain my fitness to cope with the never-ending demands of the job and so, late in May, I dusted down my old SOLO racing bike and began to pedal to work, as I did a lifetime ago in London. I also continued to trek regularly, including trips to Scotland.

The sub-standard care of a significant number of patients remained a contentious issue as a result of the frequent use of escalation wards, the misuse of the Day Care Unit and Endoscopy Ward for emergency admissions, the shortage of junior doctors and the unresolved question of under-staffed nursing shifts. Two particularly grave incidents were reported where patients had died unexpectedly and their clinicians felt unhappy with the care they had received.

***

At a forum in April 2011, the CEO gave a presentation to all employees on the financial position of the Trust. She explained that the Trust Board had commissioned corporate accountancy and international consultancy group, PricewaterhouseCoopers (PwC), to identify savings 'opportunities' and to assist with the development and implementation of a series of measures to meet the challenge. The CEO reported that PwC's key messages were that the underlying deficit for financial year 2011-12 was estimated to be £17.2 million; that, nevertheless, significant opportunities for additional cost savings existed; and that the rapid development of a robust, Trust-owned recovery plan was therefore essential, together with the appointment of an external Turnaround Director to oversee and monitor progress.

She continued by saying that eighteen areas for cost improvement programmes (CIPs) had been identified to make savings of £17.51 million. These included:

- Consultants and junior doctors: £2.91 million
- Nursing: £2.63 million;
- Capacity management (beds): £2.53 million
- Diagnostics and pathology: £2.19 million
- Workforce management £1.57 million
- A&E: 1.13 million
- Administration and Clerical: £0.98 million

The CEO explained that most of these savings had to be achieved recurrently, in other words, year on year! Her presentation did not explain the basis for these 'savings' except in respect of the proposed reduction in bed capacity which, she maintained, could be achieved by reducing patients' length of stay which was higher than the national average in some specialities. The CEO went on to say that in order to enhance governance and accountability 'internal groups' involving consultants and union leaders had been formed and also 'external groups' with Primary Care Trust (PCT), Tameside Metropolitan Borough Council (TMBC) and Strategic Regional Health Authority (SRHA) participation. However, the impression among many consultants was that the 'improvements' had already been decided.

***

The financial problems of the Trust led senior managers into taking ever more desperate measures to squeeze additional work out of the staff. A Trust review of the clerical and administrative staff, carried out without any consultation, caused an unprecedented furore amongst secretaries and doctors. Dozens of condemnatory emails circulated around the Intranet, even from pro-management consultants. This followed the arbitrary alteration by the Trust of a key document relating to the terms and conditions of the consultant body. Normally changes to terms and conditions are effected by agreement between managers and doctors, at the Joint Local Negotiating Committee. The alteration was confirmed by the Industrial Relations Officer of the British Medical Association (BMA) and I was asked to write to the Medical Director regarding this most serious matter.

Thereafter, on 14 October 2011, I was informed by the Medical Director, Dr Mahmood, that the Trust intended to appoint an independent investigator to look into continuing matters of concern regarding my personal conduct. This was confirmed by letter on 18 October 2011, indicating that guidance contained in the documents, Maintaining High Professional Standards in the NHS and The Trust's Disciplinary Policy and Procedure for Medical Staff would be followed. A narrative summary of this investigation is included in this chapter.

DIARIES 2011

10th January 2011 Monday

Today, I have sent a letter to the Personal Assistant of the Secretary of State for Health, Mr Andrew Lansley. I want to make sure that my report has been sent to Monitor and NHS North West, and to confirm that the Secretary himself was made aware of it.

14th March 2011

Received letter from David Bennett, Chair and interim Chief Executive of Monitor regarding my earlier letter to the Secretary of State dated 19 November 2010, informing me that Monitor had decided not to take any specific action against the Trust at present. He maintains that allegations are historical or not the remit of Monitor. The 'historical' argument is familiar – I've heard it repeatedly from Mrs Green. To me, there exists a fundamental flaw in the way Monitor and the CQC are required to regulate hospitals: their powers and functions do not satisfactorily or effectively cohere and failing Trusts serve only to confirm this.

24th March 2011

Libuse Ptkova, a consultant radiologist and a friend, has left. She sent me an e-card that reads, 'Tough times never last; tough people do.' I will miss Libuse, she was an excellent radiologist and one of her sessions was the mammogram clinic. Often, we lunched together and shared stories of our lives and our work cases and the frustrations caused by lack of resources.

27th March 2011 Sunday

I am in Fort William, Scotland, with my friends Richard, Dominic and Andrew. We are back at the youth hostel by the foot of Nevis after two days trekking the Ring of Steall. We had an unplanned night up in the Munroe called Am Bodach, where we bivouacked, which was a first for all of us. Altogether we 'bagged' three Munroes: An Gearanach, Stob Coire a' Chairn and Am Bodach. We are going for a nice meal tonight to recover. Earlier, Andy had all of us in stitches when suddenly he donned a red tartan Scottish cap with a bunch of ginger-hair attached to it.

11th April 2011

The financial crisis is hitting us hard. There are not enough beds and yet Ward 5 is now officially closed! Patients are being admitted into the Day Endoscopy Unit where they spend the night on trolleys. Colleagues tell me that there are plans to close an Intensive Treatment Unit (ITU) bed. To top it all, without any consultation, the locations of the Medical Assessment and Admissions Unit (MAU) will be swapped with the Trauma Unit in a few days. I will write to the Chairman to express my incredulity regarding a major decision being made without any engagement with the stakeholders.

15th April 2011

The Medical Director has responded to my concerns. He says that the £22 million gap in our finances over two years is a reality we have to face and whatever cuts we make are 'quality assured'. The ITU bed closure still has not been decided, although it has not been ruled out. He argues that the cancellation of operations due to lack of beds is the result of doctors not discharging patients or because the pathways are wrong, adding that the issues could be raised at the Senior Medical Staff Committee.

Rev. Presswood, the Chairman, has also responded to the points I made in my email: he objects to the 'wide circulation of criticisms of senior managers' and asserts that I should direct my concerns through the proper management structure – ignoring the fact that the matters I raised are beyond the remit of the Lead Consultant.

28th April 2011

Sent e-mail to all consultants explaining that I have been trying to arrange a meeting with Price waterhouseCoopers (PwC), the multi-national professional services network and independent Auditors of the Trust, to discuss the 'opportunity savings' and matters relating to their role in the financial recovery plan. I mention various examples of these 'improvement savings' that make no sense in the medical context, for instance the decision not to replace a consultant radiologist who is leaving.

16th May 2011 Monday

The SMSC meeting today was attended by the CEO, the MD and fourteen consultants. I reported my meeting with a partner of PwC who explained that the Trust had requested their assistance to secure its financial baseline and identify savings. I informed the committee that I had prepared a number of questions but I had been advised by the partner of PwC that he was not in a position to answer them. The CEO stressed that PwC were here to identify, not deliver, cost savings and highlighted the importance of lead clinicians and volunteer-consultants in ensuring patient safety when considering cost reductions.

I also reported to the Committee the Trust's plans to swap the locations of the Trauma Unit and Medical Assessment and Admissions Unit with immediate effect and without any consultation with the stakeholders of the Orthopaedic Division.

18th May 2011

Many doctors including physicians and surgeons have approached me to complain of the appalling conditions on the escalation wards. Thus, another letter to the Nursing Director, Mr Dylak, with copies to the Chairman, CEO, lead consultants, the Safety Champion and Robert Corless, a non-executive director. On these wards there is no permanent staff, no doctor in situ and not even a receptionist for most of the time. I have reminded the ND that the CQC insisted last year that the Trust must stop this practice which the Trust promised would end by August 2010! I have also said that the transcript of the current Inquiry into the Mid-Staffordshire Hospital Trust has highlighted similar malpractice.

When, in the name of God, are these managers going to understand that we need more resources and that a small, but nonetheless, significant number of vulnerable patients are dying because of poor care!

24th May 2011 Tuesday

Went to work by bicycle today, for the first time. It took me two hours to get there and one hour thirty minutes to return. The distance is twenty-seven miles both ways. I went through Heaton Park and then up the hill on Victoria Avenue. Luckily, there is a bike-dedicated lane on this avenue and, upon climbing the long hill, cycling becomes a pleasure. After passing Hollinwood cemetery, I had to stop several times to ask for directions until I finally reached Coal Pit Lane. There, in the distance, I could see Hartshead Pike, which stands high on the Pennine hills overlooking the hospital and pointing the way. From there on, it was a straight ride to work through the back roads and then the main Lees Road. Coming back was easier and quicker because I now knew the way. The racing bike that I have had for over twenty-five years did well, but I need a chain cleanser. In addition, I am rather rusty with the changing of gears and at one point the chain came off. I will need a few tools to carry with me.

25th May 20117:45 p.m.
Efficiency savings including reductions in expenditure on bed capacity, nurses and doctors, to name just three areas, are being finalised. I am already concerned at the number of serious incidents that are being reported. I have e-mailed the Regional Director of the CQC today requesting a meeting.

27th May 2011
Back at my flat and feeling pleased that I cycled to work again. About one hour 20 minutes each way. I am getting to know the route and the places where I need to be extra careful with the traffic. Going through Heaton Park is such a joy! The ride takes me by a lake which is the habitat of many wild water birds including brown geese with black necks. They remind me of the South American swans.

5th June 2011 Sunday
On call this weekend. Cycled to work – my sixth journey since I started. Beautiful weather. Saw two African couples with their children, all in their Sunday best, going to Church, by Victoria Avenue. It took me back to Tanzania, where I observed the same.

15th June 2011 Wednesday 5 p.m.
A consultant physician rang today to tell me about a serious incident that happened last night. One of his patients died unattended! He is not only distraught but also angry because it should not have happened. He was informed about it as he was starting his ward round. He asked to see the records and noticed that his patient had not been seen by a doctor of any rank. The deceased, a seventy-year-old, had been seen by a Night Nurse Practitioner, who advised intravenous fluids. He is appalled that not a single

doctor examined his patient who was clearly unwell, as attested to by the observations charts. The relatives are as shocked as he is. The physician has filled in an incident form and has contacted the Medical Director.

The sudden unexpected death of his patient explains the letter/email sent a few hours ago by the MD and the ND to all the Nurse Managers and matrons. It is a long and rather desultory letter, obviously dictated in a hurry. It has been copied to all the consultants and a senior consultant physician posted a reply within the hour writing:

'For an acutely ill patient on an escalation ward, i.e. one with no allocated junior doctors, I would recommend the nursing staff contact the on-call medical registrar.'

Within minutes another senior consultant trailed:

'Being fairly old-fashioned, I can't comprehend how an escalation ward could not have junior doctors allocated – isn't that called a hostel?'

To which the physician replied:

'I am glad you noticed! That was the supplementary purpose of my email. An unsafe hostel.'

The senior consultant added, an hour later:

'Now that the Commissioners want to re-design patient pathways, we could persuade them that directing an acutely ill patient towards a ward staffed by a doctor might be beneficial and save lives and money in the long-term.'

17th June 2011

I drove to the CQC offices in Preston today. I met with the Regional Manager and the Compliance Manager for Tameside hospital and expressed my anxieties with regard to poor nurse staffing levels, lack of beds, shortage of junior doctors and my main concern: avoidable deaths. They seemed genuinely concerned and explained to me the regulations by which the CQC has to operate regarding trusts. They say they will get back to me.

24th June 2011

Today I lodged a formal grievance against the Director of Nursing and the Medical Director for serious lack of clinical engagement and accountability concerning the re-location of the Orthopaedic Trauma Unit to the Medical Assessment and Admissions Unit (and vice-versa). I submitted it to Mrs Green, the CEO, together with a five-page report that I have been preparing and writing for the last week. It has not been an easy decision, but in my opinion it needed to be done as a matter of principle. Plans for the change-over have been rushed when what is needed is a proper period of consultation. Risk reports also need to be carried out. I recommend alternatives and suggest that an external medical advisor be engaged to advise on the wisdom of leaving the Coronary Care Unit and High Dependency Unit isolated, which is what the swap will entail. Presently the MAU is across the corridor to these Units and is staffed 24/7. (CCU-HDU has no resident doctor)

28th June 2011

An Intranet conversation among consultants is taking place regarding the implications for the workforce of the Trust's savings' plans. Many good ideas have been put forward but it is clear that to work differently we will need to invest in the short-term in order to make savings over the medium and long-term and we all agree that quality of care and, in particular, safety should never be compromised.

30th June 2011

9 p.m. and back in my flat after completing my tenth trip by bike. It has been a busy day. After work I went indoor wall climbing at Awesome Walls in Stockport with friends, Dominic and Richard. Richard is a natural and goes up the walls like Spiderman! It is excellent training for belaying and practising figure- 8 and double figure-8 knots plus a safety knot!

11th July 2011 Monday

The swap of the MAU and the Trauma Unit took place over the week-end. I am informed that a 90-year-old medical patient that could not be moved to the new MAU died in the early hours of the morning. This lady was on Telemetry which continuously monitored her heart rhythm. She could not be moved because the MAU, in its new location, still has not had telemetry installed. Her records were still on the ward and I asked to see them. I am concerned with the entry of the medical registrar that last reviewed her at 9.00

p.m. on the 10th. He wrote: 'Impression . . . deterioration secondary to missing out treatment'. He was referring to medication he had prescribed at 6.00 a.m. on 9th, (39 hours earlier) that she had not received. This lady's death saddens me because probably it could have been avoided if the medication to control the abnormal beating of her heart had been given.

24th July 2011

Another Sunday and it is my week-end on call. Commenced on Friday at 9.00 a. m. and will finish tomorrow at 9.00 a.m. I do rounds in the morning and a trauma operating list in the afternoon. I cycled to work, thus completing my 17th trip. There is a small timber merchant at the end of Coal Pit Lane, and when I cycle past, it always reminds me of my dad's timber yard in Chile. Dad passed away 5 years ago, a few weeks after mamá died. I think he let go because he could not bear to be without her. I was in England when they died and it was a very sad time for me. When I pass the yard on my bike, I whisper quietly to them: *'Buenos días mamá y papá, wherever you are.'*

5th August 2011

During my ward round in the Trauma Unit this morning, I was informed that one of my orthopaedic patients who has diabetes had been referred to the Diabetic Nurse Specialist three days ago, because her diabetes is unstable, but she has not yet been seen. She is on insulin, and she is otherwise doing well, but her discharge has been delayed due to her Diabetes. I have asked the sister to fill in an incident form because the delay is unacceptable.

Later, I sent my consultant and specialist colleagues at Tameside an email attaching an essay entitled: *'Whistleblowing and patient safety: the patient's or the profession's interest at stake?'* published in the *Journal of The Royal Society of Medicine*. It was written by Prof. Stephen Bolsin, with the collaboration of Drs Rita Pal, Paul Wilmshurst, and me.

Dr Rita Pal is an independent medical journalist, and well established evidence-based NHS whistleblower, based in the UK. Between 1999-2007, she worked as a psychiatrist in the National Health Service and was the first whistleblower to raise concerns in the Midlands hospitals run by the same local health authority. Her concerns were ignored, with the net result that many patients died needlessly. Her name was placed on the Royal Society of Medicine Wall of Honour following support from a number of doctors.

Dr Paul Wilmshurst, now a part-time consultant cardiologist, has since 1980 been involved in exposing research misconduct by individuals, pharmaceutical corporations and a manufacturer of a medical device. At some personal cost, he has championed this cause. Dr Wilmshurst believes that a public body that investigates research should be created, which has the legal powers to demand access to data; and the power to institute random checks of data submitted to journals, by experts who can verify whether it shows what the authors claim.

Dr Stephen Bolsin first raised concerns about the high mortality rate of children undergoing complex cardiac surgery at the Bristol Royal Infirmary in 1990, however managers ignored him. Dr Bolsin carried out an audit which confirmed that his concerns were justified and wrote to the Medical Director. He also informed Dr Peter Doyle, of the Department of Health. Eventually, Stephen contacted Matthew Hill, a BBC health correspondent, and the scandal was exposed on a *Close up West* regional news programme in April 1995.

The catalyst for Dr Bolsin had been the death of eighteen-month-old Joshua, one of his patients. The night before Joshua's death, a meeting of the cardiac team took place at which every doctor except Stephen agreed surgery should go ahead. The operation proceeded in spite of the fact that senior managers at the hospital had been told by Department of Health Officials to halt it. Unfortunately, baby Joshua died during surgery.

It is estimated that between 1984 and 1995 around one hundred child deaths at the Bristol Royal Infirmary may have been prevented had their heart operations been performed at a safer paediatric heart surgery unit. Dr Bolsin said at the time: *'In the end, I just couldn't go on putting those children to sleep, with their parents present in the anaesthetic room, knowing that it was almost certain to be the last time they would see their sons or daughters alive.'*

Stephen, who had been working as a consultant in Bristol since 1988, resigned from his job and, with his family, emigrated to Australia shortly after the storm broke in 1995. He maintained that he was virtually driven out of the UK by the reaction of some of his colleagues. He is now a Professor of Anaesthesia. His action led to the Bristol Royal Infirmary Inquiry, the report of which was published in July 2001. This Inquiry made a series of important recommendations and was a pivotal moment in the NHS but, as the years went by, trusts ignored many of its recommendations, as I was to find out.

7th August 2011 Sunday

Milton, my eldest son, is in training to do the Three Peaks for charity with his friend Damien. He has done Snowdon several times but never been to Scafell Pike. Thus today, I rose at 6.00 a.m. to meet with him and his brother Pablo, at Damian's place near Old Trafford. We went in Milt's car. As usual, getting to Ambleside was quick, but from there on the roads become narrower and narrower and it took us 4 hours to get there. We started up at a good pace and three and a half hours later we were down. It was a lovely day and we all enjoyed it immensely.

I am glad that Milt and Pablo have taken up trekking. Pablo wants to try indoor wall climbing.

8th August 2011 Monday 7p.m.

I was still at my Office, doing my GP referrals and other paper work when my PC signalled that I had an email. It was from a diabetic specialist nurse, who had copied me in on her email to a matron. The email is very worrying, and indicates serious governance issues regarding the care of diabetic in-patients at Tameside. Basically this hard working nurse is so overworked that she is unable to give adequate care. Her email was written an hour ago and gives an account of her work today which started at 9.00 a.m.:

'One patient seen at the ante-natal clinic with an interpreter – thirteen patients given telephone advice – three patients seen in the Trauma Unit requiring titrating oral/insulin – one patient in the Surgical Unit titrated over phone – three patients in ward 31 received telephone advice – fourteen telephone calls still to return – twelve patients referred but not yet seen, one has been waiting since 30/6/2011 – most have been advised or titrated by phone/fax but this is not best practice – Mr Peña has quite rightly complained that I did not answer phone Thurs and Fri – no cover for Dr X and Dr Y clinics - the other diabetic specialist nurse is on leave.'

This nurse says that this is not the first time she has reported her concerns. I will write to the Director of Elective Services. Clearly, the fact that I filled out an incident form for one patient is no more than the tip of the iceberg.

9th August 2011

Picked Pablo up from Timperley today and we went to Awesome Walls,

Stockport, for two hours of climbing with Richard and Dominic. He learned a lot and enjoyed the experience, although he later told me that he does not like heights!

10th August 2011
X and Y, two of the consultants who treat diabetic patients, tell me that there are major issues regarding the management of in-patients with diabetes. There are only two Diabetic Specialist Nurses, and this is clearly not enough. There is a third consultant, Z, who has not found time to meet with them yet to try to find solutions to this serious problem.

They say that they have been trying for months to arrange a meeting, but they have been unsuccessful. I believe that as the chair of the Senior Medical Staff Committee I can bring them all together. I will put this issue on the agenda for the next SMSC meeting.

11th August 2011, Thursday
I am the orthopaedic consultant on call today and at 2.00 p.m. I was asked to see a patient with a serious shoulder injury who had been left sitting on a chair in the Medical Assessment and Admissions Unit (MAU) for several hours waiting for a bed. Eight other patients were in the same situation having spent the whole night sitting in chairs, and one has been waiting since Monday! I cannot believe that this is happening. There are many risks, including the risk of clots in the legs. One was a big man with gross leg swelling and cellulitis. Earlier, I went to the surgical elective unit that is for planned operations and not emergency admissions, such as patients with infections. The sisters tell me that inappropriate admissions continue and patients that have had hip or knee replacements are consequently put at risk of cross-infection. This is happening because there are not enough beds in the hospital. All these grave issues of care, including the care of diabetic in-patients, will be raised in an email that I will send to Mr Griffiths, the Director of Elective Services, with copies to the MD, CEO, ND, Chairman and the consultants, in my capacity as chair of the SMSC.

16th August 2011
Mr Griffiths, the Deputy CEO/DES has responded to my email offering excuses for the bed crisis. He says that there is an apparent overcrowding in the MAU. Well, this is another good example of the managers not accepting reality. They

want everybody to believe that the nine patients waiting in chairs are not real. Regarding the failure of 'right patient, right bed' policy, he says he wants to obtain more information and then meet with me. This is encouraging.

Looking forward to a week away from it all, with my grandsons Elias Dylan and Tiago Sebastian, in Ambleside. Elias is keen to go trekking with me; he is three years old and already likes mountains.

31st August 2011

Met a fellow cyclist at 8.00 a.m. today. He was probably 5 years old and in tow with his mother on his way to school. As our paths crossed he looked up and proudly shouted: *'ayer'*. Like a seasoned cyclist saluting another.

Completed my 24th trip to work!

1st September 2011

After my fracture clinic, I met with the diabetic specialist nurse today. She is almost at breaking point after repeatedly raising concerns; she contacted the RCN two years ago reporting unsafe and undignified practice in the MAU. She is afraid that she may lose her job. She has been told not to email me again or other colleagues and, if she speaks to me, she will be accused of insubordination and she will be disciplined. This is unbelievable! This is another example of bullying and intimidation.

2nd September 2011

It is clear that during the last few months the Trust has been reducing the secretarial support across the hospital without consultation and due analysis of the risks. A medical secretary wrote to all consultants and relevant senior managers and Board directors today saying that in the Ladysmith building there has been a reduction in the number of full-time secretaries from six to one, and one part-time, working for four full-time consultants and their teams. She says that there is a backlog of clinical letters and discharge notes going back to May. She adds that phones are not being answered, morale is low and patient care is being affected. The situation continues despite a risk assessment form having been filled in by the secretaries.

4th September 2011

Unforgettable day. Stephanie, Pablito, Milt and I, went to Kinder Scout and did the 8 miles circuit in three hours 50 minutes. We stopped for lunch at Kinder falls and as usual the resident sheep hankered after our sandwiches. They are quite insistent! Milton's training is going well and we are all getting behind him.

10th September 2011

Showed 'Indian Head' training ground at Dovestones reservoir in Saddleworth to Milton today. So-called because from a distance, the rock formation at the top, resembles the profile of the face of an American Indian, especially the nose. The hill is probably 450 meters high, with a 35 degree gradient. Pablito was with us and both enjoyed it. We climbed it three times.

14th September 2011

A cardiology consultant raised a serious clinical governance issue by writing to the Medical Director today. He complained that the results of cardiac investigations from May 2011 are waiting to be processed due to the shortages of secretaries. This is the result of the financially-driven cuts, dressed up as 'opportunity improvement savings' by management,

15th September 2011

There is a big debate on the intranet regarding the Secretarial Review by the Trust to make savings to plug the big financial hole. This forms part of the so-called A & C (Administration and Clerical) Review. According to managers, consultants need only typists – enabling one medical secretary to be shared between three consultants. There is uproar and today I wrote the following e-mail.

Dear Colleagues:

I have kept out of the discussion concerning this matter. It seems to me that the principles underpinning the clinical work of an NHS consultant must be at the fore-front of this discussion.

Clinical NHS consultants deal with individual patients that have a mind, flesh and blood. They have physical and emotional needs; they ask questions, they have worries or may suffer an unexpected turn of events etc. Thus, patients need to be able to communicate with their NHS consultant.

Clinical NHS consultants are highly trained doctors often dealing with complex cases, using terminology in their dictations specific to their specialism.

Clinical NHS consultants do not work in a factory producing inert goods.

Thus, each NHS clinical consultant at Tameside Hospital must continue to have his/her work supported by an experienced secretary/PA who:

a. *is conversant with the medical lexicon of the specialism in question;*
b. *has a clear understanding of the consultant work pattern;*
c. *has a clear understanding of the importance of the array of investigations commonly used;*
d. *is able to answer questions from patients with serious or complex medical/ surgical problems and communicate promptly with the consultant;*
e. *is able to understand what is important on a letter that she/he types;*
f. *has the experience and knowledge to correctly prioritise workload;*
g. *has the experience and knowledge to manage the consultant diary and his/her managerial, professional, educational meetings related to his/her NHS commitments;*
h. *has the experience and knowledge to manage/organise, in liaison with the consultant, activities such as: theatre lists, extra clinics, urgent out-patient appointments, urgent admissions etc.;*
i. *has the experience and knowledge of the Tertiary Referral Centres pertinent to the consultant specialism in order to facilitate the consultant work expeditiously.*

It is extremely important to emphasise that with the demise of the concept of the "Consultant's Firm", consultants are now without a team of junior doctors and often are without a Foundation Year 2 (F2) doctor (SHO) or a Registrar. The only remaining member of the consultant's team is his trusted Secretary/PA . . . and this is now being taken away.

The hours of Medical Secretary/PA support needed by each clinical consultant can be negotiated, but not the principle.

Two whole-time Consultants sharing one PA/secretary should be the maximum allowed.

I have not discussed the secretarial needs of non-clinical NHS consultants – also highly trained doctors – but they also need hours of secretarial/PA time.

This matter will be on the agenda for the SMSC meeting on Monday 26 September.

Yours sincerely

Milton Peña

Consultant Orthopaedic Surgeon

Chair Senior Medical Staff Committee

17th September 2011 Saturday

I am in Fort William with Milt today, at the youth hostel. We arrived here at about 5.00 p.m. Later we will go for a walk in the town and a beer followed by an Italian meal. Tomorrow, we will climb Ben Nevis as part of his preparation for the Three Peaks Challenge.

18th September 2011

Milt's knees are holding! We did Nevis in 5 hours and twenty minutes. We drove back without a hitch after a stop for a quick lunch. Milt is quietly confident that he and Damien will succeed in their quest. He has now summited the Three Peaks independently and done all the right training.

19th September 2011

I am back from Tameside having completed my 26th cycling trip. In the morning I got up and thought: 'Today I will drive – after all I did enough exercise at Nevis yesterday.' But then I decided that it was no excuse and got on my bike! Having done it I feel a great sense of achievement. Straight to the shower!

22nd Sept 2011

Financial Crisis. The Trust has to find £27 million of savings – minimum – during the next three years. This is unprecedented and no-one knows the consequences for the standards of care and the safety of the patients. Today, the Secretary of State, Andrew Lansley, announced that 60 hospital Trusts are in financial trouble because of their PFI schemes. We are one of them.

26th September 2011

An important Senior Medical Staff Committee meeting took place today attended by fifteen consultants. Mr Griffiths, representing management, explained that the Trust rating by Monitor remains two out of five and is red and in breach of the terms of the Trust's authorization. Tameside is one of 11 trusts in the country in this position. I suggested that the CEO writes to the PFI partners asking for a voluntary donation to the Trust. The deputy said that the PFI annual charges are not a major factor in the Trust's financial difficulties, but I beg to differ. We will pay millions this year. Why the Trust does not admit to the big mistake it made regarding the PFI, I can only guess!

At the meeting today, we discussed the worrying situation regarding care of diabetic patients, the calamitous lack of bed capacity and continuing breaches of the 'right patient, right bed' policy.

Whilst discussing the serious problems in the Radiology Department, the Lead of the Division said that the consultant numbers in Radiology, are currently back to 1999 levels! This is partly due to the dis-establishment of a post as part of the 'recovery plan'. He said that he had opposed the dis-establishment of this post, but he had been over-ruled. I think this is very serious. There are only seven radiology consultants now, which have to cover the radiology work generated by over one hundred consultants, without counting Staff Grades and Associate specialists (SAS) and registrars.

To me, the dis-establishment of this consultant post, against the advice of the Lead Consultant of the Radiology Department, is flying in the face of what the CEO has said at forum: that all the recovery plans must have the approval of the lead consultants. The Lead of Radiology has confirmed that this is not the case.

I must raise this with the CEO.

27th September 2011

The intranet debate regarding the unacceptable delay to administrative work – lack of secretarial support – has continued and senior consultants from all the divisions have written to complain of serious governance issues.

29th September 2011

There have been fifty-one emails from consultants on the intranet regarding the consequences of the changes to the secretarial work. The emails provide evidence and they are a testament to the strength of feeling amongst the clinicians.

1st October 2011

Yesterday, at a Trust Open Forum to announce the end of the consultation period, Mrs Green gave a forty-minute presentation. The Auditorium was full, with many more people standing. At question time, nobody raised a hand to ask questions. I waited for about a minute and then raised my hand. The CEO immediately stated that it wasn't a surprise to see me there and that I would be allowed to ask a question, but not to make a statement. I replied that I understood. I said that I had asked the same question at the recent Annual General Meeting, but I had not received a satisfactory answer. I said that I would ask it again because it was an important question and the audience this time was different.

I asked Mrs Green why the executive directors had dis-established a Consultant Radiology post, bringing, in effect, the number of radiology consultants down to 1999 levels, when the total number of consultants at the Trust had almost doubled since that time. Because of the shortage of Radiology Consultants, serious issues of clinical governance in respect of patient care had arisen.

The CEO replied that the dis-establishment of the radiology consultant had been implemented with the approval of the Lead Consultant of the Radiology Division – to which I responded by pointing out that at a recent SMSC meeting the Lead Consultant of the Radiology Division had explained that he was completely opposed to the dis-establishment (abolition) of this post.

At this, the CEO became irate and lost control, shouting, 'You are only an orthopaedic consultant and have no say in the matter.'

My accusation that she was lying brought forward the Director of Human Resources who positioned himself next to the CEO and, in an intimidating manner, shouted, *'I would be careful of what you say, if I were you.'*

I simply said *'I have made my point and I am leaving, I am late for my clinic.'*

3rd October 2011

I Wrote to the CEO today. I am appealing against the decision of the Director of Elective Services, who dismissed my grievance against the MD and the DN, regarding the undue haste and lack of consultation attendant upon the reallocation of the Trauma Unit to MAU and vice-versa, (See 24 June 2011). My two-page letter complains that no explanation has been given as to why the swap took place before telemetry had been installed in Ward 2, leaving patients on telemetry on the Trauma ward. One patient had died and it had been reported as a Red incident. I read the clinical records and I found that the medical Registrar had examined this patient thirty-nine hours before she died and wrote his recommendations which, regrettably, were not followed. He happened to be on the ward – now the Trauma Unit – a day and a half later and asked to see her, when he noted her deterioration. What he recorded in the patient's file makes very sad reading.

I will contact the coroner, because there are significant issues regarding the circumstances of this lady's death.

Regarding my grievance against the directors, I do not expect much of the Stage 3 appeal that, in consequence of its dismissal, I have now invoked.

***

For over ten years there has been a shortage of consultant radiologists at Tameside and the problems that this cause have been a matter of intense discussion on the intranet throughout last week. The debate started with an email from the Medical Director advising that requests for CT scans should be made only by consultants or SAS doctors and not junior doctors, in order to reduce unnecessary investigations. This is sound advice because in any one month over 1100 CT scans, 580 MRI scans, 900 Ultra Sounds Scans and 3000 plain X-ray series (two to four or more views) are requested. These figures comprise only the non-urgent requests.

Presently, there are only seven radiology consultants and they have to rotate to be available for urgent work during evenings and week-end in a so called on-call roster. This in addition to their various individual, specialist four-hours-sessions such as interventional radiology, nuclear medicine, ultra-sound, and many more.

The consultant radiologists are extremely hard working and do their best, but the consequences of having so few radiology consultants are multiple and potentially deleterious:

- Unacceptable delays performing and reporting out-patient investigations, such as CT and MRI scans are common.
- There are no consultant radiologists on call from 9.00 a.m. to 5.00 p.m. Monday to Friday, so that if a clinician needs an urgent opinion between these hours there is no allocated consultant as their rota doesn't begins until 5.00 p.m.
- Plain X-rays for in-patients are not reported whilst scans requested for ward patients cannot be done promptly, thereby delaying discharge – sometimes for days– resulting in further unnecessary costs to the Trust.

4th October 2011

It is inconceivable! In spite of the tremendous problems of bed capacity across the whole hospital, Board directors are closing yet more beds, as part of a 'cost improvement programme' (CIP). Yesterday, an email from the most senior sister on the Trauma Ward, to the Divisional Nursing Officer, was copied in to the orthopaedic consultants saying that from Saturday 8th October the ward will lose seven beds. (from 37 down to 30). Furthermore, the email says that a recent external nursing review by an agency known as Aquity shows the ward is under-established for both qualified and auxiliary nurses. The under-staffing does not surprise me at all! Last night I stayed late to write an email to Mr Griffiths, the Director of Elective Services, because these further bed cuts will inevitably only serve to make a bad situation even worse. I copied in the CEO, MD, ND, Chairman, various managers and the Orthopaedic Consultants Once again there has been no consultation or discussion with the doctors and nurses in the Orthopaedic Division.

***

The chair of the Local Negotiating Committee (LNC), a senior consultant, has sent an urgent email to Mr Wilkinson, the Human Resources director and copied in all consultants and SAS doctors. The subject is the Administration and Clerical (secretarial) review. He explains that the current system promotes direct access to the consultant whereas the Trust's proposal will be setting a 'four stage military grade obstacle course for patients and general practitioners to navigate every time they have to query follow-ups, waiting list or emergency care'. He ends his email saying:

'There is no point legislating for our own demise. The market is more than capable of destroying foolish competitors and we do not need to assist it in doing so. The LNC recommends an urgent re-think.'

Before going home today I have sent a 'one line' email to the HR Director saying that I fully agree with the chair of the LNC's comments and, as chair of the SMSC, I also recommend a re-think.

***

On a positive note, today I completed my 31st trip to work on my bike. By my reckoning I have cycled 837 miles – more than the length of Britain! I have had one tyre blown out, several occasions when the chain has come off, and two minor falls as a result of rain, when the rear wheel skidded. Colleagues at the hospital probably think that I am eccentric, but I don't mind. I believe that a few may follow suit and take up cycling.

6th October 2011

Small battle won! A senior nurse at the Trauma Unit tells me that as a result of my letter the bed closures have been halted. Nurses are worried about it because some will be moved and others will lose their jobs. There are also concerns that the proposed closure will be 'virtual' and that, with a wave of the CEO's wand, beds will magically re-open, stretching the staff. This management ploy has been used many times in the past.

Today, eight consultants attended a second, extraordinary Senior Medical Staff Committee meeting to discuss the Administration and Clerical (secretarial) review changes proposed by the Trust. Yesterday fifteen consultants attended, including the lead of the Medical Division, the Medical Director and others from all departments. At both gatherings, it was clear that there is deep dissatisfaction and anger at the mismanagement of this matter and lack of any real engagement. It was agreed that counter-proposals should be submitted by the secretaries in each division.

***

THE INVESTIGATION

On Tuesday, 11 October 2011 at 15:52, a telephone conference took place. The participants at Tameside hospital were Dr Tariq Mahmood, Medical Director and Gertie Nic Philib, Acting Head of Human Resources, and in London, Dr Steve Boyle, Adviser for the National Clinical Assessment Services (NCAS). The conference had been organised to discuss alleged concerns regarding my personal conduct. The discussion that followed was summarised in a file note kept by the Trust and in a three-page letter from Dr Boyle to the Acting Head of HR two weeks later. Dr Boyle explained that because the Trust had admitted that there were no clinical concerns and that I was a competent surgeon, it had been accepted that the NCAS could close the case at that point. Dr Boyle also offered advice regarding the declared intention of the Trust to appoint an external investigator and made a point of reminding the HR manager that his letter should be shared with me. However, in spite of numerous written requests these documents were not handed to me for six months and then only after I invoked the Freedom of Information Act.

***

Three days later, accompanied by friend and campaigner, Paul Broadhurst, I made my way to the Chairman's office to an arranged meeting with the Medical Director and the Director of Human Resources. The MD informed me that he had discussed his concerns with Mrs Green, the Chief Executive, and with David Wilkinson, the Director of Human Resources, who had agreed that an investigation was warranted. He also informed me of his phone conference with Dr Boyle who advised that my case should be dealt with as a personal conduct issue in accordance with the requirements of Department of Health policy, Maintaining High Professional Standards – although the policy does not provide for an independent investigation, as the Medical Director noted.

The outcome of the meeting was confirmed in a letter to me from the MD a week later which stated that whilst, in normal circumstances, he himself would have been the Case Manager, this would clearly be inappropriate whilst my formal grievance against him and the Director of Nursing remained ongoing, and that David Jago, the Financial Director, had therefore been appointed. In addition, Robert Corless, a Non-Executive Director of the Trust had been appointed as the designated Board Member to the investigation to ensure that my case was dealt with fairly and promptly.

***

On 3 November 2011, I wrote to David Jago, highlighting the complexity of the case and the inadequacy of the Trust's Disciplinary Policy and Procedure for medical staff. My letter ended requesting copies of any documents sent to NCAS – or any other organisation – by the Trust, and vice-versa, in connection with my case.

Although three weeks later I received a letter from the Case Manager, it was only to inform me that the external independent investigator had been appointed. He was described as *'a highly experienced executive director with a wealth of NHS experience.'* His CV was enclosed: he had an MBE, and had been a Nursing Director and a Deputy Chief Executive at a large NHS trust in the North of England. He was making a living by providing services and conducting disciplinary investigations in hospitals, local councils and universities. (Six months later I learned that he was being paid £800 per day, plus expenses and VAT for his work.)

***

One rainy evening, just before Christmas, I was asked to personally collect from the Human Resources Department, copies of two thick files bearing the name, Hill Dickinson, the Trust solicitors and containing almost 1,000 pages of documents which had been given to the investigator. After reading the charges, I realised that I had a fight on my hands and contacted the Medical Protection Society for help and advice, but, although in 2005 they had been helpful, this time they declined to assist. I have never been a member of the British Medical Association and therefore I was on my own.

The Terms of Reference for the Investigation were three pages long and encompassed all manner of alleged breaches which I summarise below:

1. Breach of Contract referred to my alleged 'failure to cooperate' with the

Trust;

2. Breach of the Trust's 'Respect Policy' referred to my public support to patient groups calling for the Board to resign at the Annual Members Meeting in September 2010 and to the subsequent Vote of No Confidence by senior doctors in November that year. It listed the formal grievance that I had lodged with the CEO against the Medical Director and the Director of Nursing in June 2011 for 'serious lack of clinical engagement and accountability' which was still proceeding and also included the charge that I had called the CEO a 'liar' twice at an Open House Forum on 30 September 2011.

3. Breach of Trust and Confidence alleged that I had abused my position as Chair of the Senior Medical Staff Committee.

4. Deliberate misrepresentation of facts referred to my requests for information regarding the financial position of the Trust and the contents of my reports and letters over the years.

5. Creating conflicts between teams referred to my attempt to facilitate a meeting between three consultants and the diabetic specialist nurses to help resolve serious governance issues. (I had acted with caution and tact in the interests of patient care, though the consultant that had dragged his feet for months seems to have resented my involvement.)

6. Breach of Whistle Blowing Policy referred to my report of the death of a patient to the local coroner and my providing a statement. My 'behaviour' at the subsequent inquest was deemed a cause of concern.

7. Sharing information with a third party referred to an email sent by me to all consultants on the intranet on 3 February 2011. Its subject was: 'Daily struggle to find beds to admit patients and its effect on quality of care and safety . . .' It listed examples of actual patients, omitting their names but quite importantly quoting their hospital number for future reference. It was alleged that this document had been passed on to a third party who had sent it to Monitor.

***

The investigation into my conduct was not made public and I was forbidden to discuss it or any correspondence about it, with anyone. I was confident that I could defend myself against these allegations, although within a matter of only a few weeks, it became clear to me that the role adopted by the investigator was far from impartial. It became equally clear that procedurally I was being denied a fair hearing.

During the investigation, I presented the case without legal, or any other form of, representation. Not surprisingly, a large volume of letters and emails were generated but I did not involve my (shared) hospital secretary, typing all documentation myself. (One such document, a letter to Steven Dorrell, Chair of the Parliamentary Health Committee, is included as Appendix 10.)

On 21 March 2012, I wrote to Mr Jago requesting that the Trust report its concerns about my conduct to the General Medical Council or the Royal College of Surgeons. In reply, however, Mr Jago explained that: '... *I am entirely satisfied that the process will be independent and that the investigator is entirely appropriate to undertake the investigation. I do not believe it is necessary to utilise the services of the GMC or the Royal College.*'

Thus the Trust disdained from reporting their concerns to the GMC or any of the Royal Colleges, either of which would have carried out an in depth, objective and truly independent investigation.

***

On 14 May 2012, I lodged a formal grievance with the CEO against the Acting Head of Human Resources for her failure to share Dr Boyle's letter and her failure to act on my concerns, raised in five letters to her between 21 March and 1 May, where I repeatedly stated that: 'there is a real likelihood that the investigation will not be, or is not being, conducted in an objective manner.'

***

Although I had nothing personal against him – despite all that was happening – on 21 May, after a great deal of thought, I lodged a complaint against the Medical Director with the General Medical Council giving four reasons. Firstly, that he knowingly made an untrue and misleading statement against me alleging that I misrepresented facts, set consultants against other colleagues and created conflicts within teams and with management; secondly, that he failed to act with honesty and transparency during his communication with the NCAS on 11 October 2011; thirdly, that he failed to report the Trust's concerns to the General Medical Council, regarding my personal conduct and my conduct as the Chair of the Medical Staff Committee, and; fourthly, that he was in breach of the NHS managers' code of conduct when party to the altering of a document without Joint Local Negotiating Committee approval.

***

On 25 July, the Case Manager wrote to inform me that the investigator had been replaced. I replied two days later thanking him for letting me know and once again requesting that the Trust remit the matter to the GMC or a Medical or Surgical College. I also requested to see all correspondence and the statements of all the witnesses that had been obtained by the investigator. I again invoked the Freedom of Information Act.

That same day I also wrote to Robert Corless, a Non-Executive Director, and the Board Member designated to oversee the investigation, to complain about the length of the investigation and my concern that the Trust had not reported the matter to the GMC or one of the Royal Colleges for investigation. I enclosed my letter to the Case Manager.

David Jago wrote on 20 August explaining that the previous investigator had reviewed the minutes of the SMSC and JLNC meetings in 2010 and 2011, amounting to a further twenty-eight additional documents. He enclosed the CV of the new investigator and a copy of the revised Terms of Reference from Hill Dickinson Solicitors. A revealing paragraph in this document stated that: '... *one of the reasons for the investigating officer to have been changed was an impression that might have been given by some of the comments of the original investigator that he had already decided there was a case to answer and the outcome was pre-determined.*' It served as a warning to the new investigator to tread carefully and avoid the indiscretions of his predecessor who would be routinely accompanied to meetings by Ms Nic Philib, the HR manager, to take notes for him, which the hospital's solicitors considered unwise and not to be repeated, also recommending that all future meetings be recorded.

The CV of the new investigator made interesting reading and was better presented than the CV of his predecessor. The top of each page was adorned with the logo: 'Business is our language'. His qualifications included Master of Business Administration, Higher National Diploma in Production Engineering and Ordinary National Certificate in Mechanical Engineering.

His work experience from January 2000 included a large number of interim Chief Operating Officer posts in various hospitals, each lasting an average of six months. His current post was shown as deputy CEO. However his CV did not show any apparent experience in disciplinary investigations.

***

The case became even more convoluted when, on 7 September 2012, I lodged a grievance against Mrs Green, the Chief Executive Officer of the Trust with the Director of Human Resources. (In retrospect I should have lodged it with the Chief Executive of the NHS.) My stated reasons were:

1. Wilful contravention of the Data Protection Act;
2. Wilful disregard of the principles contained in the document, Maintaining High Professional Standards;
3. Failure of the Trust to report its concerns about my alleged conduct to the GMC or any of the Royal Colleges;
4. Failure of the Trust to act in March 2012, after I indicated that the behaviour of the first investigator was inappropriate and discriminatory;
5. Failure of the Trust to offer me support for stress during the first six months of the investigation.

***

I do not know exactly when the report from the second investigator was completed since the copy in my possession is undated and, throughout its 73 pages, makes reference only to the year 2013. In short, the investigator concluded that in his opinion there was prima fascia evidence to support a case of serious misconduct that should be put to an independent conduct panel on all the seven charges. He referred to alleged breaches of the GMC guidance several times but offered no explanation as to why the Trust did not report these to the regulatory body.

In the event, Mr Williams, the new Case Manager who had taken over from Mr Jago, on behalf of the Trust, refrained from acting upon the recommendation to proceed and the investigation was brought to an abrupt and totally unexpected end. After all the time, effort and resources that were so heavily invested in pursuing me, this was an unfathomable decision and the question,

'Why', remains unanswered to this day. I must confess that I have not the slightest idea and can offer no rational explanation. However, at a time when the Trust was in dire financial straits, expenditure upon this entirely fruitless exercise was not simply wasteful but perverse.

RETURN TO THE DIARIES

16th October 2011

I love Edale. I have been there many times. Today, I went with my friend Ricky and we walked fifteen miles. He is training for the Pennine Way for charity. I am proud that I got him into trekking. He is a nurse on the Trauma Unit, late thirties, wiry, very agile and strong. We have been on many treks and he has saved me from a few rather sticky situations. For example, on Snowdon when my heavy 30 kg training backpack, which was loaded with stones, was pulling me slowly down a steep section, he took a length of rope, secured it to a good anchor point, came down and tied it to the backpack, enabling me to release it and scamper up.

20th October 2011

The hospital has appointed Paul Connellan as the new chairman who will take over at the helm of the hospital Trust in November. Out-going Chairman the Rev. Presswood resigned the post at the end of his first four-year term, although the consensus of opinion amongst staff that I spoke with at the hospital seemed to be that he had been forced to stand down. The public pressure for change had been gathering rapid momentum with members of the local community flocking in their thousands to sign a petition to 'Sack the Board' organised by the Campaign for Change at Tameside Hospital. Campaign spokesperson Liz Degnen, upon hearing the news of Rev. Presswood's resignation told *Tameside Advertiser: I am delighted. It's music to my ears. It's the best thing that could happen. I just hope the others take a leaf out of his book and follow suit.*

The hospital press release says that the in-coming Chairman, Mr Connellan, spent eight years as the Director of Marketing and Customer Services at Manchester Airport before embarking on a highly successful consultancy career. He has been a Non-Executive Director of NHS Trafford PCT since 2006. The new chair said: *'I am pleased and proud to be appointed . . . My role will focus on setting the tone and culture for the entire organisation so that every member of staff – consultants, nurses, cooks or porters – understand our primary role is to provide the best health care for the local community.'* I like his statement. Hope springs eternal, as they say.

21st October 2011

Yesterday the Chairman of the Local Negotiating Committee (LNC) informed me that a document discussed at the Joint Local Negotiating Committee (JLNC), was unilaterally altered by management and the changed form of the document has been circulated to the Lead Consultants as being agreed by both sides. The meeting when the 'original' document had been discussed took place on 26th August and was attended, as usual, by the Industrial Relations Officer of the British Medical Association. The Chairman has informed the officer of the BMA, who has compared the two versions of the document and confirmed the change. This is serious and worrying because it reflects the lengths to which management is prepared to go. The Chairman of the LNC and the BMA officer, a trained solicitor, have asked me to write to the MD, which I have done today. Because the management is already using the amended document to implement changes, I have alerted all consultants and Staff Grade and Associate Specialist doctors (SAS). I am requesting urgent clarification regarding the alteration of the document and why it was circulated to the Lead Consultants as approved by the JLNC.

28th October 2011

Letter from Mr Griffiths, deputy CEO dated 17th but only arrived today, answering the nine questions I asked in respect of the proposed closure of seven beds in the Trauma Ward. It appears that meetings have taken place behind our backs, the results of which have never been discussed in the Division. The origins of the matter lie in the so-called 'financial savings opportunities' identified for the Trust. The seventh question I asked was about the money that the Trust will save by closing the seven beds. His answer was £150,000. Well, no comments there! The eighth question was why, once again, there has been no consultation and transparency. The Director admits that management failed to follow due process, including clear communication with clinicians, assuring me that lessons will be learned etc., etc. He ends by saying that the closure has been halted for now!

***

I met Mr Griffiths a few days ago in the corridor leading to the canteen and he told me that he is leaving the hospital for another job. We had a brief conversation and I wished him well. I am informed that he has been replaced by Paul Williams, who has become Chief Operating Officer.

29th October 2011

The Medical Director sent an email to the Chair of the LNC, which says that, when the offending document was discussed on 26 August, management did not aim to submit it for ratification or full agreement at any stage! It was designed simply to 'inform' the LNC – implying that afterwards management could modify it at will. This is ludicrous.

3rd November 2011

I have received a letter from David Jago, the Financial Director, confirming that the Trust has started a formal investigation into my personal conduct. I will reply asking for copies of all documents sent to, or received from, any organisation or third party in relation to this investigation. I think this is the reaction of the directors against whom I have taken grievances and complaints. This is now a David versus Goliath fight.

I have replied commenting that . . . *'an investigation under the existing Disciplinary Policy and Procedure for Medical Staff will not be a fair process, even with the appointment of an independent investigator' adding . . .' I would be grateful if you can send me copies of any document sent to NCAS by the Trust or from NCAS to the Trust regarding this matter or to any other organisation or person connected to this.'*

10th November 2011

After three weeks of waiting for a reply from the Medical Director, I wrote a Private and Confidential letter today asking eleven questions on the matter of the unilaterally amended document. I stated that directors violated the NHS Managers Code of Conduct. I asked for a reply by 21 November.

5th December 2011

Today I wrote to Robert Corless, Non-Executive Director who has also been appointed to oversee my formal complaint against the Medical and Nursing Directors, and now is the designated Board member of the Investigation into my conduct.

Dear Mr Corless

Re. Grievance against Medical Director and Nursing Director

Thank you for your letter dated 16th November explaining the decision of the Stage 3 Grievance Panel, which decided not to uphold my appeal.

I am certainly not satisfied with the decision of the Panel and I am therefore requesting that the Trust contact ACAS for arbitration and Conciliation as per Grievance Policy, Clause 8.5.5.

Yours sincerely

Milton Peña

Copied to: Human Resources Dept.

19th December 2011

Attending the Intermediate Life Support course today after reading the whole booklet on Saturday. It is a refresher course with interesting, up-dated and very important advice. A few things have changed and emphasis is on immediate cardiac massage at the rate of one hundred and twenty chest compressions per minute!

***

Yesterday, Sunday 18th, Richard, Dominic and I got up at 5a.m. and went for a trek that we have been planning for weeks. The plan was to start at Edale and hike the first leg of the Pennine Way. However, because of sudden and rather heavy snowfall, we changed our minds and began at Glossop towards the Snake Pass aiming for Edale (sort of reverse walk). It was heavy going. We had to use goggles and initially Rick and Dom had head lights. We crossed the Snake Pass road and went into the plateau towards Kinder. The trail was covered by snow and after a while we realised it was madness to continue. Visibility was about 30 metres. We decided to call it a day and retrace our steps. As we crossed the road again, a jogger on the road came out of nowhere and shouted: 'You are just as mad as me!' Later at around midday the sky cleared. We had started at 6.45 a.m. and we were in the pub by 1.00 p.m. I was driving and stuck to orange juice.

21st December 2011

As I drove to work, I heard on Radio 4 of a book called The Hardest Climb by a doctor who had climbed the seven highest continental mountains of the world, a colossal achievement. Shortly afterwards he suffered a stroke. He described his near death experience and how he heard two doctors telling his wife that she had to say her goodbyes. It was that bad! He explained that it was like being in a tube. At the bottom end of the tube he felt at peace and free from pain. However he somehow knew that to keep alive he had to climb to the top, but it was unbearably painful. He opted for the pain and the climb and survived. Later, when he recovered and saw the charts with his observations he was able to make sense of his near death experience.

This doctor has my total admiration for his courage, not only for doing the seven summits, but more so for not giving in to death and opting to suffer pain and stay alive. His story made me think of my own 'hardest climb' –my fight for safety for our patients and better standards of care.

22nd December 2011

Read the report filed by Dr X of another serious incident that happened a week ago. He was the consultant anaesthetist on call for emergencies and around midday he was asked to take over a planned list which had over-run. He tried to explain that this was unacceptable because of the possibility of being called to an emergency, but he was bullied by a manager and reluctantly agreed. Whilst finishing the routine list, a vascular emergency occurred – a patient with a femoral embolus. This patient's operation was delayed because he – the on-call consultant for emergencies – was tied up on the over-run list. Eventually – after a delay which was unacceptable – the emergency surgery took place but the patient died five days later.

***

I went to collect two bulky binders from HR yesterday regarding the investigation the Trust is pursuing with respect to my 'personal conduct'. The Trust has appointed a retired Nurse, an OBE, and ex-Chief Operating Officer from a Trust in the North West, to be the external investigator.

24th December 2011
The leading news item today: Prince Philip, aged 90, had emergency stent surgery for coronary artery blockage last night at Papworth heart hospital, London. Best wishes to him. Age should never be a factor in providing the best standards of care.

28th December 2011 Wednesday
I went to work today to do my routine all-day list in the operating theatre. On arrival, I am informed that one of my patients, due to have a total knee replacement, did not have a bed and she decided to go home and not to wait. She explained that this was the second time that this had happened recently. The first time she had waited eight hours for a bed, only to be told later to go home.

When I arrived in the UK in 1974, patients stayed in hospital for two weeks after a hip replacement. Nowadays they come the day of surgery and go home after four to five days! Big improvement in length of stay. Big savings and maximisation of earnings for the hospital. But we still need a minimum of dedicated beds for orthopaedic elective operations. The detrimental reality is that Tameside Hospital does not have enough beds. As Allyson M Pollock, Professor of Public Health, put it in her book, *NHS plc. The Privatisation of Our Health Care*:

'*The main strategies of hospitals in financial difficulties are: 1) to close wards and hospital beds and 2) to reduce the number of staff.*'

And, over the years, this is exactly what the Board at Tameside has done.

***

Another issue: an alert on the Intranet sent to all consultants by the MD regarding a Red incident that happened two years ago. It involved the death of a patient with a liver abscess. The hospital has been severely criticized for lack of communication with an Intensive Care Unit at another Trust, which did not have beds to accept the transfer of the patient.

In my view, there are not enough intensive care beds in the country and the obvious solution is to increase the number. But government administrators and their political masters would seem to take the view that this is more expensive than paying compensation. Many relatives don't know that lives can be saved by 'escalating' the care upwards – meaning moving the patient to a High Dependency Unit [Nurse/patient ratio: one trained nurse for two patents] or if their loved one is really ill to an Intensive Care Unit. [One trained nurse for one patient with doctors present around the clock]. There are specialists Intensive Care Units, for instance Neurosurgical Intensive Care Units, which offer a higher level of expertise for patients with serious head injury and a transfer to such a unit may be indicated in some instances.

Chapter Eighteen

DIARIES 2012 – 2013

INTRODUCTION

The investigation into my conduct continued throughout 2012. It was a period of stress and anguish which was made worst by the stress caused at work by the ever busy fracture clinics, lack of beds, shortage of nurses, dwindling secretarial support and other adverse effects of the cuts. In spite of all this, I did not take time off. When the investigation started in October 2011, my employers failed to follow the 'Stress at Work' policy of the Trust which provides for counselling. Eventually, I arranged to see my General Practitioner and it was only following his referral that counselling began during May at my hospital.

The Trust's need to balance the books resulted in plans to reduce 106 WTE (Whole Time Equivalent) nurses. The bed capacity crisis continued and patients were repeatedly admitted into the wrong wards and received care well below appropriate standards.

A Mortality Review Working Party (MRWP) was created by the consultants and met regularly. An anaesthetist in the MRWP designed a thorough questionnaire – aimed to find out causes of avoidable mortality – which was to be answered by nurses and doctors on the wards. I went to the wards and the junior doctors' mess and talked with many about their experiences whilst they completed these questionnaires. They seemed encouraged that a senior consultant like me was trying to do something to improve care. The junior doctors were candid and their answers shocked even the more ardent Board supporters.

At a Senior Medical Staff Committee meeting, Mrs Green surprised me when she stated that I had been right all along regarding avoidable mortality. She accepted that the questionnaire was a good idea, although the Medical Director opposed it. Ultimately, his view must have prevailed because one morning the anaesthetist who designed the questionnaire called me – sounding harassed – and asked me to stop the survey. However, it was too late as events a year later were to prove.

During 2012, following a statement from David Cameron, the Prime Minister, calling for hourly nurses' ward rounds, I tried to reinvigorate the campaign for legislation on minimum nurse/ midwife to patient ratios.

In March 2012, the General Medical Council guidance on Raising and Acting on Concerns about Patient Safety came into effect. This signified a very important change which almost immediately produced a ten per cent increase in reports to the GMC. As more colleagues report systemic failures in our hospitals, the potential for improvements in care will be so much the better. Late in 2012, I sensed a gradual change amongst senior managers at Tameside when the repercussions of the Mid-Staffordshire scandal began to filter through to the Trust. Nevertheless, the crisis at Tameside Hospital continued and colleagues privately raised their concerns, particularly regarding mortality. As a result, I made arrangements to see the new Chairman.

DIARIES 2012

1st January 2012 Sunday 8:00 a.m.

I came back from Timperley at 1:30 a.m. after a delicious ribs dinner prepared by Pablito which was very tasty and New Year celebrations with my swan family. I have been on call since Friday so I had only one glass of wine to celebrate New Year. Yesterday I operated on a 60-year-old builder with a badly broken knee. It went well. Whilst at the hospital, read email from the Medical Director following a series of questions I asked him two weeks ago. He did not answer the questions. I wrote back raising again my concerns about care and preventable deaths.

***

I just heard the news that a trekker died at Scafell Pike. He was 19 years old and from Derbyshire. He became separated and lost. What a tragedy! Reminded me of a trek in dangerous conditions that I and Ricky did at Lansdale Pike two years ago, in winter, with snow two feet deep, visibility nil, and a very steep climb in places. We were very lucky.

4th January 2012 Wednesday 4:40 p.m.

I am back at my flat because my two major operations today, a Total Hip Replacement (THR) and a Total Knee Replacement (TKR) were cancelled for lack of beds! Tameside hospital is going through a capacity crisis almost unprecedented. Patients are waiting in A&E for over twelve hours for a bed. I overheard a sister in MAU saying that today alone, sixteen patients had breached the 12 hours wait. Inappropriately, medical emergencies have been admitted into the Day Surgery and Endoscopy wards on a daily basis. These Units have trolleys instead of beds, yet elderly patients are admitted there. I understand twenty-eight such patients were there today. This means that, as a direct result, many planned day cases are cancelled regularly.

Surgical patients continue to be admitted to the Trauma Unit instead of the surgical ward. One such person admitted with acute pancreatitis died yesterday morning after he deteriorated during the night and arrested in the early hours of the morning. He should have never been admitted to the Trauma Unit. An outreach nurse has filed an incident form. I am told it is a Red incident.

Because of the capacity crisis, individuals with fractures needing operations are sent home to wait for a bed. Two such patients of mine from my recent on-call are waiting. I have written so many times before regarding these matters, in particular the poor care leading to patients' deaths. I despair because I know that some are avoidable.

On a positive note: yesterday I finally operated on Mrs X, 56-years-old, admitted with a broken hip. She came in on Friday having fallen two days earlier without realising the damage. She rested in bed after a hot bath! Yesterday after a lengthy consultation and thereafter obtaining her fully-informed consent, I gave her an un-cemented THR. It went well and hopefully she will recover speedily without complications.

5th January 2012

The *Advertiser* has a front-page article regarding the failings found by the CQC at a surprise inspection of the hospital last October. The fact is that the situation at the hospital is now worse.

7th January 2012

Just back from hospital after performing a knee and a hip replacement. Both operations went well.

Yesterday I signed up to Twitter and sent a tweet regarding my campaign for legislation on nurses/midwife to patient ratios. I am trying to revitalise the campaign having heard David Cameron calling for hourly nurse ward rounds in hospitals in England. I think this would be impossible in hospitals such as Tameside which, quite simply, have not sufficient nurses. I have also written to the *Manchester Evening News* and to the *Tameside Advertiser*.

Met with a consultant who, in private, is critical of the Board. He thinks that more than one year after the Vote of No-Confidence there is no improvement, and if anything, it is worse. Some senior consultants who were pro-management have apparently intimated to him that the CEO should resign.

10th January 2012

I have emailed the following letter to the two local papers, the *Tameside Reporter* and the *Tameside Advertiser*. I hope that they will publish it. I must promote the campaign although Julie thinks that nurses up and down the country are not signing the e-petition for fear that management could find out and they will be punished or even sacked. She is probably right.

Letter to the Editor:

Sir - I welcome the Prime Minister's direct involvement in the vital issue of nursing care in NHS hospitals in England. As a consultant for 20 years in the NHS, I agree wholeheartedly with his sentiment that somewhere in the last decade the health system has conspired to undermine one of this country's greatest professions.

I also agree that nursing must be about patients and not paperwork, although some paperwork will always be needed to document nursing care.

However, too many shifts in too many wards in hospitals across the country are left without sufficient numbers of nurses to achieve safe practice, let alone to achieve best practice. Ratios of one qualified nurse for 10, 15 or 17 demanding or acutely ill patients still occur.

In April 2010, I started an e-petition calling for legislation on the maximum number of patients per qualified nurse/midwife in hospitals in England.

This has been in practice in California since 2004 and since then eleven other states (Connecticut, Illinois, Maine, Nevada, New Jersey, Ohio, Oregon, Rhode Island, Texas, Vermont and Washington) plus the District of Columbia have enacted legislation. In California, it has been a tremendous success though there have been occasional protests from the nurses when hospitals have not adhered to the law. Legislation also exists in Canada and Australia.

I would respectfully request the Prime Minister to consider legislation to establish mandatory hospital nurse to patient ratios. Indeed, I would ask the same of Mr Clegg and Mr Miliband and the Members of Parliament of all the political parties.

Nurses, midwives, health workers and the public across the country should consider this vital matter and if they agree with legislation should lobby their Members of Parliament and sign the petition.'

Yours, etc.

12th January 2012

Yesterday, finally, I arranged an appointment to see my GP regarding stress. About six months ago, I saw the sister at Occupational Therapy at the hospital for the same reason. I phoned the surgery whilst in theatre waiting for beds for my patients. Once again, there were no beds and we – the registrar, anaesthetist and I – waited for more than two hours. Because of the delay, the list didn't finish until 7.30 p.m.!

There was another damning piece in the *Advertiser*, this time regarding a recent report from the local watchdog, Tameside Local Involvement Network (LINk), which, following its recent inspection, says that not enough has improved at the hospital since its last visit. There was a very critical reader's letter too. The Coroner's office contacted me regarding the late Mrs B – who died the week-end of the swap-over of the MAU and Trauma wards – asking me to write a report and send it ASAP. I will do so on Monday.

15th January 2012 Sunday

The lake in Darnton Road, adjacent to the hospital, was frozen this morning as I drove towards Glossop to meet with Dom and Andrew for a trek. Dom invited me last Friday and I was glad to join him and friends. The gauge in the car said it was minus 1.5 degrees Celsius outside. I stopped at a BP petrol station to buy drinks and food and could not but see the *Reporter* front page which read: *Angry MPs tell Hospital Management 'GET A GRIP'*. For a few minutes, as I drove to our meeting point, I thought about the hospital, but I quickly put it out of my mind and concentrated on the road and the 'black ice' spots.

As I got out of the car, I felt the joy and the uplift of being outdoors. There were 8 of us: Dom and his son Joshua who is 14; Andrew and his dad, Chris; Dave and his two Labradors, Pretzel and Pumpkin, and me. They were all friendly and lovely company. We started at 9.00 a.m. The ground was frozen and in places tricky. I lent one of my poles to Joshua who did well to keep up with us adults. We passed Doctor's Gate, the old Roman road, and climbed up to the Snake Pass before turning to Black Clough where we stopped for a break. There was a fell runners' race taking place and a mountain rescue tent. We descended with winter sun shining above us and thawing the grass as we walked down. I held Pretzel's leash some of the way and it brought back memories of 'Paws' the rough collie I once owned and my family loved so much, particularly Steph, my daughter.

In places, when the sheep were not close, Pretzel and Pumpkin ran free and loved the outdoors as much as we did.

16th January 2012
I attended a presentation by Mrs Green and the Nursing Director, today, for all hospital workers. The auditorium was full because of the fear of redundancies. The CEO presented the Trust Finances saying that the year-end position is very worrying and announcing job losses: 106 WTE (Whole Time Equivalent) nurses, 10 doctors and 1 manager.

Mr Dylak talked about the latest CQC and LINk reports that were critical of the Trust. His unflustered approach suggested a lack of concern at the findings. Unbelievably, the CEO said that she and the Chair had tried, but failed, to change the way in which the LINk's findings were presented. The CEO was obviously annoyed.

17th January 2012
Today, I went to Timperley, where I used to live, to see my General Practitioner. He was kind and sympathetic. We have never met before, although we have spoken on the phone in the past. He gave me good advice and thought that it was quicker to see a counsellor via Occupational Therapy at my hospital than in Salford, where I live.

20th January 2012
I slept badly. Alarm clock woke me up at 6.45 a.m. and set off to Timperley at 7.30 a.m. for my appointment at the GPs surgery for blood tests with the practice nurse. Traffic horrible, it took me one hour ten minutes to do 12 miles. Still, I arrived 20 minutes early and, as I waited, I picked up a magazine by Omega – the Swiss watch company. All articles were on the subject of the importance of water in all its forms, from liquid to solid, and how essential

it is to preserve it. There was a beautiful photo of the earth taken from space with a caption saying that from space the globe reflects all the possible shades of the colour blue. I have seen similar photos before in films, TV programs, in magazines such as *National Geographic* (my favourite) and so on, but I was mesmerised by this picture. There was also an article by Michael Phelps, swimmer and several times Olympic Champion explaining that he is making a come-back to competition which is incredible as he is now much older. He says: '*With anything you do, put natural ability into it, but the biggest thing is how much you want something. If you want something bad enough, then no matter what it is you'll work for it and get it*'. I thought about it and concluded that Michael is absolutely right.

21st January 2012

Yesterday, I attended the CEO and MD's monthly forum where they apprise consultants of developments at the hospital. They repeated the message that the Trust will use all its influence to change the way in which Tameside LINk reports its findings. The meeting started with only seven consultants with eight more arriving later. The MD re-stated his belief that admission to hospital for patients with chronic co-morbidities should be carefully monitored. At question time, I requested that suspected Red incidents should be externally investigated. I added that I remain concerned that potentially avoidable deaths continue to occur.

27th January 2012

It was raining cats and dogs as I drove to the *Advertiser* office today with the intention of talking to a reporter about the Trust's investigation of me. There was no appointment and as I waited in the car-park I thought better of it and decided that it was not the right time. Hospital issues concerning the care of patients, however, remain essentially the same. Happily, one of my patients, with serious co-morbidities, whose hip operation was cancelled three times for lack of a High Dependency Unit bed for post-operative care, is doing well, after finally undergoing surgery.

28th January 2012

The hills above the Walkerwood reservoirs between Carrbrook and Stalybridge are beautiful all year round but for me particularly during winter. They rise about 450 meters and can be seen from any south-facing window of Tameside hospital and are so close that the path to the 'Trig point' that sits on the top of the moors can easily be seen. Julie and I walked the snow covered hills today and completed a seven miles trek. It was a glorious day, sunny with blue winter sky, not too cold and we enjoyed it tremendously.

29th January 2012

To cope with the pressure caused by the disciplinary investigation, I have decided to write a book to keep my sanity. I spent some time researching Quiriquina Island, where I was imprisoned in 1973. I discovered an old photo of prisoners published in a newspaper of that time. Now memories of those months of imprisonment keep coming back. I read the description of a marine who was a witness to many of the atrocities committed, including the execution of prisoners.

30th January 2012

Excellent news for patients and public treated at British hospitals. The General Medical Council has published a new guidance for doctors, entitled: *Raising and Acting on Concerns about patient safety,* I have read this 16-page document. Clauses 7 and 8 read:

7: All doctors have a duty to raise concerns where they believe that patient safety or care is being compromised by the practice of colleagues or the systems, policies and procedures in the organisations in which they work. They must also encourage and support a culture in which staff can raise concerns openly and safely.

8: You must not enter into contracts or agreements with your employing or contracting body that seek to prevent you from, or restrict you in, raising concerns about patient safety. Contracts or agreements are void if they intend to stop an employee from making a protected disclosure.

In essence, doctors that report or whistle-blow must not agree to gagging orders imposed by their employers. This is exactly what TH management did to me in 2005!

Under the sub-heading: Making a concern public in Clause 17, the guidance reads:

17: You can consider making your concerns public if you:

a.   *have done all you can to deal with any concern by raising it within the organisation in which you work or which you have a contract with, or with the appropriate external body; and*
b.   *have good reason to believe that patients are still at risk of harm; and*
c.   *do not breach patient confidentiality.*

But, you should get advice (see Clause 18) before making a decision of this kind, the Guidance adds.

I will circulate this guidance on the Intranet. It comes into effect on March 12th. I have no doubt that the main reason why the GMC has published this guidance is the serious criticism it received after the Mid Staffordshire Inquiry. I wonder if the article on whistle-blowing by Steve Bolsin, Rita Pal, Paul Wilmshurst and l, played a part.

2nd February 2012

I am the consultant Orthopaedic Surgeon on call today. Day started with Children's fracture clinic in the recently-built new wing of the hospital. At 10.30 a.m., I moved to Clinic 10, the adult fracture clinic. I was on my own as my Registrar is on annual leave. It was a busy clinic. I finished at 12.30 p.m.

According to the organisation known as Dr Foster, last year we were the second worst Trust in the country for mortality rates! Afterwards I hurried to the consultants Mortality Review Working Group meeting at the Post-graduate Centre. After the meeting, I moved to the operating theatre to do a Trauma List that I finished at 5.00 p.m.

One patient who had accidentally crushed his leg between two cars was in casualty, waiting for a bed. He was sent to the Medical Assessment and Admissions Unit (MAU) where he remained on a trolley in the corridor until midnight, as there were no beds in the Trauma Unit. He was eventually sent to the Endoscopy Ward that had been opened as an escalation ward for acute admissions. He was not the only patient who had been waiting for a bed today. MAU was full and patients kept coming hoping that eventually a bed would become available. Nursing staff were rushed off their feet and frustrated because today was not an exception; it is a daily occurrence.

At 7.00 p.m., I went to the MAU to review patients admitted under my care.

A factory worker with a deep cut on the index finger of his right hand, which he had sustained at around 2.00 p.m. was seated in a crowded sitting room in MAU. There was no room for examination, so I walked him to theatre to examine him there, following which I arranged for an operation under local anaesthetic – ring block – that I did at 8.00 p.m. He went home two hours later, from the theatre. Never had a bed!

I decided to sleep in my office, where I keep a mat, a sleeping bag and a pillow. I drafted a letter that I will send to the Chairman tomorrow.

3rd February 2012
Busy day! After Trauma Meeting with junior doctors I went to see the dozen or so patients under my care. They were in various inappropriate wards. Several patients with complex injuries requiring lots of work needed to be reviewed and processed. At around 4.00 p.m., I went back to my office to review a draft email to the Chairman and CEO that I sent an hour later and which I copied to Board members including Non-Executive Directors and to Lead Consultants. It is a long email giving specific examples of patients where care was well below accepted standards including the case of a patient with *pancreatitis* – a very serious surgical condition – who was admitted to the Trauma Unit and who arrested and died within twenty-four hours of admission. In the email, I say that *the first step to a solution is to recognise that there is a problem* that, at its worst, is costing lives. The sad fact is that the underlying projections and plans for the surgical re-design – have failed to meet with expectations and we need more beds. I, therefore, asked the Chair to put on the agenda for the next Board meeting a request to the shareholders of the Private Finance Initiative Consortia for a voluntary 10 per cent donation from the Trust's PFI Annual Unitary payment, which the Trust could re-invest in patient care. (See Appendix 9)

10th February 2012
My secretary contacted me at lunch to ask if I was free to see the new Chairman on Thursday regarding my concerns.

The CEO sent me two emails: one long one trying to explain the problems of capacity and for the first time acknowledging that we need more beds! I was told by a senior nurse that the first thing that Paul Williams, the newly appointed Chief Operating Officer, told the Board, after he had settled into his new post, was that we urgently need more beds – which perhaps explains the CEO's 'U- turn'. The other email states that she will forward my email to the external investigator because according to her I did not follow the Reporting Concerns policy when I wrote directly to her!

On call this weekend. As usual, there are many patients needing surgery and too few beds and little theatre time. As a result they wait for days at home or on the wards.

12th February 2012

Whilst I was in the surgeons' room in the theatre, this evening, waiting to do emergency surgery, I heard of the tragic death of the singer Whitney Houston at the age of 48.

Afterwards I did a difficult operation on a forty-year-old woman who fell down a ladder last night. She sustained a fracture dislocation of the talus, the large bone that makes the ankle joint. These injuries threaten the survival of the foot and need to be treated before the skin and foot circulation suffers permanent damage. Closed manipulation failed and I had to expose the bones to put them in place and fixed them with screws. The operation took ninety minutes. The anatomy looked nicely restored in the end. Hope she makes a good recovery. While I write this I am watching the Top 20 Whitney in Music 4 Freeview Channel. Her death has made me so sad! It is almost mid-night, time to hit the pillow.

15th February 2012

I will meet the new Chairman and the CEO tomorrow. I will take my laptop. Here is what I will say to him:

MORTALITY

Mortality at Tameside Hospital is linked to:

a. Lack of beds for immediate admission for suitable periods of observation and prompt investigations;
b. Lack of junior doctors to asses these critically ill patients, especially at night and at week-ends;
c. Seriously ill patients admitted to inappropriate wards, resulting in them

being nursed by non-specialist nurses and making the review by medical staff more difficult and less frequent;

d.   Patients are sent home from A&E when they should be admitted. Sometimes they are sent home twice whereupon, following a third admission, they are too ill and die;

e.   Patients being moved from ward to ward resulting in a lack of continuity of both nursing and medical care;

f.   Low nursing staffing levels on many shifts. For example ward 31, the cardiology ward has 30 patients, yet the night shift has only two qualified nurses, giving a ratio of one qualified nurse to fifteen patients;

g.   Patients who become critically ill not being transferred promptly to the Medical High Dependency Unit due to its lack of sufficient capacity;

h.   The fact that it is not always clear which consultant is in charge of a medical patient transferred from the MAU to the Medical HDU;

i.   The shortage of ITU beds and surgical and medical HDU beds. As a result, patients who need admission or transfer to these beds are often subject to potentially fatal delays. The Trust's solution of managing these patients in the recovery room in theatre is sub-standard and inappropriate and also disrupts planned theatre activity.

The Trust still has plans to close an ITU bed, in spite of the fact that it is obvious that this will be detrimental to patients. There have been several patients who have died at Tameside where one or more of the issues stated above have been mentioned at the Coroner's Court as being a contributory factor.

Review of medical records shows that when doctors, outreach nurses and other team members recommend escalating a critically ill patient to a Medical High Dependency or Surgical High Dependency bed, the decision is often blocked or delayed due to lack of capacity.

THE MEDICAL ASSESMENT UNIT

This clinical area has been an example of poor management for many years: reports by the Royal College of Physicians, the Deanery, and the CQC testify to that. I have written many letters quoting examples of mismanagement because, regrettably, some patients have suffered as a result of it. In its present location it was meant to have 38 beds, which has now been increased by the addition of a further 14. This, however, has left no rooms free for assessment. Clearly the services provided at Tameside hospital in respect of admissions to the MAU and the transfers of patients from A&E to the MAU have, too often, fallen well below accepted standards.

17th February 2012.

The meeting with Mr Connellan, the new Chairman, took place yesterday. The CEO was present. We sat around a small table. No note taking. He began by asking if my concerns arose from a system failure. I replied that they did and that my main concern was the continuing number of avoidable deaths linked to such failure.

I had my laptop open and I read from my prepared document. Mrs Green spoke several times, arguing, as usual, that Tameside Hospital is not performing any differently to other hospitals regarding, for example, admitting patients to the wrong wards, delays in admission etc. I said that sub-standard care in other hospitals was not an excuse for poor and unsafe care at our hospital. The Chairman interjected saying that he had had discussions with the CEO on this subject and found himself in disagreement with her.

I informed the Chairman that I had publicly, and also in writing, stated that in my view one to two patients per one hundred dying at Tameside Hospital, owing to a combination of factors, could in fact be saved.

The issue of lack of resources was discussed, the Chairman agreeing that the Trust needed more. He said that he will fight for them with the Primary Care Trust and Consortia and, if unsuccessful, will contact the local MPs and ask for their help.

I sensed an incipient power struggle between the Chair and the CEO. He appeared dominant and gave the impression that he is trying to understand what is going on at the Trust, having apparently not been fully informed. At one point I handed him an eight-page list of *incidents of misidentification* at the Trust during the year 2010/11 – some of them very serious. The CEO tried to take the list away from him but he very quickly put it under his papers. The meeting lasted two and a half hours. I promised on departing that I would email what I brought to the meeting on my laptop to him. I did it today from my office at 7.00 p.m.

22nd February 2012

I took Stephanie to Birmingham University today, by car. She has been offered a place to do Classics at the Archaeology and Antiquities Institute. On the way, she edited the introduction to my book and then read it to me. Listening to it out loud for the first time was quite an emotional experience for me.

We attended a presentation for prospective students and parents. The lecturer, a lady, was a little nervous. She finished her power presentation with the words - *'We can offer you a course that will release the life of the mind, your mind'.* I thought it was a brilliant ending. Afterwards we went for tea at a small departmental library, where we were able to question some of the other lecturers.

Later, we were taken on a tour of the campus by Georgina, a first-year student of Classics. The setting is nice with some green areas and squares. There was a farmers' market offering produce and goods which seemed an excellent idea. Also, several commercial banks were scattered about together with a Waterstones bookshop, where I bought Steph a book. Before returning home we went to a fair for post-graduate students to ask about progression to law after her Classics degree.

25th February 2012

Yesterday the CEO and the MD attended the Senior Medical Staff Committee meeting. Incredibly, Mrs Green openly admitted that I have been right all along in my view that one to two patients for every one hundred that dies at Tameside could be saved with better care. She went on to explain that Professor Keogh, the Medical Director of NHS England, is concerned with avoidable deaths in NHS hospitals.

The chair of the Local Negotiating Committee (LNC), who is a member of the MRWP (Mortality Review Working Party), has designed a thorough four-page questionnaire which consultants will take to the wards to ask nurses and doctors to complete. It will be anonymous and strictly confidential.

28th February 2012

I was up at 7a.m. to go trekking with Richard today. On the way to Edale, we stopped for petrol at Glossop Caravans Sales' Offices. As I was paying, Scot, one of my patients recognised me. He owns the sandwich bar and café next door and he gifted us egg and bacon sandwiches which we needed for later. He said to the young lady cooking: *'This is Mr Peña, who sorted out my knee after my motorbike accident but, more importantly, he diagnosed my damaged kidney as well'*. He then proceeded to demonstrate how I noticed this potentially lethal injury when I examined his tummy! He also recognised my friend Richard, who nursed him in the Trauma ward.

We started the trek at 9.50 a.m. from Edale. The weather was foggy all day and windy till 2p.m. We went up Jacob's Ladder and then into Kinder Fall where we had a hot drink. Scot's egg and bacon sandwiches were excellent! From there we followed the sandy bed of the river that feeds the Fall up to Bleaklow moors. Initially, the trail was easy to see, but as we got higher we became lost in the deep trenches that the water has cut into the peat – some of them over twenty feet deep and so narrow that we had to climb out on to the boggy moors. Even with Richard's GPS we found it hard to navigate. Eventually the streams began to flow in the opposite direction and we knew that we had reached the highest point and eventually would come to the edge of the Edale basin. We were well prepared to camp overnight but I am due to operate all day tomorrow. We were back at the car by 3.30 p.m. It was excellent preparation for Rick, who is training for the Pennine Way.

29th February 2012
Back to Tameside for a full-day elective list which is going quite well. Waiting for the last patient. A colleague has sent comparative mortality data for all NHS Trusts. The HSMI, Hospital Standardised Mortality Index, for our hospital, is 119, which remains one of the highest in the country.

2nd March 2012 Friday
A beautiful, big, red and orange sun hung in the sky as I drove back to my flat this evening. It was twenty-to-six and as soon as I got to the brow of the hill in Moor Lane I saw it, partially hidden by the trees initially–but then revealing itself in all its glorious majesty. I felt a peculiar sense of loss when our star disappeared from view as I turned on to the car park of the flats where I live.

I have been to the consultant's Mortality Meeting at the hospital today. Seven of us turned up and we made important modifications to the questionnaire, which was then approved.

4th March 2012 Sunday

For two months or so I have been typing, correcting and researching for my book. I am discovering facts and stories about people that left their mark on the history of South America, and Chile in particular. For instance, the Clark brothers, two British men that financed and built the railway line between Buenos Aires and Valparaiso in Chile in the 1890s – a feat of engineering which required a tunnel under the mountains at over 10,000 feet and hazardous work in the most inclement conditions. Initially a success, maintenance proved too costly over the years and the last trains to run between Mendoza and Valparaiso were in 1980. Likewise, the trains between Mendoza and Buenos Aires –which we once boarded – have also been discontinued.

7th March 2012 Wednesday

Three cases of another consultant, all major operations, were cancelled due to lack of beds. My own three patients had priority because all had been cancelled previously for the same reason.

Went to the MAU and discussed the mortality review questionnaire with a physician colleague and a senior sister which they afterwards completed. Also went to Ward 3; found out that the sister there had already filled out the questionnaire.

12th March 2012 Monday

Have been working hard on the book I am writing. In the meantime, two letters came, to do with the 'investigation into my conduct,' yet I have not received a formal response to my request to see all documents regarding this matter, which is my right.

14th March 2012

A tragic day. A bus carrying Belgian children from Switzerland to Belgium crashed in a tunnel resulting in twenty-four deaths, including the two drivers. They were returning after a skiing holiday.Their young lives have been cut so short; I hope that all the survivors make a full recovery and those families that lost a dear one, eventually find peace and solace.

21st March 2012

Wrote a long letter to the Case Manager of the Investigation, the Financial Director, saying that my request to see all pertinent documents, four months ago, has been ignored. I ask who is paying the investigator and how much it is costing. In the letter, I formally request that the Trust report the matter to the General Medical Council and ask it to investigate my conduct. Alternatively, I suggest that the Trust should report me to any one of the Royal Colleges for investigation.

24th March 2012 Saturday
It is a beautiful, early spring day, sunny and quite warm, with a bright blue sky. I would rather be trekking but I am at the hospital in the operating theatre. I have done one total knee replacement but we are unable to proceed further because there are no beds for the other two patients, who are also listed for knee replacements. Even the lady I have just operated on has not got a bed. So we wait!

29th March 2012
Busy fracture clinic this morning. It is 3.00 p.m. and we have been waiting in theatre since 1.30p.m. to start the operating trauma list. As a result, one patient with a hip fracture will be cancelled, and her chances of surviving her injury will be reduced.

6.00 p.m. I am back at my flat. The hospital is in the news again, this time for serious breaches of security regarding the storage of Saline IV bags. A manager has anonymously told the Manchester Evening News that open crates with bags of this fluid are kept outside the goods entrance, unprotected and without security cameras. A reporter approached them unchallenged and took photos. Bearing in mind the current fluid contamination investigation by the police at nearby Stepping Hill hospital in Stockport, the lack of security at our hospital is worrying.

On a more positive note, I learned today of the brilliant work of Chester Zoo, that has a project in Tanzania where every week they take school children by bus on safari. There, for the first time these youngsters see the wild life of their own country. I have been fortunate to visit this beautiful country and this project is really commendable.

My colleague, Nick O'Mullane rang to tell me that he has received the preliminary draft of the book I sent him and will read it soon. Today, on a course, he met with another colleague who is very supportive; they are both my trusted friends.

31st March 2012

Back from Exeter. Yesterday I went to pick up Pablo from university. He needed to empty his room for the Easter holidays. He showed me around the city and the University campus which is hilly with very pretty lawns and gardens. As we paused by a flowering camellia I showed him how to recognise this evergreen plant with shiny leaves and showy flowers.

Later we walked by the River Exe which had many pairs of mute swans and lots of wild ducks but alas, not black-necked swans.

11th April 2012

It has been tough and I am taking it day by day. On Sunday Pablito and I went to Edale and walked about seven miles. It was good to be with him. He is very fit and climbed the 460m to Edale Head without effort. There was a lot of snow, two feet deep in places.

The bed crisis at the hospital persists and patients continue to be inconvenienced by it.

I have been asked to attend the inquest of Mrs B, the patient that died the week-end of the wards swap, in June.

20th May 2012

Julie and I have been to Martin Mere bird sanctuary near Ormskirk today, to see the only black- necked swans in the British Isles. There was one couple and five cygnets about three months old whose feathers were gradually changing colour. Simon, one of the keepers told us that, of the original couple, the male had sadly died and the female rejected two potential partners especially brought from South America. She accepted the third, but it was not until this year that she hatched little ones. Took lots of photos. The male was very territorial. We saw Andean Geese, Corcoran swans and Chilean flamingos in addition to several species of South American ducks.

It was an unforgettable day and I was happy to see my cousins, but I sensed their isolation; they feel alien, like me.

***

Last week, I sent a letter (See Appendix 10) reporting the Trust for breaches of Article 6 of the European Convention on Human Rights – the right to a fair trial – to the Chair of the Parliamentary Health Committee, and copied in the Secretary of State for Health, the Chair of the Audit Commission, the Chair of Monitor, the Regional Director of the CQC (See Appendix 11), the Chair of Tameside Hospital Board and the Case Administrator of NCAS.

27th July 2012

It has been a long time since I wrote in my diary. Reasons? Probably depression, but I really do not know. It is the stress of having to live under the cloud of a disciplinary investigation, hanging like a sword of Damocles above my head. Nevertheless, to stop it crushing me I am working harder than ever in my job as a consultant. Received replies from the chair of the Audit Commission saying that it is not within their remit to investigate individual cases. The Chair of the Health Select Committee has not yet replied. I may ask the local Labour MPs to look into it.

I have been having weekly, one hour counselling sessions to combat my depression with a nice lady called Irene, for the last six weeks. They take place on Fridays, at 1.00 p.m. and to get there I have to walk in front of the new Trust Headquarters and enter a small building called 'The Lodge' by Darnton Road. I wonder if the CEO or any of the Directors have, by chance, seen me enter the building, which is used almost exclusively for counselling. The sessions have been extremely useful and Irene is a good listener. I told her about the book and how writing it has been therapeutic and has allowed me to keep my sanity. After the fourth session I asked her if she would like to read it, so she can understand the issues and me better. The last two sessions have been about the book and her comments have been invaluable. She is of the view that it should be proof-read and published.

Until two days ago I had not heard from David Jago, the Case Manager of the Investigation, for three months! On 25th I received a letter advising me that the Trust has appointed a new investigator. The letter does not say why or who this person is. I replied to the letter asking for clarification. I also wrote to Mr Corless, the non-executive director appointed to the Investigation by the Board, sending copies of all the correspondence so far and requesting, once again, that the Trust should report their concerns to the GMC and ask a Royal College to take over the investigation.

28th July 2012

Oscar (not his real name) is a 33 years old patient admitted on 15th under the medical team for a severe infection of his left leg, misdiagnosed as *cellulitis*, who was treated with intra-venous antibiotics. He did not respond and on 20 July he was referred to the general surgical registrar who contacted me at midnight to ask for my advice, explaining that his own consultant could not help. Half-an-hour later, I found an extremely ill patient suffering from *necrotizing fasciitis*, affecting the whole of his left leg. An immediate operation was needed to save his life. The young surgical registrar was eager to learn and stayed to assist me. I had to do the largest surgical wound of my career, on the outside of his leg, from the waist to the foot. Upon opening the *fascia* (the tough layer that envelops the muscle compartments) there was pus everywhere and the fat and fascia, that were a hideous black colour in places, had turned to jelly. The smell of putrefaction was overwhelming. Painstakingly I cut out all the dead tissue and used litres of normal saline fluid to clean the wound. After dressing it, I was subsequently told that Oscar's condition had improved.

We didn't finish until after 3.00 a.m. and so I slept in my office. I got up at 8.00a.m. and went to see him in the Intensive Care Unit. He was better but he needed to return to theatre for further inspection and debridement, which I did at about 4.00 p.m. I was not surprised to find that, just hours after leaving a clean wound, lots of further tissue had become necrotic and I removed it. After I finished, I contacted the microbiologist to ask for an up-date on the findings from the numerous tissue samples we had sent hours earlier. Further antibiotics were added and Oscar began to respond.

Since then, I have operated on him daily and he will survive, but whether he will keep his leg remains in the balance. Altogether, I have worked a good twenty-four hours on him since I was asked to take over eight days ago. He is a drug addict including opioids and alcohol. I have spoken to his sisters who obviously love him dearly. Their mother committed suicide when he was seventeen, his father was addicted also and died at age 42, one year after his right arm was amputated, apparently as a result of a serious infection.

Oscar's is the most serious case of necrotizing fasciitis I have seen. Three years ago, I managed to save the life and the leg of a young woman, an actress, who was also an addict, but who is now clean, as I discovered a few months ago when I saw her in my clinic. It was a pleasure to see her – a transformed and happy human being. I hope Oscar does well, too.

29th July 2012 Sunday

We have a new Director of Nursing: John Goodenough has replaced Philip Dylak who left the Trust in June. His departure was felt by many to be a consequence of the unabated public demand for a wholesale change of management and follows the resignation of the Chairman, the Rev. Presswood, only a few months earlier.

***

I checked on Oscar today. He is still sedated but awake enough for his eyes to be open and obey simple verbal commands. The good news is that he feels pain when I prick his left foot, which means that his sciatic nerve is still functioning in spite of the infection. The dressings were changed yesterday but they are soaked and must be changed again today. About eight assistants are needed to accomplish this and must be done in theatre.

***

I am doing a Waiting List Initiative today. One total knee replacement and one total hip replacement and two other cases. Mr P, the registrar on call tells me that there are no beds in the hospital and patients are being admitted to the day surgical ward to keep things moving.

***

This coming week I will contact the three local Labour MPs to inform them of the Investigation. I will also write to the GMC.

***

Last Friday I sent an email to Consultants and specialist doctors attaching the minutes of the last SMSC meeting. I remind them that, after occupying the position for six years – two full terms – my tenure as Chairman finishes in October and a replacement will be needed. The constitution of the committee does not allow for a third term and none of the consultants has so far put their name forward. There is no payment of any kind and apart from a secretary attending the meetings to take minutes and type a summary of the deliberations, the chairman has no other secretarial or administrative support. The secretaries (there have been several) work for the Human Resources Director and Medical Director in the Trust Headquarters and like all their colleagues they are always extremely busy – overworked is perhaps a better description. I have got on well with all of them. I wonder what they really think about us doctors and managers?

1st August 2012

Oscar is moving the toes of his left foot and this is excellent news. Today, I tried to contact the plastic surgeons – who are based at Wythenshawe hospital in south Manchester – but they are away on leave and their secretary is not contactable! I finally succeeded in leaving a fax referral form via another secretary. I am hopeful that they will admit him over next week as he will require extensive skin grafts.

***

I am in theatre waiting to do my last case, a total hip replacement on a lady about my age. She has segmental collapse of the femoral head due to avascular necrosis, a condition which has many causes, including prolonged intake of medication such as steroids or as a result of trauma.

***

Sent letters to the three local Labour MPs today enclosing the letter to Stephen Dorrell, the chair of the Parliamentary Select Committee on Health that I sent in May and that has not yet been answered. The MPs are Jonathan Reynolds, Andrew Gwynne and David Heyes. I honestly do not know what they can do, but they need to be informed of this Investigation.

8th August 2012 Wednesday

What a past seven days! Been so busy that I feel drained. Last Thursday a sixteen-year-old girl with complex needs was admitted under my care with a painful leg, after waiting twelve hours in Casualty for a bed. She has a *mental age of two*, cannot talk, has epilepsy and fits, Crohn's disease and a Peg tube. That day, I was informed about her at about 6.00 p.m. and I went to the emergency Department immediately, where I stayed for two hours making phone calls, awaiting answers, and even pleading in person with the consultant paediatrician, but to no avail. My registrar was a witness to my efforts. The girl was denied admission to the Children's Ward by the lead paediatric consultant and the paediatric divisional nurse manager, because chronologically she is six weeks over sixteen. Now, she is in the elective surgery adult ward and I am doing the best I can to take care of her. I have written to Dr Mahmood, the MD and Mr Goodenough, the new ND, a letter of complaint and to ask that she be moved to the Children's Unit – so far without success. This shows a rigidity and lack of compassion that, to me, is incomprehensible.

15th August 2012 Wednesday
Another seven days of frustration and utter despair due to lack of resources to treat my patients to the standards of care they deserve.

23rd August 2012
At last I received a letter from Mr Jago, the Case Manager, regarding the investigation into my conduct, informing me that the investigator appointed by the Trust has been sacked! New Terms of Reference have been produced by the Trust's solicitors who have commented that one of the reasons why the investigator was replaced was the comments he made that 'he had already decided there was a case to answer and the outcome of his work was pre-determined.'

The Trust – allegedly for legal reasons – is not releasing any of the documents I requested, including the statements from 'witnesses' that the investigator had interviewed: Mrs C Green, CEO; Dr T Mahmood, Medical Director; Mr P Dylak, Director of Nursing; Mr D Wilkinson, Director of Human Resources; Mr A Griffiths, Director of Clinical Services (former); Mrs K Shingler, Divisional Nurse Manager; Mrs A Baxter, Divisional Nurse Manager; Mrs A Prendergast, Quality and Risk Manager and the Ward Manager of the MAU.

8th September 2012
Important developments in the saga of the investigation. I hand-delivered a letter to the Human Resources Director yesterday regarding a formal grievance against Mrs Green, the Chief Executive Officer. My reasons for it

are: 1) Wilful contravention of the Data Protection Act; 2) Wilful disregard of key principles contained in the document entitled, Maintaining High Professional Standards in the Modern NHS; 3) Failure to report concerns about me to the GMC; 4) Failure to request that an investigation into my conduct is carried out by any of the Royal Colleges; 5) Failure to act in March 2012 after I indicated that the behaviour of the previous investigator was inappropriate and discriminatory; 6) Failure to offer support for stress during the first six months of the investigation.

I have now submitted two formal complaints for failings on the part of the Trust and, therefore, there is an overlap between the investigation against me and the grievances that I have lodged. It is now a very complex state of affairs. The more I look into this situation, the more certain I become that procedurally the Trust has acted erroneously. Whether she likes or not, the CEO has a lot to answer for concerning how this affair has been handled.

The new investigator sent me his mobile number; he wants to talk informally. The fact is that the Trust has put him in a difficult situation because they have given him the same data going back to 1997 contained in the nearly 1,000 pages of previously accumulated documents. I pointed out months ago that this is prejudicial and unfair and furthermore in violation of several sections of the Data Protection Act.

***

My counsellor has been wonderful. Yesterday I had another one-hour session and I told her that Julie and I went gathering blackberries and rose hip by the banks of the River Irwell and made blackberry jam and rose hip syrup. The syrup is special and I have never made it or tasted it for about 55 years! The jam tasted better than the Bonne Mammon in the supermarket! Rose hip syrup is unfortunately no longer found in supermarkets.

***

Went cycling in Waterdale Park this morning for 90 mins. Day was perfect, and I cleared my head. More determined than ever not to give in to the pressure. I have defended myself, without any legal advice and I am still working, head high and bearing it all, despite the immense stress.

***

Oscar, the patient who had necrotising fasciitis and on whom I carried out the more extensive fasciotomy I ever done – beginning on his foot and ending at waist level – continues to do well. He had skin grafting at Wythenshawe last Wednesday! It was all worthwhile. He has survived and hopefully will not lose his leg!

10th September 2012

Today I sent the CEO an addendum to my grievance against the Human Resources manager in charge of the investigation against me. This manager, like the two external investigators, has blatantly ignored the precepts laid down in the policy document, *Maintaining High Professional Standards* and the Trust Policy for disciplining medical staff, as I have repeatedly pointed out.

19th September 2012

It is another Wednesday and I am in theatre. I am doing two major operations: one hip and one knee replacement and two minor cases.

The investigation into my conduct is now eleven months old. The new investigator is not medically trained but has a business degree.

16th December 2012

I live close to the River Irwell which meanders towards Salford and Manchester. There is a path known as the Irwell Sculpture Trail because it has seventy works of art on it. It starts in Salford Quays and roughly follows the river all the way up to Summerset and beyond. In Radcliffe the path runs alongside a disused canal and it was on it that today I found a solitary white swan. As he saw me approaching, he swam towards the bank and asked me:

'Where do you come from, strange swan with such dark feathers on your neck?'
'I am from Chile a country at the other side of the world,' I responded.
He looked at me and smiled. 'Why are you in these lands?' he continued.
'It is a very long story, brother, but would it suffice to say I had to leave?' I added.
'Ah,' he said, and gesturing with his head, he sent me on my way.

DIARIES 2013

INTRODUCTION

The disciplinary investigation continued into 2013 although it appeared to have stalled. The second investigator appointed by the Trust failed to send me the witness statements he had obtained from the CEO, the Medical Director, the Human Resources Director, various other managers and a nursing officer, (who has since been dismissed). It was my right to see the statements before meeting the new investigator who, it transpired, proved to be no more impartial than his predecessor. Meanwhile, I saw my counsellor on a regular basis until May.

In February, I had a meeting with the Chairman and asked him if he shared my opinion that the CEO should resign. He informed me that he had appraised her and was satisfied with her performance. At that time, however, Tameside had been named in Parliament by the Prime Minister as one of five failing Trusts nationwide (subsequently extended to fourteen) that would be subjected to full inspection by a review team under the auspices of Sir Bruce Keogh, Medical Director of NHS England. In May, the findings of a Rapid Responsive Review by the team were released and were a damning indictment of governance and the safety and quality of patient care at the hospital. The unfolding of events is described in the final chapter.

26th February 2013

The meeting with the Chair of the Trust today lasted almost two hours. I had requested it, once again, to discuss the high mortality rates at Tameside (relative to the average across all trusts) and also to express my concern regarding the length of time it had taken to conclude the ongoing Investigation into my conduct. I expressed my view that the Investigation was a matter of public interest and should be discussed by the Board. Formal notes were taken. With regard to avoidable deaths, I explained to him that they continued to occur, in response to which he indicated that an external professor had conducted a review in 2012 and found no links between the quality of care and patients dying at Tameside hospital. I mentioned the case of a 70-year-old patient, critically ill with a life threatening condition, who was inappropriately sent from A&E to the Trauma Ward, where he died within six hours. He asked for more information, which I will send tomorrow. Concerning the disciplinary investigation he said that he could not interfere with the process.

During the meeting, I asked the Chairman if he thought that the CEO should resign. He replied that he had recently appraised her and was satisfied with her performance. I informed him that I would be writing to Prof. Keogh, Medical Director of NHS England, who is leading an investigation launched by Prime Minister, David Cameron, into the hospital, to inform him that I wish to give evidence during his Review. (Appendix 12)

19th April 2013
I formally reported to the Coroner my concerns regarding the death of a patient in the Trauma Ward on 22 February. His medical/surgical condition was serious and he should have been admitted to a high dependency unit. This was the patient about whose death I had spoken to the Chairman on 26th of this month.

3rd July 2013
The CEO has resigned! This comes in the wake of the shocking findings of the Keogh Review and follows the resignation of the Medical Director. A colleague tells me that there was a major article in The Guardian yesterday about recent events at Tameside hospital and another one today.

10th July 2013
Met with Susan Watts, Keith (cameraman) and John – the team from *Newsnight* from BBC 2 – to film an interview regarding Tameside. It was fine, although I was rather tired, having woken up at 5.00 am with my mind racing, full of thoughts and unable to get back to sleep!

12th July 2013
The front page of Tameside Advertiser has the headline: *'As hospital chief quits, whistleblower insists. . . . 'Lessons must be learned'.* It carries an interview with

me by reporter, Sue Carr, which was conducted a few days ago and which is a well-balanced account. It has been a long, stressful and lonely fight for better standards!

14th July 2013

Header on the front page of *the Sunday Telegraph*: 13,000 died needlessly at 14 worst NHS Trusts! In my view, a more realistic figure is 1300. Nonetheless, it is still utterly unacceptable and an unconscionable number of avoidable deaths, even though they occurred over a period of ten years.

27th July 2013

After several days of reflection on the momentous events of the past few weeks, I sent an email to the senior doctors, directed in particular at those that have joined the hospital recently. I attached the letter that I had sent to Sir Bruce Keogh back in March and the various enclosures (seventeen additional documents). The email was copied to the recently-appointed Interim CEO, the new MD, the Chairman of the Board and the Chief Operating Officer/ Director of Elective Services.

I pointed out that the majority of the failings noted by the Rapid Responsive Review Panel were highlighted in my report to the Secretary of State for Health in 2010. Amongst these were the panel's findings that:

- the chairman had not fully considered the impact of the CEO's leadership style on the ability of the other executive directors to fulfil their functions;
- there were clear gaps in Board to Ward communication, including assurance of quality and safety;
- the Trust was reliant on external reviews, but did not have a history of delivering improvements based on them;
- the Quality Impact Assessments carried out following the implementation of 'efficiency savings' did not contain quality indicators for the monitoring of either an improvement or deterioration in care quality;
- the quality of mortality reviews was poor;
- the culture appeared to be one of managing targets rather the ensuring overall quality and patient experience;
- there was evidence of sub-standard practice that was frequently accepted

by the Trust;
- the care of deteriorating patients was sub-optimal;
- there were a number of concerns on nurse staffing levels; the nurse ratio per bed at Tameside was 1.31 compared to the national average of 1.91;
- there was inadequate senior medical supervision of patients and inadequate junior medical staff supervision and cover; and
- it was not clear how the Trust was using serious incident reports to learn lessons and to improve care.

I continued my letter by saying that instead of spending hundreds of thousands of pounds on reports from consultancy and accountancy firms, the Trust should use the money on intelligently-devised schemes to incentivise staff to work happily and efficiently towards a common goal: the best possible care for every patient. I maintained that we urgently require an injection of money (something that I had been saying to the previous CEO for years) and stated that the Board must commit to nursing levels of a minimum of one qualified nurse for seven patients. I added that the Board must consider financial incentives to attract consultants and junior doctors, for instance an initial bonus, which would surely be less expensive than paying agency fees for years on end.

I ended by saying that I am now optimistic for the future of the hospital and by thanking those colleagues that stood by me.

2nd August 2013

Nick O'Mullane has sent me an email with his comments on the Keogh Review; they are important coming, as they do, from a man who was the most senior physician at the Trust at the time of his retirement two years ago. He says:

1. MRSA and C-Diff infection rates are not helped by the unnecessary movement of patients from ward to ward around the hospital;
2. Care of patients in A&E and MAU is not always consultant-led;
3. Over-reliance on Night Nurse Practitioners is not good practice for medical emergencies and not good for training junior doctors;
4. There is no resident Surgical Registrar leaving F2-year doctors unsupported;
5. High agency expenditure on staff is linked to escalation wards which

once opened are difficult to close due to continuous demand;

6. Under-staffing on medical wards with regards to both nurses and doctors is common;

7. Nurses on the wards, including MAU, are over-burdened and unable to meet patients' needs owing to deliberately assigned low staffing levels. As a result, stress-related sickness levels are high amongst nurses and replacement agency nurses have to be employed causing additional heavy expense and disrupting continuity of care.

8. Dummy clinics are not a satisfactory way to arrange follow-up appointments. (Dummy clinics are virtual or non-existent future clinics where 'shadow' bookings are made but no real appointment date is given to the patient who, as a result, can become lost in the system and may never get a follow-up appointment)

Nick worked at Tameside for thirty years and tenaciously pursued managers to obtain the best standard of care for his patients.

3rd August 2013
Received a letter from the Head of Regional Compliance (North-West) of the Care Quality Commission. It says that following the Keogh Review, he has been reviewing the records of Tameside hospital and noticed that in May 2012 I had sent a letter to the CQC detailing staff shortages and incidents of poor care. He says that the information I gave was used but apologises on behalf of the CQC because I had not been sent a reply!

5th August 2013
Met with community campaigners Liz, Rod, Derek and Paul to discuss Rod's Charter for Change, which is a superb piece of work. It has seven points. The first is to grant an automatic right to a patient's spouse, relative, carer or next-of-kin to be in attendance at daily doctor's rounds. In my opinion, this point alone will bring about an almost certain improvement in patient care. It is costless for the hospital and can be implemented immediately. We agree that when I meet the interim CEO, I will present her with the Charter.

7th August 2013
Took time to write a short email to Mrs James, the interim CEO to thank her for meeting with me last Friday. Mrs James is a trained nurse and the meeting was to discuss nursing issues such as staffing, career progression, motivation and

recognition of their work. I explained that regarding the matter of nurse-to-patient ratios, the recent report from the National Advisory Group on the Safety of Patients in England, by Don Berwick, 'A promise to learn – a commitment to act' supports all the recommendations in the Charter for Change.

I mentioned that having read the document, Tameside Pathway Accreditation process, submitted to the Board by Mr Goodenough, the ND, it is not conducive to safer patient care as it reduces the number of qualified nurses and nursing auxiliaries by ten in each category.

9th August 2013
Paul Williams, Chief Operating Officer of the Trust, came to my office two hours ago. He took over Finance Director, David Jago, as the Case Manager of the Investigation. My secretary was present – at my request because the agenda of the meeting was the Investigation that had begun 22 months ago. Paul explained that the independent investigator had concluded that there was a case to answer, but the allegations were historical and should have been dealt with contemporaneously. He told me that, in consequence, the investigation would be terminated and no further action would be taken as a result of the allegations.

20th August 2013
I saw the piece in the *Manchester Evening News* and the local papers regarding the Charter for Change, including advice to the public on how to obtain copies. I am happy that the third point of the Charter calls for minimum staffing levels of one qualified nurse to no more than seven patients on all acute wards.

There was also an article reporting the inquest on the death of Philip Goodeve-Docker on April 28th this year. He was from Chilbolton, Hampshire. He and two companions were caught in a sub-zero storm during a charity trek in Greenland. He was raising money for nursing care. He died just two hours before a helicopter rescued his friends. What a tragedy!

9th September 2013
I have seen the video of the Risk Summit Meeting of the Keogh Review Panel with the CEO, MD and ND back in July before the CEO and MD resigned. The demeanour of the CEO and MD speaks volumes as they listen to the accounts of the panellists.

Chapter Nineteen

THE FALL OF THE ANCIEN REGIME

Mrs Green's régime lasted fifteen years. I recall my first encounter with her one evening in 1998 at the old Post-Graduate Centre where, together with other candidates for the post of chief executive, she informally met consultants. We talked for a while and she explained that she had risen through the ranks and this would be her first job as a chief executive. At that time, I would never have predicted that in years to come she would be so reluctant to listen to my concerns. I had only been at the hospital for a year and was still finding my feet and for the next few years my focus was almost exclusively confined to meeting the demands of my new appointment. At first, I missed Rochdale and agonised over whether I had made the right decision, but gradually I warmed to Tameside. Four years on, I became increasingly conscious of the deteriorating situation with regards to patient care resulting from poor nurse staffing levels and the lack of junior doctors. Mr Dunningham, the Medical Director at the time, was also an orthopaedic surgeon and therefore it was easy to convey to him my uneasiness and worries. In response, he confided that he shared my concerns and naively I thought he meant it. But in meetings and confidential letters about me he behaved differently and could not accept any criticism of the Trust.

During most of the long years of her régime, there were two key directors who served the CEO with unswerving loyalty: the deputy CEO, Mr Griffiths, who was also the Director of Elective Services, and Mr Dylak, the Director of Nursing. Together with successive Medical Directors and half a dozen key consultants they were part of her 'inner circle'. They commissioned many external reviews into the Trust's performance but often the reports were either not submitted for a full discussion at Board level or else watered-down findings would be tabled and passed to one of the many Trust Committees to prepare a ritualistic 'action plan', which would have a time-table for action that would be circulated, discussed and, if necessary, made public. However, in the event, nothing or very little would change. One important document that was effectively suppressed without reaching Board level was the Invited Service Review by the Royal College of Physicians. This was a comprehensive report, compiled late in 2008, which slated the emergency patient pathway: Accident and Emergency, the Medical Assessment Unit (MAU), the Medical Wards and Medical High Dependency/Coronary Unit. It also criticised the appalling lack of supervision of junior doctors. (I sent this report to the Keogh Review panel.)

Upon announcing her resignation, the CEO was quoted in the press as saying that she cared passionately about the hospital, its staff and its patients. She certainly cared about the infrastructure – the new building in particular – but in my view she did not exhibit the kind of empathy or compassion that becomes the CEO of a hospital trust and that the position necessitates. Had she been capable of understanding and identifying with the people to whom she owed a duty of care, she would have taken remedial action in 2003 when I first sent her a draft of my report and letter to the Commission for Health Improvement, which provided incontestable evidence of the suffering and neglect of human beings on the wards. Her pure blind complacency in respect of the welfare of patients, nurses and employees characterised her régime. She became a devoted and forceful advocate of the prevalent view that the delivery of healthcare can be regulated by market forces and its corollary, that hospitals have to be run as a business. She was fervent about it and pursued the promotion of Tameside Hospital as a brand – like *Puma* or *Coca Cola* – to attract 'customers'. The principal goal every year was to deliver efficiency savings and keep within budget.

The propaganda techniques became very sophisticated and messages were played into our computers frequently to convince us that all was well. Even as late as 28 February 2013 the hospital website stated that the CQC had given Tameside a 'clean bill of health'. Slogans were employed, such as *'Everyone matters'*, which was not what most people experienced. Photos of smiling employees appeared everywhere – who knows at what cost – for public consumption and to remind us of our 'contentment'.

For years – on a routine basis – I read the minutes and papers of the Board meetings and noted the lack of leadership of successive chairmen and the weakness of the non-executives who seldom challenged the papers submitted by the CEO or other executive directors.

Staff Forums served Mrs Green well. They allowed her to be seen as meeting regularly with her employees whilst providing little opportunity for dissent. The Forums were also a platform from which she could keep her managers happy by lecturing them on how the Trust's problems or various crises were being resolved. Many of these managers would show their loyalty by leaping up to defend her against critics who dared to raise awkward questions.

Why was the CEO forced to resign? What caused her downfall?

I believe, in retrospect, that the crisis she faced in 2010 wounded her régime badly, if not mortally, and the support of such a large number of senior doctors for a vote of no-confidence signalled the beginning of the end. Another damaging blow was delivered by the junior doctors who courageously reported their serious and un-remediated concerns to the Head of the North-West Deanery, Professor J Hayden. They had been reported to the Trust's directors for years and were recurrent in the Deanery reports and other documents, but shamefully the situation continued unabated until 2013, at which point the Dean formally raised her concerns directly with the CEO in writing. The initial response of Mrs Green to the Dean's letter, according to press reports, was a brief and largely dismissive reply, provoking a strong reaction and causing a second, more hard-hitting letter to be dispatched, inflicting yet another wound to the embattled Chief Executive. It could have been avoided, if in 2008 the *Junior Doctors' Charter*, which enumerated their concerns and which Nick O'Mullane presented to the Human Resources Director, had been taken seriously and acted upon.

Early in 2013 the Trust requested the Emergency Services Intensive Support Team (ESIST), based at the NHS's headquarters in Leeds, to review the hospital's Emergency Pathway to identify any areas of concern and make recommendations to improve performance, in particular against the 4-hour standard. ESIST's subsequent report was uncompromising and delivered some stark and unpalatable messages to the Trust, finding that:

- Consultant leadership in A&E, MAU and core medical wards was not evident during the review;
- Consultant input to ward rounds was extremely variable;
- Several wards advised that their main daily medical input was only from junior medical staff;
- Estimated Discharge Date was not being used as a proactive tool to drive community and social service and there was limited consultant input to dates;
- Inter-action between consultants and nursing staff was limited;
- Effective consultant supervision for trainees was lacking with some senior members unwilling to assist trainees with patient care.

The report concluded that 'delays in assessment, treatment and admission' from A&E are adversely affecting the 'individual patient experience' and, critically, 'patient outcomes'. A separate report by the North West Utilisation Management Unit (NWUMU) which helps hospitals in Greater Manchester improve their performance, was equally critical.

Not surprisingly, these reports led to a series of meetings chaired by Mrs Green and supported by the Medical Director, Dr Mahmood, and Chief Operating Officer, Mr Williams, and involved the A&E and medical consultants. An action plan addressing both external reviews was prepared which was submitted to the Trust Board at their meeting in May. This plan had been in the making for a few weeks and a revised version was submitted to the Board under the heading: *Recovery plan based on the ESIST & NWUMU Reviews at Tameside, April 2013*. It had thirty 'actions' to be urgently implemented which were submitted to the regulator, Monitor, for approval.

But it was to no avail. The national newspaper, *The Guardian*, got wind of what was going on and ran the story extensively, dealing another wounding blow to the moribund régime which was now visibly teetering.

In February 2013 the Chairman, Mr Connellan, had told me that he had full confidence in his CEO. We now learn that he met with Mrs Green on 27 June 2013 and she tendered her resignation. The Guardian story appeared a week later on 2 July. The following day, Mrs Green issued a statement making public her resignation.

The role played by the General Practitioners (GPs) who form the Tameside and Glossop Clinical Commissioning Group (CCG), was also crucial. The CCG had commissioned the review by NWUMU. According to Denis Campbell, the Health Correspondent of *The Guardian*, quoting from the minutes that he obtained of a private meeting of the CCG's board held on 1May: *'Because Tameside's "shortcomings" were "currently having an adverse impact on patient care [and] some were serious enough to require immediate attention",* the hospital's bosses needed to be replaced.' The minutes add that, *"Although there had been some progress in a number of areas more recently, opportunities to address others had been missed over a number of years. Many of the key failures reflected on executive and medical leadership."*

According to *The Guardian*, the GPs also found that nurses reported that, *'Should the registrar [middle-grade doctor] be very busy over the week-end, patients transferred to the ward on a Friday night might not receive a senior review [by a consultant] until the following Tuesday, perhaps 84 hours later'.*

Wounded and under increasingly heavy bombardment, Mrs Green remained at her post until the Keogh Review delivered what was effectively the coup de grâce, leaving the CEO with little option but to fall on her sword.

The immense and unquantifiable tragedy of her tenure of office is that the pain and suffering of hundreds of patients and their relatives over the course of at least twelve years could have been avoided or mitigated. It remains my view that between one to two hundred deaths were preventable.

We now know that foundation trusts in England will be required to make annual efficiency savings of four per cent of their budgets until 2020. The public may have noticed that the announcement is no longer made by the Secretary of State for Health because he has relinquished his responsibility to the Chief Executive of the NHS Commissioning Board, re-named NHS England, since the 2012 Health and Social Care Act came into effect. My contention is that these levels of 'efficiency' are not possible without affecting quality in any of its three dimensions: clinical effectiveness, patient experience and safety. I hope that this book gives the reader an insight into what could and does happen when they are implemented at local level.

PART 3

EPILOGUE

Regarding issues that arose in Part 1: Chapters 1 and 2

What is the current political situation in Chile?

After the free elections in the year 1990, the first for almost twenty years, Chile has returned to a stable democracy. Since then there have been six presidential elections. Much has changed for the better concerning civil liberties, all of which have been restored, although the freedom to assemble and to protest has on several occasions been trampled.

Have the perpetrators of the atrocities been tried in a court of law?

The Law Courts have since sentenced some of the perpetrators responsible for the atrocities committed. Regrettably, many have not been brought to justice because of the amnesty laws passed by Pinochet, which gave immunity to him and his murderous agents for crimes committed between 1973 and 1977, laws which the Chilean National Congress has so far failed to repeal.

Who is the current President of Chile?

The current president is Dr Michelle Bachelet who was elected to a second term of office in 2014 by sixty two per cent of the people. A socialist and the first women elected Head of State in Chile, she suffered at the hands of the Dictatorship. Her father, Alberto Bachelet, was a general in the Air Force, who refused to support the *coup d'état* and died of a heart attack whilst under torture in 1974.

In January 1975, then a medical student, she and her mother were arrested and tortured for one month by DINA agents at Villa Grimaldi. Upon release she went into forced exile in East Germany, returning to Chile in 1979, when she completed her medical studies.

After she qualified as a doctor, she treated children of the tortured and missing under the fascist regime. She specialised in Paediatrics and Public Health and worked in various posts until the return to democracy in 2000, when she re-joined the Socialist Party. She served as a Minister of Health and later as a Minister of National Defence. Her first term in office was very successful and her popularity rose by the end of it; however the constitution did not allow for her immediate re-election.

Was General Pinochet ever brought to justice?
The answer is no. However, when he returned to Chile after being arrested in England for 503 days he was a broken man. In January 2001, Chilean Judge Juan Guzmán Tapia questioned Pinochet on the circumstances surrounding the Caravan of Death, whose agents carried out more than 70 killings in the immediate aftermath of the *coup*. It was the first time the former dictator had been legally called to account for the human rights abuses of his regime. As a result Pinochet was charged and placed under house arrest in his Santiago mansion, on 30 January. He was released on bail on 11 April and later his lawyers successfully appealed that he was mentally unfit for trial, due to dementia.

However, in 2004 the Chilean Supreme Court ruled that he was no longer immune to prosecution and soon faced more than forty law suits for his involvement in the sequestering, torturing and murdering of thousands. In one notorious case, in August 2004, he was ordered by a judge to testify in the case of the murder of Victor Jara, a legendary composer and folk singer, executed in the Chile Football Stadium after the coup. [He was one of the sixty one artists killed during the Dictatorship.] In 2006, his henchman, the sadist colonel Manuel Contreras, the man that had been head of the DINA, was arrested and turned against him, declaring that Pinochet received daily briefing about the activities of the secret police, as confirmed by contemporary records from the CIA and the US embassy in Santiago.

In addition to numerous lawsuits for crimes against humanity, the dictator's finances were investigated by Chilean authorities and the USA senate. It had become known that during his arrest in England, he had set up secret bank accounts, under false names, in Washington-based Riggs Bank, to the tune of $ 8 million, to avoid taxes. In September 2009 Judge Manuel Valderrama put an exact value on the figure, saying that shortly before his death the accounts of Pinochet and his family totalled US$25,978,602. The University of Chile estimates that less than 10% of this amount could have been sourced from his military salary. A possible explanation of the source of some of Pinochet's wealth surfaced in July 2006 when former DINA commander Manuel Contreras claimed that Pinochet was involved in manufacture, smuggling and sale of cocaine during the 1980s. According to 'The New York Times', Contreras also accused Pinochet of 'embezzling money from secret government accounts.' Pinochet was never brought to justice, but died a diminished and humiliated man, a figure of hate for the majority of Chileans, who was denied a State Funeral.

Has a process of peace and reconciliation taken place?

In July 1990, President Patricio Aylwin established the National Commission on Truth and Reconciliation which produced a report nine months later. Although undoubtedly this was a positive step, there were many limitations, not least because the armed forces, in most cases, refused to provide information, even in those few cases were they had executed victims after a military tribunal. The report was made public in March 1991. It strongly criticised the Supreme Court for not defending the human rights of individuals during the Dictatorship. Conversely, it praised the work of the Committee for Peace and its successor, the Vicariate for Solidarity, for lending legal and moral assistance to victims and keeping invaluable records of each case.

An English version of the report can be found at: Chile90-Report.pdf

What is the economic situation in Chile now?

Economic indicators put Chile as the leading economy in Latin America. The neo-liberalist economic policies, started by the Dictatorship, continued after democracy was restored and indicators for foreign trade, mining, agriculture, tourism, services, and foreign investment have all continued to grow. Chile's Gross Domestic Product (GDP) in 2015 is forecasted to be $280 Billion, three times that of 2006.

Chile's population is 17.6 million. The percentage of people living in poverty has halved from 29 percent to 14 per cent in this period of time.

Nevertheless, why are a significant number of Chileans unhappy and, regularly, protesting in the streets and in particular the young and the students?
They protest because, regrettably, the gap between the poor and the very rich has increased.

According to the Organization for Economic Cooperation and Development (OECD), Chile has the highest income inequality among countries that are part of the OECD. The richest 20 per cent of Chileans receive 61 per cent of GDP compared to 3.3 per cent of GDP for the poorest 20 per cent. Although the figures regarding people living in poverty have improved, still five per cent live in extreme poverty.

Some of the reasons why poor people find it almost impossible to escape poverty are clear: the existence of *oligopolies,* corruption and tax evasion, poorly regulated credit and the privatization of a large part of superior education. Oligopoly markets are markets dominated by a small number of suppliers. They pervade the Chilean economy and operate like cartels which control prices, e.g. medicines, bus fares etc. Oligopolies also exist in others sectors such as the media where the reporting of news-worthy issues is ditched or it shows strong bias in favour of the political elite. Students leave university with a mountain of debt and only to discover that jobs are given to graduates of more established universities. The present government has promised reforms which hopefully will narrow the inequality gap. Incidentally, amongst the worst 10 countries for highest income inequality Chile is the worst, the USA is fourth and the UK seventh.

What is currently happening to the native Chilean Forest?
It continues to be wiped out, for fast woodchips profits, although the rate of destruction has slowed. The plantation of fast growing radiate pine and eucalyptus uses an enormous amount of water from the soil and this has caused severe drought and rivers that once carried torrents of water are now trickles.

What is currently happening to the Mapuche people?
During her presidential re-election campaign, President Bachelet promised a

new treatment of Chile's Mapuche population. Her programme looks good on paper but she needs to regain the trust of the indigenous people, lost after long years of ill treatment including, regrettably, during her first term in office. It is also a shame, that since 1990, successive governments, including her own, are using Pinochet's anti-terrorist laws, against the Mapuche.

Concerning issues that arose in Parts 2 and 3. The NHS and Tameside Hospital

Was what occurred at Tameside – the chronic nursing and junior doctors understaffing, the collapse of bed capacity, the death of between 100 and 200 patients – avoidable?

In my opinion the answer is yes. There was enough evidence in my report to the CHI in 2003 for the regulator to investigate the hospital. Its failure to do so was compounded by a parallel failure to act on the part of the Regional Health Authority. From 2007, after I became the Chairman of the Senior Medical Staff Committee (SMSC), I repeatedly asked the CEO to allow me to make representations to the Health Department, on behalf of the Trust, to put the case for more equitable funding for Tameside. I made clear to her the support for such special pleading that existed amongst large numbers of consultants in order to reinforce the request. We fully understood that the so-called efficiency savings were imposed on the Trust by government, but, alas, she remained unforthcoming on the matter, arguing that we had to manage with what we were given. Since the Keogh Review in 2013, however, 'contingency' funds have been made available to Tameside hospital twice and this could perhaps have applied earlier had the case been made, although that would have required the CEO and Board to have admitted that there was a problem which is not something they were prepared to do. In the final analysis, their reputations, it would appear, were of greater concern to them than was the quality of care for patients.

Official figures show that during the ten-year period 2001/2 to 2011/12, *10,476* died at Tameside Hospital. As I have already said, in my opinion, one to two per cent might have survived with safer care, and this would mean between one hundred to two hundred patients. As I said on a BBC Panorama programme in March 2010, this is a conservative estimate and we will never know the precise number. This figure is, of course, less than the 1,300 'excess deaths' reported by Dr Foster, which represents the difference between actual and expected and unsafe care, particularly at night and at week-ends. A lack of high dependency beds for deteriorating high-risk patients, lack of overall bed capacity, use of 'escalation' wards, admission of patients in wrong wards and an inadequate number of doctors and nurses would, in my opinion, constitute the main contributory factors.

What about the future of Tameside Hospital?

Having declared that the Trust was financially unsustainable in the summer of 2013, Monitor announced in September 2014 the appointment of a Contingency Planning Team (CPT). The aim was to develop an Integrated Care Organisation (ICO), bringing together health and social care, hoping that the combined deficits of the Tameside Hospital Foundation Trust (THFT) and Tameside Metropolitan Borough Council (TMBC) could be addressed. Following a procurement process in which the three principal organisations – THFT, the Clinical Commissioning Group (CCG), and TMBC – were involved, PricewaterhouseCoopers (PwC) were appointed at the behest of Monitor to facilitate this process.

PwC ran a number of Care Design Groups (CDG) made up of few clinicians, social care professionals and patient representatives during a very brief consultation period in November-December 2014 and submitted their conclusions in a Report to Monitor in July 2015. Figures released by PwC put the population of Tameside at 241,919. The costs of services at current levels are projected to be as much as £443 million by 2018/19, equal to £1,831 per capita.

The model of care proposed in the report, by the Contingency Planning Team under the aegis of PwC, is based on a reduction of 246 acute beds and an increase in day-care beds by thirty. The model is based in the creation of 'extensivists' which the authors define as 'hospital based clinicians who would focus on a cohort of high risk patients in the community' and five multidisciplinary Local Community care teams who will focus on keeping patients out of hospital.

I am all in favour of integration of hospital and community care, but not in this manner, which is in my view an experiment, not evidence based, and I fear is a recipe for disaster.

Whether the proposals of the Contingency Planning Team are implemented, the minutes of THFT board do not make it clear. However, we know that in the Greater Manchester Region, the hospital and community care health budget will be devolved to a proposed Mayor and the combined Authorities from 2016, which means that strategic decisions are already no longer solely in the hands of the Board or the Council of Governors of the hospital.

With the introduction of the Health and Social Care Act in 2012, the NHS as we know it is under existential threat as never before. Market forces will increasingly have a decisive influence on the way that healthcare is provided to the people of Tameside and Glossop and I fear that the rationing that already exists will become ever worse, not least because of the 'efficiency savings' needed.

What about the campaign for legislation on nurse and midwife to patient ratios?

I hope that this book will raise awareness of the vital importance of this matter. I urge the reader to sign any of the e-petitions calling for legislation on mandatory nurse and midwife to patient ratios in English NHS hospitals. Perhaps one day legislation will be enacted that will bring to an end under-staffed shifts, which continues to adversely affect quality of care in hospitals throughout England.

In 2013, the Department of Health and NHS England asked the National Institute for Health and Clinical Excellence (NICE) to develop evidence-based guidelines on safe staffing for hospitals in England, with a particular focus on nursing staff. This request followed the publication of the following reviews and reports:

- The Francis report on Mid Staffordshire Hospital Trust (Francis 2013);
- The Keogh review into the quality of care and treatment provided in 14 hospital trusts in England (Keogh 2013);
- The Cavendish review, an independent inquiry into healthcare assistants and support workers in the NHS and social care setting (Cavendish 2013);
- The Berwick report on improving the safety of patients in England (Berwick 2013).

The first guideline of the NICE work programme made recommendations on safe staffing for nursing in adult in-patient wards in acute hospitals and was published in July 2014. Although it does not support minimum nurse staffing levels, the guidance, complex as it was, was thorough and was welcomed by the majority of nurses in Trusts across the country.

However, in June 2015, Simon Stevens, the Chief Executive of NHS England, announced that he had asked its Chief Nursing Officer to incorporate work on safe staffing levels into her NHS England reviews of urgent and emergency care, maternity and mental health services. In this way, the NICE programme for the development of guidance on safe nurse and midwife levels was abruptly brought to a halt.

This transfer of responsibility away from NICE amounted to a U-turn by the Department of Health which aroused widespread criticism, including from Sir Robert Francis, who, in an interview with the Health Service Journal, declared that he was 'surprised and concerned' by the move and pointed to the fact that NICE was set up to be independent of the NHS and the wider policy structures. Defending the government U-turn, the Chief Nursing Officer of NHS England stated that she had the support of many directors of nursing – which should come as no great surprise to anyone. Acting on behalf of Trusts that are finding it increasingly difficult – and for many, near impossible – to operate within their allocated budgets, directors of nursing are unlikely to welcome constraints imposed by legislation upon their capacity to make savings by maintaining a 'flexible' approach to ward nursing establishments in their hospitals. Unfortunately, the effect of such 'flexibility' upon patient care should be abundantly clear to the reader from the catalogue of evidence revealed in the preceding pages in Part 2 of this book.

Despite all its rhetoric and protestations to the contrary, it now seems clear that the present government has set a course upon containing expenditure on the NHS, notwithstanding the impact on care quality and despite the pledges contained in Patient, First and Foremost, announced in ringing declarations in the wake of the Francis report on the Mid Staffordshire scandal. At that time, a Statement of Common Purpose issued by Health Secretary Jeremy Hunt in Patient, First and Foremost proclaimed that, 'Blind adherence to targets or finance must never again be allowed to come before the quality of care'. With every day that now passes, however, that commitment looks increasingly hollow.

Finally, what happened to the family of swans with ebony necks?
The original couple remain good friends. The four cygnets have grown up and flown to various lakes around the country, following which new cygnets have been born.

APPENDICES: LETTERS AND REPORTS

INTRODUCTION

I thought long and hard about whether this chapter was really needed. I concluded that it was. As I have said I believe that knowledge empowers users of the health services. These are a small fraction of the letters I wrote during this period. (2002 – 2013)

1. LETTER TO THE CHIEF EXECUTIVE OFFICER TAMESIDE GENERAL HOSPITAL

17 October 2002
Mrs C Green
Chief Executive
Darnton Building
Tameside General Hospital
Dear Mrs Green
Re: Lead Consultant – Orthopaedic Division

Thank you for your recent letter of 4 October 2002. At our last divisional meeting attended by Mr Dunningham, Mr Muddu, Mr Ebizie, Mr Obeid and myself, this matter was discussed. Unanimously my colleagues asked me to take up this post.

I note that in your letter you explained that the Lead should be acceptable to management but I do not know the meaning of this. However, I have read the role description enclosed and I agree with it.

I note that, concerning Clinical Governance, it is mentioned that one of the responsibilities of the Lead was to ensure effective systems to implement it. I also note, however, that the quality of the service has not been mentioned. I would put this on top of the list.

I would like you to know that I passionately believe in the National Health Service. As you can see from my enclosed CV, I was born in Chile where we also have a National Health Service which was created more or less at the same time. Indeed, the study of the British NHS was part of our curriculum. It was then considered to be an excellent model.

During my career since 1974, I have seen many advances in all branches of medicine, surgery and radiology to mention just three. Unfortunately, planning to be able to meet with these advances in terms of capital investment, funding and provision of human resources, has been inadequate. Regrettably, there are today hundreds of unfilled consultant posts in many specialities including orthopaedic surgery, radiology, oncology etc. The same can be said concerning shortage of nurses, radiographers, occupational therapists and many other health professionals.

As a result, in my opinion, the NHS is now in crisis. We are all so used to the daily problems that this great institution is experiencing, that nobody mentions this rather dreaded word. We are now immune to the anguish and suffering experienced by the general public. We read and hear about patients with terminal illnesses waiting for their investigations and treatment, patients waiting long hours in the Casualty Department etc., patients, who, when they are seen by a specialist, have to wait months for investigations which, in other developed countries, are done within days.

Who is responsible for this situation?

It would be reasonable to say that over the last 30 years, advisors to successive governments failed to really understand the significant changes occurring in the world of medicine and provision of health care. As a result many of the high standards established at the time of the creation of the NHS have deteriorated.

This, in my view, is reflected in our Orthopaedic Department on a daily basis.

The signs are there for everybody to see:

- Complaints concerning inadequate nursing care in the wards;
- Resignation of many qualified nurses from the orthopaedic wards. This has meant that now there is a need for a regular supply of agency nurses. This is obviously more expensive for the Trust (minutes of Elective Services Directorate Management Team meeting, 7 October 2002), and does not necessarily solve the point mentioned above;
- Complaints about waiting times to see a specialist being addressed by a policy of waiting list targets. I believe planning for expansion of the Department is the long term answer;
- Patients with fractures and other injuries being sent home to wait for a bed (sometimes for several days) before being admitted for the necessary treatment; and
- Orthopaedic surgeons having to operate with inadequate instruments. For instance, presently there is a shortage of power drivers in theatre. Those which are still working are old and their performance is poor. This lengthens the operations to the detriment of the patient.
- These are five examples. I could mention many more.
- To be fair, over the last few years, improvements have been made. As you know I have introduced into the Department many changes to utilise our human and material resources more efficiently. For instance:
- Fit patients for elective surgery walking to theatre, rather the being placed on trolleys. This is now a standard policy at this hospital;
- Rationalisation or pooling of the out-patients being referred to our Department;
- The screening of X-rays and casualty records of all patients referred to our fracture clinics, in order to prioritise and categorise their appointments. This pilot scheme started the first week in September in conjunction with the A&E department.
- The use of the Transfer Lounge to process patients going to theatre to have operations under local anaesthetic. We are rapidly approaching the 100th patient since this was commenced a few months ago. This has saved the Trust several thousand pounds because none of these patients has been admitted into a hospital bed.

If I become the Lead Consultant I would like to make it my first priority to improve the quality of the nursing care on the orthopaedic wards. This will be in accordance with the spirit of the definition of clinical governance and in due course I wish to submit a development plan which will aim to increase the number of qualified nursing staff on wards 2, 3 and 4.

The Trust should commit to develop a clear career policy for qualified orthopaedic nurses (to retain them) and these policies should be patient-focused which means based always in the best interests of the patient.

I believe that unless the true spirit of Clinical Governance is followed through, with clear lines of accountability to safeguard a high standard of care for our patients, we will not be able to improve our delivery of care,

Furthermore, serious consideration should be given to an increase in the present level of funding allocated to our Department.

I hope this letter will form the basis for an understanding between us concerning how I see my role as the Lead Consultant of the Orthopaedic Division.

I am looking forward to meeting with you.

Yours sincerely,

M A Peña FRCS (E)
Consultant Orthopaedic Surgeon

Copy: Mr T H Dunningham, Medical Director, TGH
Mr A Griffiths, Director of Elective Services, TGH
Mr A B Woodyer, Lead Consultant Surgical Department, TGH
Mr P Dylak, Director of Nursing, TGH
Mr A Ebizie, Consultant Orthopaedic Surgeon, TGH
Mr B Muddu, Consultant Orthopaedic Surgeon, TGH
Mr E Obeid, Consultant Orthopaedic Surgeon, TGH

2. LETTER TO THE COMMISSION FOR HEALTH IMPROVEMENT

10th October 2003
Ms L P
Enquires Office
Commission for Health Improvement
Finsbury Tower
103-105 Bunhill Row
London EC1 Y8TG

Dear Ms L P

RE: PATIENTS AT RISK DUE TO NURSING UNDERSTAFFING AT THE ORTHOPAEDIC/TRAUMA WARDS AT TAMESIDE GENERAL HOSPITAL

I am a consultant orthopaedic surgeon, employed by Tameside and Glossop NHS Trust since March 1997.

For over a year, I have been increasingly concerned with the risks to patients admitted to the adult Orthopaedic/Trauma wards at Tameside Hospital due to poor nursing staffing levels.

The Orthopaedic/Trauma Wards

The wards, 2, 3 and 4, have 28 beds each.

Ward 3 is the ward for planned orthopaedic surgery.

There are 2 elective theatre lists (schedule) every morning Monday to Friday and one every afternoon Monday to Friday.

Major joint replacements are carried out routinely at an average of twelve per week and some weeks more. Joint revision surgery is also carried out. There are six orthopaedic consultants.

Epidural anaesthetic and Patient Controlled Analgesia (PCA) are routinely given by the anaesthetists.

Ward 3 houses a seven-bedded bay for Day Case Surgery and thus this ward is normally staffed for only twenty-one in-patients. Due to chronic demand for beds, often the Day Surgery bay is transformed into an 'in-patient bay' during bed crises, regardless of the often inadequate number of nurses to care safely for the extra patients.

Wards 2 and 4 are for Trauma. There are Trauma lists every afternoon and evening from Monday to Friday and during the afternoons of Saturday and Sunday. During the week, these three wards are extremely busy with the planned orthopaedic admissions and the trauma patients, particularly the early and late shifts. Below I will explain the additional activities of these three wards.

Additional Ward Activity

Medical patients. The three adult Orthopaedic/Trauma wards have been a de facto medical ward for the last year. Although the numbers of the medical outliers in each has declined, there are always a variable number of purely medical patients in the three orthopaedic/trauma wards. Following the last Commission for Health Improvement visit, each ward has been allocated a named medical consultant to cover the medical patients in the ward. This has helped. At any time patients with medical emergencies may be transferred from the Medical Assessment Unit to the orthopaedic wards with serious conditions such as; angina/acute chest pain; stomach and bowel bleeding; diabetes, strokes, etc. These patients may be stable initially but they can deteriorate suddenly. When this happens and the ward has two or even only one qualified nurse, the understaffing may have serious consequences for the other patients. In my view, the practice of moving nurses from other wards to come and help has to be condemned as it leaves the other wards under-staffed. The nurses have reported instances of inappropriate transfer of critically ill patients from the Medical Assessment Unit to the orthopaedic/trauma wards. This is a separate issue and needs to be addressed. The patients known as 'medical outliers' generate extra ward rounds by medical consultants and their junior doctors and other staff. Their relatives, quite rightly, demand high standards of care, but the quality of the nursing care of these patients is often hindered by chronic nursing under-staffing. The care of these medical patients is further compromised by the low staffing levels of doctors at Tameside. This includes junior doctors. The medical wards are physically far away from the orthopaedic wards and even with the best will in the world, sometimes it takes considerable time for the junior medical doctors to come to orthopaedic wards to see these outliers. This is sometimes frustrating for the patients and their relatives. I have witnessed some relatives losing their patience and venting their anger on the nursing staff.

Head Injuries. Patients with head injuries who do not require to be transferred to a Neurosurgical Unit are admitted to the Orthopaedic/Trauma wards from the Accident and Emergency Department. Any of these patients can very rapidly deteriorate. Even those with a normal or near normal Glasgow coma scale. If the symptoms of headache or vomiting are missed or not acted upon, it may be extremely serious. This is why, in my view, regular observation of these patients by experienced trained nurses is vitally important. Similarly, patients with serious head injuries are discharged from the Intensive Care Unit or from the Neurosurgical Unit at Hope Hospital to the orthopaedic wards. They are often disoriented, have tracheostomy tubes etc. These are still seriously ill patients and ideally require being in a High Dependency Unit or at least having one-to-one nursing care. Frequently, these patients remain in the orthopaedic wards for many weeks. Often they are still unaware of time and space and wander off the ward.

Patients with Polytrauma. In addition, patients recovering from multiple fractures, some of them with chest injuries are also eventually transferred from the Intensive Care Unit to the Trauma wards. Often they are still highly dependent with tracheostomy and chest tubes in situ.

Background Information
I have put my concerns in writing to the Chief Executive of the Trust and to the Director of Nursing, with copies to the Medical Director and the Director of Surgical Services. I have also expressed my worries repeatedly during orthopaedic Divisional Meetings and Clinical Governance meetings. In February, I requested a meeting with the Director of Nursing to ask for an urgent solution to the under-staffing apparent during many shifts. This was repeatedly leading to nursing care that fell below accepted best practice for my patients. Around that time the Orthopaedic ward nurses were so concerned with the safety of their patients that they too requested a meeting with the Director of Nursing which was also attended by the Divisional Nurse Manager

and me. The nurse managers agreed that given the number of beds and the high level of activity in these wards it was completely unacceptable to have only one qualified nurse on any shift. The ward nurses and I explained that even with two qualified nurses, best practice could not always be achieved and patients were at risk. I explained that the qualified/trained nurses' establishment for the wards was inadequate, even if the vacancies were to be filled. At this meeting, related issues, such as the movement of Orthopaedic ward nurses, unexpectedly, to another ward, the use of agency staff, international recruitment of nurses, the medical outliers, patients and training, were also discussed. The Nursing Director explained that the Trust was conducting a Ward Staffing Review. He was not convinced that the Orthopaedic wards were under-staffed or needed more trained nurses. However, he acknowledged that he had not seen reports written by the nurses and passed to the Divisional Nurse manager over the preceding months. The Nursing Director wanted more evidence with factual detail such as: a) number of nurses planned per shift; b) actual number of nurses on each shift; c) familiarity of the nurses with the ward; d) how the under-staffing affected the care of the patients etc. It was agreed that the nurses should design a pro-forma that they would complete whenever their shifts did not have a minimum safe number of nurses and safe mix of qualified and unqualified nurses. These reports were to be passed to the nursing managers with a copy to myself.

By 28th March 2003, the content of the nursing staffing pro-formas confirmed, in my view, extremely serious staffing problems. I wrote to the Director of Nursing and part of the letter reads: 'These forms, which have been completed by the nurses, indicate that we are seriously compromising the quality of care of the patients and also, in many instances, putting lives at risk.' I was informed that ward staffing matters would be decided after the Team Work Study (conducting the ward staffing review) had been completed and that the Trust could not in any case spend more in orthopaedic ward staff as there was already an overspend due to the need for agency nurses.

Review of the Pro-formas (Staffing Level Reports)
I have reviewed copies of fifty pro-formas for shifts when the registered nurse in charge felt that the number of nurses, especially qualified/registered nurses, was insufficient for the needs and safety of the patients. (February to August 2003). The reports show the following data:

There were twenty-four instances of shifts when there was only one qualified nurse working with a variable number of support staff.

There were six shifts when there was only one qualified nurse and only one support staff member.

There were twenty-two shifts with two qualified nurses who felt that they could not provide adequate nursing care in spite of having support staff during the shift.

There were six shifts when only two qualified nurses worked without any support staff.

There were fifteen shifts staffed by nurses unfamiliar with the ward.

Below I will give some specific examples, as recorded in these pro-formas.

5 March 2003 Ward 2. Late shift
Two qualified nurses. Three support staff. Three unfamiliar with the ward. Should have been three qualified staff and three support nurses.

Ward full with 28 dependent patients. Two have had blood transfusion. Patient with epidural infusion requiring recorded observations every fifteen minutes. His observations not carried out as per protocol. Anaesthetic staff informed prior to commencement of epidural that ward was under-staffed. Told to inform Nursing management. Same done.

Nurse signature

9 March 2003 Ward 3. Late shift
Two qualified nurses (one unfamiliar with the ward) two support staff (one unfamiliar with the ward) Shift originally planned for three qualified nurses. Ward full with 28 patients, including seven day-care beds being used for in-patients.

Head injury observations not recorded regularly – Sliding scale insulin not checked for over four hours – Pressure relief not provided – Clinical observations not recorded all shift – Intra-venous antibiotics not given on time. Patient admitted from A&E with dislocated cervical spine and potential for tetraplegia. Poorly surgical patient admitted to ward then transferred to Ward 17. (Surgical Ward). Four other patients transferred to Ward 17. Escort nurse needed for patient to X-ray Department.

Manager informed. Consultant on call informed.

Nurse Signature.

14 March 2003 Ward 2 Early shift

Two trained nurses. Four support staff, two of them unfamiliar with the ward. Shift originally planned for three qualified nurses and three support nurses. One medical patient was critically ill (had deteriorated overnight). He required one-to-one nursing from the commencement of the shift, until transferred to the Coronary Care Unit at 11.30 am. This effectively left one qualified nurse responsible for twenty-seven patients. Nurse in charge bleeped the Nurse on Block and the Clinical Nurse Leader several times to report situation and request a qualified nurse but had no reply. During the shift, staff from another ward wanted to transfer another poorly and unstable patient into the ward. Advised this was unsafe so they transferred a day-case patient so two patients could be discharged earlier in order to admit new patients.

Specific problems reported:

Late administration of medication (up to two hours late) – Lack of time to record vital signs – Regular pressure area care not done – Dressings not done – Inadequate monitoring of food and fluid in-take – Inability to document and up-date care plans – Inability to refer patients to Chronic Rehabilitation and Discharge Team.

16 March 2003 Ward 2 Late shift

Two qualified nurses. Three support staff. (Two off them unfamiliar with the ward) Shift initially planned with three qualified and two support nurses.

Patient had cardiac arrest. Both qualified nurses needed – Three post-operative patients got basic care – Unable to give time and attention to one poorly patient needing TLC (tender loving care) –Nurses unable to give time and compassion to relatives of deceased patient – Pressure area care not done

– Four patients needing meals, this affected as well.

This shift had been originally staffed with three qualified nurses but one of them was moved to cover another ward.

Nurse signature

4 April 2003 Ward 3 Late shift
One qualified nurse. (Should have been three) Two support nurses. Twenty-five patients in the ward. All aspects of care at risk.

Nine post-operative patients, two of which with knee replacements. One of these patients is suffering from Alzheimer's. Closer supervision needed but not able to be given.

One qualified nurse to administer all medications and IV antibiotics, arrange discharge of day-case patients and in-patients – Staff had no time for meal breaks – Delay of discharge of day-case patient – Observation of post-operative patient not performed as often as needed – Observations of second and third day post-operative patients not recorded at all – Delayed administration of post-op IV antibiotics and maintenance IV fluids – Theatre staff asked to bring theatre patient back without ward escort – Three ENT patients in day-case bay. Orthopaedic nurses have limited experience of ENT surgery and ENT protocols. Clinical Nurse Leader aware of staffing problems.

Nurse writing this report left ward at 23.20 hours.

Nurse signature

17 April 2003 Ward 3 Late shift
One qualified nurse on duty with periods of help by two other qualified nurses, unfamiliar with the ward. Three support staff. (Should have been three qualified nurses the whole shift)

Care of patients immediately post-operative not given to an acceptable level – Delay to commence blood transfusion on post-operative patient –Unable to collect patient from theatre – Unable to escort Consultant on Ward round.

Nurse signature

19 April 2003 Ward 4 Late shift

One qualified nurse. Three support staff (one unfamiliar with the ward) Should have been three qualified nurses and two support nurses).

General patient care affected – Unable to check intravenous fluids and intravenous antibiotics – Unable to accept certain admissions.

Nurse signature

1st May 2003 Ward 3 Early shift

One qualified nurse. Three support staff (one unfamiliar with the ward).

All areas of nursing care affected – Theatre staff had to bring patients to the ward (against protocol) – Post-operative recovery attended by student nurse (unsupervised and against protocol) – Medication round for 28 patients interrupted by doctors several times – Doctors becoming agitated as no qualified nurse available to do ward rounds with them – No time to answer physiotherapist and occupational therapist questions.

Nurse signature

31st May 2003 Ward 2 Night shift

One qualified nurse. One support staff. For 28 patients (shift planned for two qualified nurses).

All areas of nursing care affected as well as safety of patients.

Nurse signature

27th June 2003 Ward 3 Early shift

Two qualified nurses. Two support staff (two unfamiliar with the ward). Should have been three qualified and three support nurses).

All areas of care affected including clinical observations – Delays in transporting patients to and from theatre – No documentation done in breach of Nursing and Midwifery Council Rules.

Staff late off duty (going home later than they should).

Nurse signature

11th July 2003 Ward 3 Night shift
One qualified nurse. One support staff (shift planned for qualified).[???]

The overall level of care on the ward was below acceptable standards and dangerous at times – Immediate post-operative patients did not receive adequate care and observation for PCA's (patient controlled analgesia) and epidural infusions were affected – Two risk events were reported. One patient fell twice – Another patient with learning difficulties set the fire alarm off.

Nurse signature

26th July 2003 Ward 2 Late shift
One qualified nurse. Two support staff. (Should have been two qualified and three support staff.).

Observations i.e. neurological observations not done at planned time intervals – Turning of poorly patients performed less frequently than planned.

Nurse signature

27th July 2003 Ward 4 Late shift
Three qualified staff (two unfamiliar) one support staff.

The general nursing care of patients affected due to the unfamiliarity of the bank staff with the ward, complicated by the high number of high dependency patients.

Nurse signature

3rd August 2003 Ward 4 Early shift
One qualified nurse. Should have been three. Four support staff. (One unfamiliar with the ward) The ward as a whole was affected because safe nursing care could not be achieved effectively – Temperature, pulse and respiration not done in Bay two.

Nurse signature

3rd August 2003 Ward 3 Late shift
One qualified nurse. Should have been two. Two support staff – Unable to check injections, IVI, PCA'S etc.

Nurse signature

6th August 2003 Ward 3 Late shift
One qualified nurse. Should have been three, one support staff –Post-operative observations affected – PCA observations affected – Potential risk of patients deteriorating without adequate observations – Lateness of administration of medicines – Theatre staff returning patients to ward (contravening protocol).

Nurse signature

16th August 2003 Ward 2 Late shift
One qualified nurse. (Should have been two). Two support staff. (Should have been three).

Several poorly patients requiring total care – Nurses unable to spend time with patients due to poor staffing levels.

Nurse signature

25th August 2003 Ward 2 Night shift
One qualified nurse. One support staff.

Some of the poorly patients not monitored as required – No break taken by staff during this shift.

Nurse signature

26th August 2003 Ward 3 Night shift
One qualified nurse. Two support staff (one unfamiliar with the ward) Should have been two qualified nurses.

Post-operative observations of patients affected – One patient with chest pain

– One confused patient with diarrhoea on intra-venous antibiotics – Three post-operative patients on intra-venous antibiotics – These patients could not be observed (or cared for) as well with just one trained staff – Three new patients were admitted during the shift.

Number of Staffing Level reports

The fifty pro-formas that qualified/registered nurses from the three adult Orthopaedic/Trauma wards have completed, in my view, do not reflect the total number of shifts which have been under-staffed. In some instances, nurses have told me that because of the lack of improvement in staffing levels, they felt that completing these forms was not worth the effort. They have become disillusioned. On many occasions, the single qualified nurse in charge of a shift has simply been too tired and stressed to complete a pro-forma. Occasionally, I have sensed that nurses are too apprehensive to complete the staffing level report, which has to be signed, for fear of jeopardising their careers.

Analysis

Analysis of these pro-formas shows than when the orthopaedic wards are under-staffed, the following facts are reported by the nurses:

1. Post-operative patients following major operations such as hip or knee replacements are not being clinically observed as frequently as they should be. (Patient's life may be at risk).
2. Recording of vital observations (pulse, respiration, temperature etc.) is not carried out or is carried out less frequently than advised. (Patients' lives may be at risk).
3. Intra-venous fluids prescribed are not given or given later than required due to lack of a second qualified nurse on the ward. (Serious risk).
4. Intra-venous drugs, including IV antibiotics and painkillers not given on time due to the lack of second qualified nurse for the shift. (Serious risk).
5. Nurses' drugs' rounds running late. (May seriously affect the outcome).
6. Patients falling. Sometimes due to the lack of nursing supervision. Sometimes patients falling twice on a shift. (The Trust reported over 330 falls per each quarter between July 2002 and June 2003).
7. Feeding and assisting patients who are unable to feed themselves has been sub-standard. (It causes suffering and may seriously affect the outcome).

8.   The administration of oral fluids has been sub-standards (serious risk of de-hydration).

9.   Record keeping, for example fluid balance charts, has not been done (extremely important in elderly post-operative patients).

10. Dependent patients requiring turning have not received this care as often as needed (risk of pressure sores, a serious complication if large and deep).

11. Patients with epidural catheter in-situ have not been monitored according to the protocol (patient's life is at risk).

12. Patients with patient-controlled analgesia (PCA) in progress have not been monitored according to protocol (serious risk).

13. Diabetic patients on sliding scale insulin have not been monitored, on one occasion for as long as four hours (patient 's life is at risk).

14. Patients admitted with acute head injuries have sometimes been left unobserved when the staffing level is inadequate and the activity of the ward is high (patient's life is at risk).

15. Nurses are on many occasions unable to join doctors on their ward rounds causing loss of continuity of care that may jeopardise outcome.

16. Delay in escorting patients back to and from the theatres, resulting in disruption of theatre activity. Theatre porters having to wait for a nurse to become available.

17. Theatre personnel escorting patients back to the wards, resulting in delay of theatre activity, which may result in cancellation of a case.

18. Nurses do not have time to answer queries of other members of the team, such as pharmacist, physiotherapist, occupational therapist, social worker, speech therapist, dietician etc.

19. Nurses are unable to plan the discharge of patients and complete the necessary documentation.

20. Teaching and training of student nurses by qualified and support staff is inadequate due to the lack of time.

21. Student nurses asked to work without or at best with inadequate supervision when ward is under-staffed.

22. Nurses have no time to give patients advice regarding their care when needed.

23. Nurses have no time to give poorly patients all the care they need.

24. Ward staff not able to have meal breaks.

25. Nurses late finishing their shifts, sometimes by two or three hours.

26. At the start of, or even during a shift, nurses are being asked to work in a

different ward, which is often unfamiliar to them. This practice disrupts continuity of care and reduces the number of nurses on the wards from which they are transferred.

27. Nurses are being asked to stay for a second shift when a crisis occurs.
28. Nurses report high levels of stress, often going off sick with that diagnosis.
29. Nurses resign and leave the orthopaedic wards or the hospital.
30. Nurses, who have only recently qualified, are left in charge of the ward because many of the more senior qualified nurses have resigned.

Hand written letters/reports
Over the last year, several lengthy fully hand-written reports by senior nurses have been passed to the nurse managers (in addition to the fifty completed pro-formas mentioned above) highlighting the serious risks for the patients which have been summarised above.

In my view, these nurse-reported facts' show that the Board of Tameside and Glossop Acute Services NHS Trust is in breach of regulations from: Clinical Governance – Clinical Negligence Scheme for Trusts – Improving Working Lives – Essence of Care – Nursing and Midwifery Council Code of Conduct – Code of conduct for NHS Managers

The Trust's response
Nursing managers of the Trust have received copies of the staffing level reports (pro-formas) and of the handwritten letters/reports.

In spite of the seriousness of the facts reported, the Nursing Managers, the Director of Nursing, the Medical Director and the Chief Executive, in essence the Trust Board, have not, in my view given these issues the degree of urgency they clearly deserve.

The recruitment of 25-trained nurses from Singapore to fill the vacancies across the whole hospital, welcome though it is, will not resolve the under-staffing in the orthopaedic/trauma wards.

The development of Assistant Practitioners in the orthopaedic wards at Tameside General Hospital, intended to ease the burden of qualified staff, in my opinion, will not significantly improve the quality of nursing care and the treatment of the patients.

On the Team Brief (a bulletin distributed by the Trust summarising the monthly Trust Board meetings) May 2003, it is mentioned that a major external review of ward and nurse staffing levels was commissioned last year. That some initial results from the 'Team Work' (the name of the document produced by the private firm called Newburgh Technologies) study had then (May) been received and that the 'data need to be carefully checked and further analysis will be required'.

On the Team Brief, September 2003, no mention was made of preliminary results of this analysis. It is clear after reading this brief, specifically under the headings CHI Action Plan and Staff Survey, that the Trust has no plans to increase the qualified/registered nursing establishment of the Orthopaedic/ Trauma wards. This is confirmed by reading the 2003/2004 Delivery Plan.

In the May Team Brief, the Chief Executive mentioned that the Dr Foster Hospital Rating publication in the Sunday Times, 6th April 2003, showed deterioration in the mortality index for Tameside Hospital. She explained that: 'The Trust is undertaking further analysis to explain the reason for the deterioration of the mortality index'. To the best of my knowledge, this analysis has not yet begun.

Mortality index
The mortality index is one indicator of the quality of clinical care in a hospital and is based on the average mortality expected in England and Scotland, which is defined as being 100. Trusts with figures lower than 100 are doing better than expected and vice versa. It is based on the 80 diagnoses associated with the highest mortality. It is standardised for age, sex, primary diagnosis, emergency admission and length of stay.

For instance, Bedford Hospital has a mortality index of 73. This hospital has 146 nurses for 100 beds and 44 doctors for 100 beds. Huddersfield Hospital has a mortality index of 93. It has 162 nurses for 100 beds and 32 doctors for 100 beds.

In comparison, Tameside General Hospital had a mortality index of 116.2 between 1999 and 2001 with an increase of 5 per cent during 2002. It is the seventh worst in the country and the second worst in the region. Tameside has 115 nurses for 100 beds and 27 doctors for 100 beds. The mortality index shows that the Trust has approximately 20 per cent higher deaths than expected.

The higher mortality is probably multifactorial. In my opinion, two important factors contributing to it are the lower number of doctors and nurses compared to other trusts.

Only recently, on 12th September, at the Chief Executive's Open Forum, it was acknowledged by the Trust that the medical and orthopaedic wards are under-staffed.

In my view the seriousness of the under-staffing and how it adversely affects the outcome of the patient's treatment has been ignored by the Trust Board for too long.

According to Dr Foster, the mortality for patients admitted with a broken hip at Tameside is 29 per cent higher than expected. I accept that many of these patients have serious co-morbidities and die of natural causes, having received good medical and nursing care. However, there are instances of patients who have received care below accepted nursing best practice and this has been noticed by patient's relatives and the coroner at the patient's inquest.

In the October 2003 Team Brief hand-out which summarises the items discussed at the Trust Board Meeting on 26th September 2003, it is stated under the sub-title Ward Staffing Review that: 'In the case of Orthopaedics, it does appear that internal movement can resolve the staffing issues and the Divisional Nurse Manager is currently completing an action plan to achieve this. Two additional qualified posts have already been assigned and more will follow.'

These two additional posts, which of course are welcome, could have been created six months ago if the evidence provided in the Pro-formas had been considered.

I believe there has been a failure of the management systems in place. I believe there has been prevarication, to the detriment of the patients. It is very worrying that the Director of Nursing does not see that unless the Trust seriously commits to an overall increase in Qualified/Registered nurses in the Orthopaedics/Trauma wards, the nursing care provided to patients during poorly staffed shifts will be below best practice and sometimes so poor, that patients' lives will be at risk.

Over the last month I have, unsuccessfully, tried to see the Chief Executive to personally discuss my concerns, but the CEO has repeatedly declined to meet me.

On 25th September, I handed a draft copy of this report to the CHI to the Director of Clinical Services after an hour-long meeting with him. I wanted my secretary to be present to take accurate notes of our discussion but he objected. His own notes from the meeting, in my view do not reflect my concerns on these issues. I urged him to read the information entered in the fifty pro-formas filled by the nurses and to discuss them with the CEO and Nursing Director.

I also asked him for any evidence-based study backing the Nursing Director's philosophy with respect to Nursing Staffing. In particular, evidence that it will improve the outcome of patients.

I understand the Nursing Director, a trained nurse, has written a thesis on the subject of ward staffing with 'mixed skill' nurses, in each ward, taking into consideration the planned activity on the day. As a Director of the Trust Board, he advises on nursing issues. It appears to me that the Trust has accepted his solution to the under-staffing at face value, because it minimises the Trust's spending.

Qualified/Registered Nurses
A Qualified/Registered nurse is personally accountable for her practice. This means that she/he is answerable for her/his actions and omissions.

A qualified nurse has a duty of care to named patients who are entitled to receive safe and competent care.

If one considers the potential workload of a 28-bedded ward, as explained above, and that only Registered nurses on a shift have statutory responsibility for:

a. Care of named orthopaedic and trauma patients.
b. Care of named patients admitted at any time during day or night with head injuries.
c. Care of named patients with acute medical conditions.
d. Care of named patients recovering from operations, many of them major operations, some with important pre-operative medical history, some with necessary but risky equipment attached to them.
e. Care of named patients returning from theatre safely.
f. Care of named patients going to theatre adequately checked.
g. Care to complete proper and adequate documentation on each patient.
h. To do ward rounds with junior doctors and consultants.
i. Drug/medicine rounds conducted safely without interruption and on time, with sufficient time for explanation to the patients, as recently highlighted by the CHI, following its in-patient survey.
j. Giving intra-venous antibiotics and parenteral painkillers safely.
k. Giving blood transfusions and intra-venous fluids on time and safely to named patients.
l. Answering phone queries from relatives etc.
m. Liaising with other health professionals.
n. Ward administration duties etc.
o. Planning and acting on ward discharges etc.

Upon seeing this list one would conclude that, unless the Trust is prepared to relinquish responsibility for named patients to support nurses, a ratio of one qualified nurse responsible for seven named patients during the day and one for 9/10 patients during the night would be the minimum to achieve best practice levels of nursing care. In addition, three support nurses during the day shifts and two for the night shifts would be needed.

I would like to state that this report is not intended to criticise the dedication and professionalism of the existing support nursing staff. I firmly believe that they have an important role to play.

In my view, the Qualified/Registered nurses and the support nurses in the Orthopaedic/Trauma wards are extremely hardworking, dedicated and caring and take great pride in the care of their patients, sometimes in very difficult circumstances. This also applies to all the nursing staff throughout Tameside General Hospital.

My main concern is the wellbeing of the patients coming to Tameside General Hospital. I firmly believe that sometimes the outcome of their care could be better and that often they could have had better care.

CHI Investigation

I believe that the Commission for Health Improvement should carry out an investigation concerning the chronic under-staffing in the Orthopaedic wards at Tameside. In my view, there has been a failure of Management and little accountability concerning these issues, to the detriment of the public.

The reasons for the increase in spending on agency staff from £2.6 million (2001–2002) to £3.6 million (2002–2003), necessary as it was, need to be investigated.

I am concerned by the use of £1 million of capital funds, necessary for essential medical equipment, to cover the Trust's overspending. The overspending was due largely to payment on Agency nursing staff, in turn caused by absenteeism due to sickness and stress caused by under-staffing in the first place. To me this is an obvious vicious circle.

I am concerned that the Trust spent nearly half a million pounds on Consultancy fees. Yet the capital expenditure available for essential medical equipment for the whole Trust was only £827,000 in 2002–2003. This ratio appears to be disproportionate. The orthopaedic nurses have highlighted the need for medical equipment on the wards for years.

I am concerned with the continuous request by the Trust for Cash Efficiency Relief Savings on nursing expenditure on the one hand and the increase in management costs, year after year, on the other.

The June financial report stated that there has been a £90,000 cumulative under-spending on nursing so far this year. This needs to be investigated.

The nursing under-staffing was clearly articulated by a stakeholder at the recent Annual General Meeting of the Trust. This man had noted, after his mother was admitted with a hip fracture and during her four months period of hospitalisation, how poor the nursing levels in the orthopaedic wards very often are. He explained to the Board that he was making the point not only on behalf of his mother, but also on behalf of all the patients, which he had observed, had suffered during that time.

He wanted to say more but he was obliged by the Chairman to stop, due to lack of time and told by the Chief Executive that his 'complaint' could be taken up later with the appropriate employee of the Trust whom she identified for him in the audience.

I felt that there was insufficient time for questions from the floor and hopefully the Trust Board will allocate more time next year.

Yours sincerely

Milton A Peña

Copy:
Chief Executive Officer
Tameside General Hospital
HM The Coroner
Coroner's Office, 10 Greek Street, Stockport

3. LETTER TO CEO, MD AND ND OF THFT

To: Green Christine; Mahmood Tariq; Dylak Philip
Cc: # All Consultants; Black Mary; Griffiths Adrian; Wilkinson David; Gardner Stephen; Shingler Karan; Keogh Joanne; Rice Carol; Ashworth Stephen; Brown Karen (Finance Director)
2nd June 2009
Mrs C. Green, Chief Executive Tameside Hospital NHS Foundation Trust
Dr T. Mahmood, Medical Director Tameside Hospital NHS Foundation Trust
P. Dylak, Director of Nursing Tameside Hospital NHS Foundation Trust

SUBJECT: HEALTH COMMISSION INVESTIGATION INTO MID STAFFORDSHIRE NHS TRUST. IMPLICATIONS FOR TGH

Dear Mrs Green, Dr Mahmood, Mr. Dylak,

I have read your letter dated 18th May and the action plan to address the main issues arising from the Healthcare Commission report following the investigation into Mid-Staffordshire NHS trust.

I am deeply concerned that the analysis by the Trust Executive Group, and the action plan arising from it, not withstanding its endorsement by the Corporate Clinical Management Group, fails to address fundamental issues affecting TGH which in my opinion are:

Inability by nurses to provide adequate nursing care on many shifts.

This happens for many reasons, the main being a low ratio of Qualified Nurses per 100 beds compared to other trusts.

a. Simply too few qualified nurses for too many patients. For instance Ward 4, with 17 highly dependent patients, with one qualified nurse and one auxiliary nurse for the early and late shifts. This has happened many times and has repeatedly been reported to the Divisional nursing manager and at Divisional and Governance meetings.
b. Qualified nurses being moved from one ward to another at the last minute, leaving the ward short of a qualified nurse. For instance, sometimes, from Ward 30 to escalation Ward 41 when it opens, leaving Ward 30 with only 2 qualified nurses for thirty patients on an early or late shift. From Ward 2 to escalation Ward 4 leaving Ward 2 short of one qualified nurse during busy day shifts.
c. Patients being moved from ward to ward due to chronic lack of bed capacity. Examples: patients numbers ***039, ***363, ***873, ***382 among others, were moved five times during their stay. Many more are moved 2, 3 or 4 times between wards. This common practice seriously disrupts nursing care and is undignified and sometimes dangerous.
d. Patients being admitted to an inappropriate ward due to lack of bed capacity. For instance this week-end surgical patients were admitted or transferred to Ward 5 and placed among elective orthopaedic patients
e. Investigation results not being checked or acted upon when patients are moved to other wards. Furthermore this leads to poor record keeping and the documentation, both medical and nursing, becomes disjointed. Fluid charts become incomplete and the standard of nursing care becomes poor or dangerous.

f.   Nursing care is on many occasions disrupted when a doctor of any grade visits a patient who should not be on that particular ward, and requires a nurse to accompany him or her.

g.   Qualified nurses leaving the Trust due to demoralisation and inability to provide the standard of nursing care they aspire to. Current case in Ward 2; with countless other examples having occurred in the past.

h.   Accepting that a safe and adequate standard of nursing care for a thirty beds acute ward at night – Wards 30 and 31 for example – can be delivered by only 2 qualified nurses supported by 2 auxiliaries, leaving one qualified nurse having responsibility for 15 patients..(Same or worse ratio applying to other acute wards).

1.   Low number of junior doctors.

a.   Inadequate number of Junior Doctors on some shifts. Medical registrar cover not available some nights. Tameside Hospital NHS Foundation Trust has a lower ratio of doctors per 100 beds compared to most Trusts.

b.   Doctors having to go round chasing patients admitted to the 'wrong ward' wasting valuable time.

c.   Inadequate number of doctors at weekends. Most divisions have a junior doctors' rota which provides mainly for emergency cover at weekends and, not all patients are reviewed on Sat or Sunday. The potential for a serious or fatal deterioration going undetected is high.

d.   Serious problems with recruitment of junior doctors in almost all specialities across the whole country. Junior doctors are working in specialities first on call without adequate experience and training. This is especially dangerous at night, when registrar or second on call is not resident in hospital. (With some exceptions such as maternity and anaesthetics etc.)

e.   Often there are long delays going to see a patient in a 'wrong' ward, after being asked to by nursing staff, simply because the junior doctor is too busy attending to a patient somewhere else and there is nobody else free.

f.   Often there is a delay in speciality doctors going to see patients in the A&E department, mainly due to being busy elsewhere

2.   Low number of beds in the hospital.

The reduction of bed capacity has led to patients being admitted to the wrong clinical areas on a daily basis, e.g. Patients with infections being admitted to Ward 5 designated as an elective orthopaedic and ENT ward.

The escalation Ward 4 permanently opened without proper nursing staff, proper managerial structure, and proper receptionist cover.

Patients who need admission being sent home to wait for a bed, causing delays in treatment.

Some patients, who for medical reasons need to be admitted the day before their planned operation, are prevented by bed shortages. As a result, they come the day of surgery and are ill-prepared, resulting in a cancellation.

Patients wait in offices or rest areas whilst a bed is vacated. This is not good practice for many reasons, hygiene being but one.

Disruption and delays of operating lists because patients are not ready when they are collected in the ward by the porter/ nurses.

3. The Trust System for Governance is not adequate.

Presently to be "green" in any particular issue of Clinical Governance, Tameside Trust has set itself a minimum target of 70% compliance.

In my view, this is too low and fails to ensure that acceptable standards of care are delivered at this Trust. No other industry would operate with such a wide margin.

4. The Trust is more preoccupied with finances and strategic objectives than in the quality of care to the patients.

In my view, the actions of the Trust over the years and recently speak for themselves: here are some examples:

Closure of Children's Ward in the Hartshead Building, resulting in more disadvantages than advantages for the children admitted with fractures and orthopaedic and ENT conditions. Particularly at night for emergency operations.

Closure of Ward 4, only to open under another name and without proper Nursing or managerial structure.

Closure of Ward 3 as an independent elective orthopaedic unit, placing ENT and elective orthopaedic patients in the same ward and now admitting patients of any other speciality without assessment of risk for patients undergoing Total Hip or Knee replacement.

Closure of Ward 41 only to open it as escalation ward.

Acceptance, year after year, of a high Hospital Standardised Mortality Ratio [HSMR]; an issue which I brought to the attention of the Trust and the Healthcare Commission in October 2003.

Not allowing consultants direct communication with the non-executive directors on important clinical issues which have not been resolved by line management channels. (Bristol Inquiry Report finding that all too often these directors were kept in the dark on important clinical issues) and stating that all communications with non- executive Directors have to be authorised by the Chief Executive or the Chairman.

Finally I wish to point out that the Chief Executive and the Board of the Trust have a corporate responsibility to maintain adequate standards of patient care. The issues of manpower are not addressed by the action plan. The Chief Executive is ultimately responsible for any harm that comes to a patient as a result of bed shortages, patient being admitted to the wrong ward or due to shortage of nurses or doctors.

Yours sincerely

Milton Peña
Consultant Orthopaedic Surgeon
Chairman SMSC

4. LETTER TO ALL CONSULTANTS AND SENIOR DOCTORS

06 November 2009
cc: Medical Director; CEO; Chairman of the Board; Director of Planning;
Deputy CEO; Director of Nursing; Human Resources Director; Care Quality
Commission
Subject: Care Quality Commission North West Region

Dear colleague,

On 20th October, I contacted the Care Quality Commission to raise my serious concerns over issues undermining the standards of care to our patients.

The main worrying issues are:

1. Inability of nurses to provide adequate nursing care on many shifts due to low staffing levels, compounded by borrowing of nurses, escalation wards, sickness etc. [This occurs on wards across the hospital: medical, surgical, orthopaedic etc.]
2. Inadequate number of Junior Doctors. This continues to be a serious problem, in particular the Medical and Orthopaedic Division.
3. Lack of bed capacity. This is an extremely serious issue, the consequences of which put patients at grave risk.
4. The Trust is more preoccupied with finances than quality of care to the patients.

These matters were explained in my letter to the CEO, the Medical Director and the Nursing Director on 2nd June 2009, also circulated to all consultants. As I explained in that letter I raised similar concerns to the Healthcare Commission in October 2003, in particular due to our high Standardised Mortality Rate [HSMR].This was almost six years ago and in many respects, sadly, little has changed.

I will keep all of you informed of any developments from the Care Quality Commission.

Yours sincerely

Milton Peña
Chairman of the Senior Medical Staff Committee

5. LETTER TO CHAIRMAN OF THE BOARD THFT

From: Peña Milton
Sent: 28 January 2010 15:01
To: The Chairman of the Board
Cc: CEO; Deputy CEO; Director of Nursing; Medical Director; Director of
Planning; # All Consultants; Matrons;
Subject: safety of patients at TGH

Dear Mr Presswood,

I am extremely concerned for the safety of patients being admitted to TGH.

In many clinical areas, it is clear, to any patient or visitor, that practices currently enforced by managers are extremely unsafe. Incidents are happening daily. The reasons are many and I have mentioned them in numerous letters to the Chief Executive and other senior managers and board members over the last 8 years.

In my letter to the CEO, dated 02.06.09 I listed the following causes:

- Inability of nurses to provide adequate nursing care on many shifts.
- Low number of junior doctors.
- Low number of beds.
- Inadequate system of Trust governance.
- The Trust is more preoccupied with finances and other non-clinical objectives than with the quality of care and safety of patients.

In an earlier letter to the CEO dated 23.01.09, which I copied to you, I politely requested that these issues should be discussed at Board level. The shortage of beds goes back many months and was highlighted at an extraordinary meeting of the SMSC. Now the situation is worse. Patients are being admitted to Escalation wards or into the 'wrong' wards. These escalation wards have no permanent nursing establishment and nurses are borrowed from other wards. The MAU, which I visit daily, has patients waiting in chairs for a bed sometimes for up to 12 hours. Where is the care, compassion, and dignity for patients?

I would like to be given the opportunity to discuss my grave concerns with you and other members of your Board urgently.

Yours sincerely

Milton Peña
Consultant Orthopaedic Surgeon

6. LETTER TO ALL CONSULTANTS AND SENIOR DOCTORS

27th October 2010

Dear Colleagues

I wish to explain why I am asking all of you to participate in a confidential ballot to establish if the SMSC has a mandate to proceed to a Vote of No confidence in the Board, or not.

The main reason is my firm belief, shared by several other senior doctors at our hospital that over many years the Board has placed its Finances over and above the safety, quality of care and dignity of the patients and the mental and physical wellbeing of its staff, when making its decisions. This 'ethos' in the collective Board thinking will not change now or in three months.

Financial pressures have been at the forefront of management thinking during the last 10 years. Top down proposals asking all divisions to identify cuts to achieve the CRES (Cash Relief Efficiency Savings) or CIP (Cost Improvement Programmes), as they are now called, have been implemented every year.

Many of you who have worked here for a few years have experienced the detrimental effects of various policies such as ward re-configurations aimed to meet the CRES/CIP targets. These policies have reduced our bed capacity to such an extent that our bed admission system has been sub-standard for a very long time – on many occasions chaotic and unsafe.

In the past, I have asked senior managers at the Trust to request to the Department of Health to make our hospital a special case because our resources have always been less, proportionately, in comparison to other Trusts. I volunteered for the task. The management answer has always been, 'no'.

I asked for transparency and openness to the public and patients regarding CRES. The Chief Executive has never agreed to it.

Meanwhile, as the 'cost improvements' continue year after year, the majority of employees at this Trust, particularly those working in the acute adult divisions, experience the consequences. For the doctors, from senior to junior, these 'improvements' have led to tremendous difficulties in delivering an acceptable standard of care in the clinics and theatres and during ward rounds.

Searching for patients across the hospital, not finding a nurse to do a ward round, overbooked clinics, lack of secretarial support etc. are now a common occurrence. Some colleagues are under the impression that THFT may be taken over by another Trust. In my view, with the Health Investment in Tameside Project, our hospital's future is assured.

Finally, I would like to reiterate that I am always available to discuss these matters with any of you, individually or as a group, at any convenient time.

Yours sincerely

Milton Peña
Chairman SMSC

Enclosed: A Factual Report on the Systemic Failure of Integrated Governance and Leadership by Tameside Hospital Foundation Trust Board, containing seventy references (Draft).

7. LETTER TO SECRETARY OF STATE FOR HEALTH

Note: This letter together with the enclosed report is important because it shows how the government has devolved power to the regulators. Twenty years ago, it would have led to an investigation by the Secretary of State.

19th November 2010
The RH Andrew Lansley CBE
Secretary of State for Health
Department of Health
Re: Concerns about Tameside Hospital Foundation Trust (THFT)

Dear Mr Lansley,

I am the chairman of the Senior Medical Staff Committee at THFT. I enclose a report [See below] stating the reasons why I no longer have confidence in the Board of this Trust; I also attach the response from the CEO of the Trust.

In my view, from the period 2002 to 2009, for every 100 deaths at Tameside Hospital, at least two or three occurred because of lack of care and could have been prevented. In her letter, the CEO stated that 'the Medical Director acknowledges that the recent improvements in HSMR were also due to improvements in care'. The question is: Why has it taken seven years to bring about these improvements in care?

The CEO acknowledges that many issues raised in the enclosed report are real, but claims they 'are nobody's fault but reflect the pressure experienced widely in urban hospitals throughout the NHS'. Many of my senior colleagues and I profoundly disagree with the CEO's justification for, and acceptance of, sub-standard and dangerous care – because, apparently, it is happening elsewhere!

Because of the issues raised in the attached report, the senior doctors at the Trust were balloted regarding whether there was a mandate to proceed to a vote of No Confidence in the Board of THFT. This vote took place against the background of the opening of the new PFI wing of the hospital, lower mortality figures, and, not surprisingly, a formidable PR and Intranet campaign against the motion.

This was a confidential postal ballot over two weeks. Ninety-four votes were received out of 121 votes distributed. The counting panel included the Medical Director and the Director of Human Resources. Three votes were considered invalid; forty-six voters supported the motion to proceed to a vote of No Confidence in the Trust (34 consultants plus 12 Speciality Doctors) and forty-five voters were against the motion to proceed (All consultants).

For the sake of the unity of the senior doctors' body, I chose not to proceed to a formal vote of No Confidence in the Trust Board.

Tameside Hospital Foundation Trust must make savings of £30m over three years and I am concerned that patient safety and quality of care will continue to be seriously compromised. My concerns are shared by more than 43 per cent of the consultants who voted and 100 per cent of Specialist doctors.

THFT has historically been under-funded and this has been acknowledged by the CEO but according to her, it can never be remedied. I have read the whole of the Francis Inquiry report into Mid Staffordshire Hospital and I have found many similarities between the two Trusts.

I firmly believe that the Board has not learned the lessons from Mid Staffordshire hospital and that this Trust Board should be made accountable for its failings over the last seven years.

Yours sincerely,

Milton Peña
Consultant Orthopaedic Surgeon
Chairman Senior Medical Staff Committee
Tameside Hospital Foundation Trust

8. REPORT SENT TO ALL CONSULTANTS, SENIOR DOCTORS AND THE SECRETARY OF STATE FOR HEALTH

A Factual Report on the Systemic Failure of Integrated Governance and Leadership of Tameside Hospital Foundation Trust Board (THFT)

Milton Peña
SMSC Chairman
Consultant Orthopaedic Surgeon
Tameside Acute NHS Trust
MP/26/10/2010

INDEX

INTRODUCTION

This Document aims to show that the Board of Tameside Hospital has consistently failed in its duty of delivering Integrated Governance.

Of the five pillars of Integrated Governance, the Board, pre- and post-Foundation status, has placed Finances and Performance way above Clinical Governance and Quality. The 5th domain, Strategy, has been 'top down' driven year after year. (1)

The author is of the opinion that the Cost Improvement Programme of nearly £5m every year for the next three years, plus the £5m reduction in income from Demand Management contracts with the PCT will lead to further deterioration of the quality of care and safety of our patients.

Three key Executive members of the Board: the Chief Executive Officer (CEO), the Nursing Director (ND), the Deputy Chief Executive Officer/Director of Clinical Services (DCEO) have been in post for over ten years and they must bear the brunt of responsibility for the failings listed in this report.

The period referred to in this report begins in January 2003 and continues to the present day (October 2010). During this period there have been two previous Medical Directors (MDs), one previous Finance Director (FD), one previous Human Resources Director (HRD) and one previous Chair. The present Chair was appointed in November 2007. The previous Chair of the Board was in post for ten years and he is accountable for failures during his tenure. The present MD was appointed in April 2009.

During this period, the author of this report, in his capacity as a Consultant Orthopaedic Surgeon at the hospital since 1997, has reported the Trust to the Commission for Health Improvement (CHI) in 2003 (2) and to the Health Commission in 2005 (3) (4) In his capacity as a Chairman of the Senior Medical Staff Committee, he reported the Trust to the Quality Care Commission in August 2009. (5)

The reasons for contacting these external regulatory organisations in 2003 and 2005 were mainly concerned with unsafe care to patients due to poor nurse staffing levels in the orthopaedic wards.

The author wrote to the CEO of THFT in June 2009 (6) and explained that he was seriously considering writing to the CQC.

The reasons for contacting the CQC may be summarised as follows:

1. Poor/unsafe nursing levels in the Medical/Surgical/Geriatric and Orthopaedic wards;
2. Low number of junior doctors per 100 beds;
3. Low number of beds due to closure of wards without considering the consequences;
4. Failure of the Board in its delivery of Clinical Governance;
5. The Board has historically placed finance over the safety and care of patients.

The three successive Health Commissions failed to formally investigate the Trust as requested by the author. The failure of the present Commission, the CQC, to investigate the Trust is extremely worrying.

1: High Standardised Hospital Mortality Rate (HSMR)

Despite the repetitive indications by Dr Foster Hospital Guide between 2002–2009 period, during which Tameside General Hospital was one of worst 10–20 performing NHS Trust in England for mortality out of 153 NHS Trusts, the Board has failed to responsibly act on this alarmingly high Standardised Hospital Mortality Rate.[7]

In 2006/2007 Councillor John S Bell chaired a local authority Scrutiny Panel to study the high Standardised Mortality Rates at Tameside General Hospital. [8] By and large, his recommendations were not put into practice. Close observation of the Trust's handling of this matter shows an evident confusion on the part of the Board leadership. For example, in a letter to all consultants in April 2009 the MD and the CEO explained that: the high SHMR is not caused by 'bad coding' – although the quality of the diagnoses may be strongly implicated... the Shipman effect is of relatively small influence... this leaves the clinical pathway and care of the patients as the main area of interest. However, when the Trust was alerted to the high mortality in relation to urinary tract infections in 35 patients [9], a questionable review was conducted by the MD which concluded that no more than six patients had died from UTI and that the coding had been wrong in the rest.

Thereafter, the Trust Board, at its meeting on 30th September 2010, reported that [10]: it is clear that clinical documentation and coding have played the largest part in the reduction seen, following the dramatic fall in Trust HSMR for 2009/2010 to 103.5 from 119 the previous year.

The Board of THFT has failed to learn from recent history when it ignored the recommendation of Robert Francis QC (11), that:

'There is a clear preponderance of opinion that, whether or not coding practices at the Trust Mid-Staffordshire] were weak, all the statistics taken together indicate strongly that mortality was higher than expected and that a search should be made for the reason. While it was not unreasonable to review coding, this was no reason not to look searchingly as a matter of urgency at the standards of care being provided in all areas where the figures were high.'[Francis Report page 369, section 55:]

To add to the prevailing confusion amongst Tameside's senior management, comes the suggestion by the MD that the recent improvement in HSMR is due to improvements in care!

This ambiguity shows a lack of clarity in the collective thinking of the present Board and it is reasonable to conclude that this improvement of the figures may have resulted from revisions to the coding process [which were carried out] rather than improvements in clinical and nursing standards of care [for which there is no evidence].

This conclusion is supported by reservations expressed in the Francis Report that:

. . . much scepticism has been expressed to this Inquiry about the apparent leap of the Trust in one year from the bottom of the "league" to somewhere near the top. This does not mean that all matters for concern have been removed – far from it. Therefore there is a danger that the current information could create a misleading favourable impression of hospitals, including Mid Staffordshire.'[Francis Report, p369; section 60]

At THFT, the MD has failed to show what steps were undertaken by the Trust Board to improve the HSMR for acute myocardial infarction, stroke and broken hips.

Moreover, the Trust has continued to give conflicting messages regarding the relative importance of the different factors contributing to the high mortality rate. After the Board meeting of 30 September 2010, Team Brief reported that: *'it is clear that documentation and coding have played the largest part in the reduction seen.'* The Right patient Right bed policy, heralded 18 months ago as one of the five main planks of the Action Plan to reduce HSMR, has not merited a single mention in Team Brief.

The Review of contemporary deaths in adults has been carried out by a consultant paediatrician. This is worrying because he is outside his area of expertise. He has found several cases where there were questions concerning the management of these patients. No answer, however, was given to the author of this report when he raised questions concerning two cases. Furthermore the monthly report distributed to all consultants regarding the Review of Contemporary Deaths is no longer circulated.

The author of this report acknowledges that other actions taken by the Trust to tackle HSMR have helped to reduce the total number of deaths in the hospital. In this respect, the MD should be congratulated following his latest announcement. (12)

The questions that arise are: why it has taken so many years to address an issue first raised in the report by this author to the CHI in 2003; and why the Trust waited for years before funding extra nurses for the Critical Outreach Team?

2: Lack of bed capacity

2.1: The collapse of the Bed Management System and consistent failure to admit patients to the right bed under the right consultant.

2.1.1: Despite its clear condemnation by the Royal College of Physicians Invited Service Review (13) [p.9, section 8.3], the Trust continued to adopt the very short-sighted policy of bed management where patients in the Medical Assessment Unit (MAU) are distributed arbitrarily to the next available bed regardless of medical specialism required, for example, the admittance of gastroenterology patients onto the chest ward and accommodating chest patients in gastroenterology.

2.1.2: The continuous failure of the effective management of acute medical admissions due to the insistence of senior management on being involved in the minute by minute running of MAU, depriving the patients of the expertise and knowledge of trained consultants and nursing staff. (Currently, MAU is effectively run by the director of clinical services – who is not medically trained – supported by the medical divisional nurse manager).

2.1.3: In the absence of available medical and surgical beds, doctors and nursing staffs have to deal with patients in inappropriate areas during admission when the process of clerking, consenting, surgical marking and so forth is performed. This can have an adverse impact upon patient safety with case notes not infrequently getting mixed up, patients' blood pressure rising and the result in some instances leading to the cancellation of the operation. Example: incident 26286 dated 09/01/10: 'Ward is disorganised and understaffed. Unable to locate patient's notes... '

2.1.4: Not uncommonly, due to lack of bed capacity, patients in MAU – often hooked up to drips – wait in chairs or on trolleys for many hours and sometimes the whole night. Conversely, to make way for them, post-operative patients are obliged to vacate their beds prematurely and sit in chairs for long hours awaiting discharge. This appalling way to care for patients has been repeatedly reported to the CEO and other senior managers; numerous complaints from relatives have simply been ignored. It is a scenario which continues on a daily basis.

2.1.5: Some patients find that, whilst in theatre, their bed has been taken by another patient and recovery nurses have to keep them in the recovery ward until a replacement bed is found, thus delaying the operating list.

2.1.6: Closure of the Orthopaedic/ENT/surgical Children's Ward in the Hartshead Building (Ward 1) has meant that children requiring surgery have now to be transported over a long distance to theatre exposing them to unnecessary serious risk during transfer, especially at night. (Thankfully, this risk will cease with the opening of the new wing of the hospital, but this does not mean that the managerial decision was right.)

2.1.7: Presently the Trust is operating 'winter emergency' contingency measures which include deploying an 'admission avoidance practice' in MAU and A&E. (See Trust Board minutes, August 2010) This Policy has never been properly explained to the doctors and nurses working at this hospital.

2.1.8: The lack of bed capacity and consequential admittance of patients to inappropriate wards - a patient with a fractured hip may, for instance, be admitted to the gynaecology ward – does not lend itself to safe and effective care. Such outliers can easily be missed in ward rounds, or be seen not as early, or not as often, as they should. Example: incident 26215; Patient was left over 30 hours after procedure without review.

2.1.9: The chaotic admission system continues to admit some stroke patients in wards other than the Stroke Unit. Likewise, patients with complex cardiac conditions are admitted under a non-cardiologist consultant whilst the Cardiac Unit may have a number of patients who should be in a Care of the Elderly Ward.

2.1.10: Lack of bed capacity at the time of admission causes serious disruptions to the running of the operating schedules, causing delays, unplanned changes to the order of the list, overrunning and ultimately putting patients at risk.

2.1.11: The lack of bed capacity also means that some patients are moved two, three, or four times from ward to ward. This is sub-standard bed management and can be dangerous, due to lack of continuity of nursing and medical care and may be a significant factor in spreading infections. (14)

2.1.12: On numerous occasions, patients arrive to ward from A&E precipitously without the ward having accepted them, in order to meet the four-hour waiting-time target. Sometimes no bed is available and porters are dispatched around the hospital in desperate search for one. (15)

2.1.13: Ward 5, the designated elective Orthopaedic and ENT ward, is commonly used as a Medical and Surgical ward, admitting patients with infections, including MRSA, and thus placing Orthopaedic patients at grave and unnecessary risk (See monthly incident report spreadsheet). This practice continues regardless of the fact that it has been repeatedly reported to the Divisional Nurse Manager. In addition to which, the ward invariably suffers from poor staffing levels. Example: incident 28828: 16/06/10. The CEO and other senior executives of the Board have repeatedly been notified of this dangerous practice. Part of an email by an orthopaedic surgeon two years ago reads: The following patients have been admitted to the joint replacement Unit yesterday and I have confirmed this with Sister X: one patient with tuberculosis of the ankle wound, one patient with an abscess in the shoulder area due to Anthrax, one patient with a peri-anal abscess put next to patient recovering from joint replacement surgery, one patient with chest infection put next to patient recovering from joint replacement surgery.

In reply, however, the DCEO (16) confused the elective Orthopaedic ward (Ward 3) with the Trauma Unit (Ward 2), therefore missing the point completely. Furthermore, his express hope that these will be an 'exceptional circumstance' that should not be repeated, has proven forlorn.

2.1.14: The Surgical Elective Ward (SEF) is used as a medical, acute surgical, orthopaedic facility, with complete disregard for its originally intended use and often leaving only one qualified nurse supported by an Assistant practitioner for 17 patients. Example: incident 28757; dated 02/08/10.

2.1.15: Thousands of medical patients who have their initial assessment in outpatients clinics are thrown into a black hole called a 'dummy clinic', leaving them unattended – 3,700 patients in cardiology alone and 800 in diabetes and endocrinology.

2.1.16: Patients coming to TGH for a planned procedure or operation will very often, upon arrival to the designated ward, find there is no bed ready at the time of admission. These patients wait in inappropriate areas, corridors, communal offices, waiting rooms etc. until a hot bed is vacated. (17) This is a regular occurrence on ward 5.

2.1.18: The catastrophic failure of the launch of the 'right patient, right bed' policy owes much to the failure to engage front line staff.

2.2: The escalation wards.
2.2.1: Failure to provide adequate bed capacity has for many years, been the result of repeated Ward reconfigurations (closing beds and whole wards) (18). For example, we have witnessed the closure of most beds on Wards 3 and 4 only for these wards to be reopened later as escalation wards. The reorganisation of the beds for the orthopaedic and ENT departments has been an abject failure, with the management plan unachieved and promises unkept.

Other wards in the hospital have also been closed.

In June 2009, a consultant physician wrote to his colleagues, copying in the CEO and Directors, amongst others:

'Despite an increasingly larger elderly population, our complement of elderly patient wards has been reduced by over 100 beds: Ward 43 is closed, Ward 40 is now a chest ward, and Ward 41 is intermittently an escalation ward and Ward 46 the short stay ward.'

2.2.2: Escalation wards remain open for months, are closed for a few days, only to be reopened again. Ward 4 is a typical example. Trust Board Policy of opening escalation wards remains in place despite a clear condemnation of these kind of wards in the Department of Health Report, An Organization with a Memory, as long ago as 2000. Currently, the Trust remains in perpetual breach of its Compliance Action Plan, promising the Care Quality Commission that: by the end of August 2010, there will be a total (or virtual?) elimination of medical outlying and the use of escalation facilities.

2.2.3: Escalation wards are opened at very short notice. They do not have a regular nursing establishment and therefore lack nursing continuity. Nurses are frequently moved from their usual bases in other wards to these escalation wards, leaving their shift understaffed – despite the Trust's pledge to the CQC in its Compliance Action Plan to eliminate unplanned staff movements. The Director of Nursing has made similar promises many times since 2003 in previous actions plans.

Analysis of the minutes of the monthly meetings of the Board over the last seven years reveals that the issue of escalation wards appears to have been discussed rarely and, in one instance, when it was apparently discussed, was omitted from the minutes! Thus:

'The CEO apologised for not including in the minutes the report of Mrs X, a Non-Executive Director, regarding a visit to the Ladysmith wards and would make an appropriate record as follows: Mrs X... has noted the increased number of admissions, the complexity of some of the case mix and the work involved in safely staffing escalation wards.'(19)

2.2.4: The escalation wards, not untypically, have appalling nurse/patient ratios. One qualified nurse for 14, or even worst, for 17 patients has repeatedly been reported in writing to the Director of Nursing, the Divisional Nurse managers and executives of the Board by senior nurses and senior consultants of the surgical, medical and orthopaedic Divisions. (20)

2.2.5: Escalation wards often also lack vital equipment and medication; when patients deteriorate this can put them at serious risk. (21)

2.2.6: The lack of beds has led to the current practice of sending patients with fractures and needing admission from A&E, back to their homes, instead of admitting them, as they should, for pain control, elevation of limbs and rest. They are now offered an appointment to busy fracture clinics, from where they are often sent back home yet again to await a phone call.

2.2.7: Thus, the admission of patients on numerous occasions has been delayed for many days. This has caused substandard care as a direct result of a lack of beds. Patients with fractures wait at home sometimes for many days with the result that the bones begin to set in the wrong position making their subsequent operations more difficult than would otherwise be the case.

3: Persistent lack of Dignity in Care
3.1: Discharge of patients becomes a hurried and undignified process because the bed is needed without delay. This can lead to mistakes, such as giving patients the wrong medicines or inadequate advice and information. The evidence for this can be seen in Patient Advice and Liaison Service (PALS) reports as many patients complain as well as in the monthly incident reports.

3.2: Some patients attending A&E and MAU with, what later transpires to be a serious complaint, are sent home, sometimes more than once. The lack of beds influences the decision of the attending doctors. PALS reports and monthly incident reports again provide examples of this.

3.3: Patients coming to TGH for a planned procedure or operation, upon arrival to the designated ward, find there is no bed ready at the time of admission. These patients are assigned to wait in inappropriate areas: corridors, communal offices, waiting rooms etc. until a hot bed is vacated.

3.4: Many complaints in respect of the Trust's failure to honour its Dignity in Care pledge are related to rushed discharge and the movement of patients from ward to ward. Example: incident 26169; dated 29/01/10.

4: Persistent high incidence of in-patient falls

Failure to provide safe levels of nursing and auxiliary care has been a contributory factor to the high number of falls, particularly at night. Many of these patients have sustained head injuries and fractures, including hip fractures. The last six months statistics showed that a large number of falls continues to be reported to the Clinical Governance Committee, yet no effective action plan to improve this dangerous problem by the Trust Board has been announced. Some of these falls victims have not survived. Although there has been a decrease in the total number of falls compared to data from 2002/2003, an unacceptable level of falls persists, particularly in the Emergency and Critical Care Division.

Earlier data from quarter 1 (April – June 2009) shows that 183 incidences of falls were reported, an increase from the previous quarter (152). Two aspects of the analysis of the data are worrying:

Eleven patients account for 45 of the 183 reported falls. Of 37 injuries, three fractures were graded moderate; the remaining 34 were low grade.

More recent data from the same quarter (April – June 2009) show that, in fact, 253 falls for that quarter were reported.

From Jan 2009 to Jan 2010 ten falls resulted in Hip Fractures. (22) Hip fractures sustained after a fall in hospital are regarded as a moderate injury!

Two recent examples (23) of falls resulting in serious injury occurred in MAU and Ward 2.

The PCT appointed a 'Falls Co-ordinator' a few years ago but, regrettably, she works only one day a week. Presently the 'fall clinic' is dysfunctional after the physician who ran it left the Trust.

The Trust's lack of concern regarding falls can be seen in the minutes of the Risk Management & Corporate Governance Committee (24) in July 2010. The Chair (an NED) expressed concern about 71 falls in the month. He was reassured that the majority of falls are not serious and are more likely to be slips or trips, the Director of Finance adding that this number of falls equates to about two a day in a hospital of over 2,000 staff and a large number of patients, so she does not feel the committee need be overly-concerned (sic).

5: Long stay Patients: Trust Board lack of leadership, capability and interactions with external organisations.

The Trust Board has displayed catastrophic failure in resolving the issue of increased length of stay in general (one of the longest in the north-west region and, in particular, 'the social long-stay patients' where patients have been medically discharged but remain in hospital., Successive Chairmen and the CEO have not addressed this issue with sufficient firmness with counterparts from the PCT, Strategic Regional Health Authority and Social Services over the past 10 years.

Only very recently the Board has decided to escalate this issue to CEO level with the local authority, Tameside Metropolitan Borough Council (TMBC), and the PCT. (August 2010).

As a result of a failure of leadership and capability at Board level to find a solution to the issue of long stay patients, together with the closure of whole wards, there has been a total collapse of the Bed Management System (25), resulting in a daily/weekly outcry by senior middle-ranking managers for extra ward rounds by consultants, whose planned clinical activities are, thereby, consequentially disrupted.

Over the years the Trust has created posts such as Discharge Facilitators and Transfer Teams in order to manage bed capacity. Regrettably these measures alone have not resolved the issue of long stay patients who have been medically discharged.

The CEO's Report to the Board in August 2010 states (26):

The hospital has experienced very unseasonal acute demand in August. Patients' admissions and discharges have not been in balance and have resulted, over the last fortnight, in considerable capacity and performance problems for the Trust. The height of the problems was experienced in the week commencing 9th August during which:

a. Up to 38 escalation beds were opened;
b. Over 30 elective procedures were postponed or cancelled to create capacity for emergency admissions;
c. The list of medically fit patients waiting for assessments or interventions from the community health and social care rose to over fifty patients;
d. The A&E four hour wait performance fell to below 92 per cent on two occasions; and
e. Average ambulance turnaround times on occasions exceeded 40 minutes.

In effect, winter contingency responses have been enacted in summer for two consecutive years.

6: Not acting on Patients' Complaints

There has been an egregious failure of the Trust Board to recognise the serious nature of the complaints raised by patients and relatives in letters to the Chief Executive and via PALS over the years and a concomitant failure to resolve the real cause of many complaints: lack of beds and lack of human resources.

A sample of the PALS Report, February 09, provides some examples of the nature of the complaints:

- Father discharged from MAU and collapsed at home following day. Ambulance returned him to A&E but discharged again. Later in day nurses attended home and admitted again by ambulance. Now transferred to Alexandra Hospital where nurses discovered had lost two stones in last two weeks.
- Patient left sitting in MAU for eight hours as there was no bed for her.
- Client concerned because elderly patient discharged from MAU at 2 am.
- Client unhappy that elderly patient discharged in evening (adult medicine ward). Also that he was very unwell and had to be readmitted a few day later.
- Concerns with care given to grandmother. Grandmother sick over three nights and left to relatives to clean up (adult medicine ward).
- Patient left sitting in chair all night because staff did not come to put her into bed (adult medicine ward).

It is believed that some patients and relatives who have complained about the poor standards of care at this Trust have been branded by management as individuals with psychological problems. (27)

7: Unsafe/sub-standard Nursing Care due to poor Staffing Levels

Failure to provide safe levels of nursing care during many shifts in medical, geriatric, surgical, orthopaedic and A&E wards since 2003 and Escalation wards and the Medical Assessment Unit since its creation is an on-going and extremely serious matter.

Hundreds of low staffing reports from nurses (28), Incident reports (29), letters (30) and emails written by senior nurses (31) and consultants (32) from various Divisions since 2003 up to the present time bear witness to this failure. (33)

In spite of the dangers to the patients during shifts with inadequate nursing staff, in her August 2010 report to the Board (34), the Director of Finance listed two actions to be implemented with immediate effect in order to improve/recover the Trust's position with respect to CIP delivery (Cost Improvement Programmes):

1. Divisional Nurse Managers have been advised of the (financial) position including the level of bank nurse utilization and will review request to ensure appropriateness...
2. A detailed review of a ward with high bank nurse utilization will be carried out...

These two actions were approved by the Board without a discussion of the implications for the patients in wards with inadequate levels of nurses. (35)

In the Risk Management and Health and Safety report of 2nd August 2010, the Director Of Nursing gives the following statistics for Quarter 1 (April – June) (36)

Month	Number understaffed shifts	%
April	157	9.8 %
May	172	9.1 %

| June | 136 | 7.4 % |

These statistics are clearly unacceptable, equating to around 1,500 understaffed nursing shifts per year!

An independent Report (37) in 2003 found the levels of nursing staffing in an Orthopaedic Ward at a dangerous level. The findings of this report were never fully revealed to the Board at the time. (38)

Careful review of all the documentation produced by the Board and its different committees over the years explains how the Trust Board continues to fail to understand that even a single under-staffed shift is putting patients at risk.

8: Failure of the Board to analyse, discuss and act on important reports:

8.1 Royal College of Physicians Report 2009.
Failure of the Chairman to put on the Agenda and discuss a Royal College of Physicians report (39) at Board level denied the non-executive directors access to its contents and the opportunity to consider it. Parts of the Report read:

Page 9: 8.1 *'Movement of patients from the MAU appeared to be dictated by bed pressures rather than clinical need and this may have been worsened by the recent substantial bed cuts by the Trust'...*

'We found little evidence of a formal mechanism for handover of care'...

'We were not made aware of the modelling upon which this decision (for Ward re-configuration) was determined, but the majority of those we interviewed felt that they were not sufficiently consulted prior to the changes and the outcome was largely financially driven and required by the Private Finance Initiative development. Subsequent to the bed reduction, the Trust has to open Escalation Wards . . . this issue is quoted as an example of what they (the interviewees) perceive as disengagement with the senior management.'

'The College has advised the board about the urgent need to establish appropriate cardiac cover for the CCU/A&E/MAU out of hours and over the weekends.

Leaving this high-risk group of patients with cardiovascular emergencies unattended for up to 72 hours is unacceptable. There is no mention of this very important issue in any of the minutes of the Trust Board or even the Division of Medicine.'

8.2 Deanery Report May 2010.

The North West Deanery Report (40), following a visit on 28 May 2010, highlighted areas of good practice in O&G, and commends the anaesthetic department and Respiratory and Cardiovascular Physicians. However it is also highly critical of the Trust, in particular on issues of patient safety, staffing levels and lack of supervision of trainees.

The Deanery report, 18 months after the Royal College of Physicians' Invited Acute Medicine Service review on 13, 14 & 15 October 2008, highlighted once again many of the failings of the Trust.

For Example:

Page 3, 1.8: *'The Trust must urgently review the process of handover'*...

Page 4, 6.6: *'The Trust must urgently review the staffing levels'*...

Page 12, 8: *'The trainees... said that if patients were going to exceed the four hour wait they were sent to the MAU resulting in poor quality of care.'*

Page 12, 13: *'They also found it problematic that GP referrals were admitted straight to MAU, as the waiting area within the unit was small and often crowded. They described very ill patients (some with drips up) sitting in chairs waiting for beds. Although the trainees have tried to divert GP referrals to the A&E when the MAU was overly full, this had been refused.'*

Page 14: *'Trainee said that they had attended a Staff Open Forum where they had tried to highlight some of the problematic areas but said that their observations were not well received. The trainees felt that the problems across the Trust arose from lack of staff and poor organisation of services.'*

Pages 15, 16: *'the Trainees were disappointed that the 12 areas for improvement identified in the Junior Doctors Charter had not yet been addressed'.* (41)

8.3 *Junior Doctors Charter*

Failure of the Human Resources Director and the Deputy CEO to bring to the Board Agenda the Junior Doctors Charter (42), denied the NED's the opportunity to discuss this important document released in 2008.

Furthermore, the subsequent review of this report (43) from the trainees' perspective, published in July 2009, was never distributed outside the Division of Medicine and was never discussed by the Trust Board. (44)

An email by the Chair of the SMSC concerning this document, copied to the CEO, DCEO, MD reads in part: *'This is a worrying document. Urgent action is required.'*

Exactly the same failings were noted in the RCP report following their invited visit in Oct 2008 and the North West Deanery report, concerning the Medical Division and MAU, more than two years after the launch of the Charter.

The recently released action plan by the MD is two years too late. The subject of inadequate number of junior doctors at THFT will be discussed by the author in a future report.

8.4 *Review of Integrated Governance: Report by KORN/FERRY/WHITEHEAD MANN, June 2010.*

KFWM was jointly commissioned by THFT and the foundation trust regulator, Monitor, to undertake a review of the Execution of Governance and the Delivery of Integrated Governance from Board to Ward.

Among its conclusions the report noted that, *'The Board has provided the oversight and level of governance that has supported delivery of a solid financial track record and delivery to the national targets as a FT.'*

In the opinion of the author of this report, this has been achieved at an enormous cost to patient safety and quality of care.

The KFWM report noted: *'As the leader of the Board, the Chair has not yet fully utilised and developed the skills, experience and capability of all the Board directors.'*

The report went on to highlight important failings regarding integrated governance:

Page 25. B75: *'The Board does not demonstrate strongly the consideration of the impact of decisions being taken in one area on another or the strategic , future or risk implications for the THFT.'*

Page 29. C11: *'The Corporate Management Group is used by the Executive Directors to consult the Lead Consultants regarding major operational projects or changes and there are staff engagements forums, which are used to consult on proposed changes to policies and working practices. The Board, however, has no direct means to assure itself whether the strategic messages are understood and bought into by frontline staff.'*

Page 29.C12: VALUES. *'The Board has defined its values through four pillars in the form of the THFT aims for the patients, public, staff and partners. The values are expressed as standards and behaviours these stakeholders should experience in interacting with the THFT...'*

Page 30.C13: *'There is no clear definition of how the implementation of the values will be measured or monitored by the Board, and therefore how the Board will be assured of the B2W (Board to Ward) delivery.'*

Page 32.C27: *'The Board is provided with the level of resources overall within the THFT through the annual Planning process and the quarterly statistics, but does not have a clear view of:*

a. *The resources supporting the operational divisions or services to evaluate their adequacy from a business basis; and*
b. *The extent to which the THFT is adjusting the capabilities and capacity to sustainably deliver services over the next 2/3 years.*

Page 34.C42: INTER-CONNECTED THINKING. *'To deliver integrated governance requires an understanding of the interdependency, an identification of the inter-connections between the key domains (i.e. Quality, finance, performance, clinical and strategy). For example it is clear that the processes for delivering complaints are overseen by the Board and audited by Internal Audit. The level and general themes of the complaints need to be used more* *by the Board and DMT's to focus management attention on delivering service improvements...'*

This report highlighted two other important issues:

The board meetings are not discussing urgent clinical matters in depth and not conducting rigorous debate on key issues (page 6, A.19, c).

The Chairman and CEO *lack* the leadership qualities required (page 9, B7).

It is worrying that KFWM did not observe Divisional meetings and this is a major flaw in their report.

8.5 Francis QC Mid Staffs Report.
The action plan of the Trust Board of THFT reflects that it has failed to understand the recommendations from the Francis report on Mid Staffs., particularly concerning putting numbers and targets before patient safety and quality of care. The Report summarised it, thus:

'If there is one lesson to be learnt, I suggest that it is that people always come before numbers. It is the individual experiences that lie behind the statistics and benchmarks and action plans that really matter, and that is what must never be forgotten when policies are being made and implemented.'

The Francis report also makes the point that Trust Boards should engage with clinicians at all levels, yet the Chair of the Board of THFT recently denied a request by the Chair of the SMSC to be allowed to attend the monthly Trust Board meetings as an observer. (45)

On a written reply to the Chair of the SMSC, who was requesting a meeting to discuss concerns regarding patient care, the Chair of THFT replied: *'Although it is highly irregular and improper that you have asked to meet with me ...!'* (46)

8.6 NHS staff survey
The Board of THFT has repeatedly failed to critically discuss the appalling findings of the annual NHS staff survey, year after year. Example: Minutes of Board Meeting, 30th April 2009, Item 68/69:

The results of the NHS Staff Survey were disappointing . . .

As in previous years, the Board quoted meaningless surveys such as Healthcare 100, or the Employers Federation table to conceal the fact that when employees give their views anonymously – as in the NHS Staff Survey – in general, they give vent to their feelings more openly about the way the Trust treats them, although, even here, because of low staff morale and the widespread feeling that the staff survey makes absolutely no difference – nothing changes – participation rates are low.

At the last Annual Survey the response rate from the Emergency & Critical Care Division was 26 per cent (54 out of 208 employees returned the Questionnaire). Responses from the Women and Children's Division were at a similar low level.

8.7: Failing to follow recommendations from Bristol Inquiry (47) regarding non-executive Directors (NEDs)

Written instructions have been issued by the CEO of THFT that all communications with NEDs must be conducted only via the offices of the CEO and DCEO, (48) thereby preventing individual consultants from interacting directly with them.

In this regard, the Bristol Report reads:

As for the non-executive directors, a very clear message to emerge from Bristol is how readily the Board's non-executive directors (and even to an extent the Chairman) can be prevented from exerting the authority expected of them, simply by not being let in on issues. A strong chief executive, with support from executive directors, can seek to control what comes to the board and in what way. Once this approach takes place, it is hard to overcome. Its consequence is that the board cannot effectively serve the public interest.

The CEO re-affirmed her instructions on the matter at a meeting nine months later. (49)

9: Coroner's criticism about the hospital.

HM the Coroner's criticism of the standard of care of many patients at TGH over the years has often been portrayed as a personal crusade, instead of addressing the significant issues raised repeatedly in his court.

10: Finances and Resources: Waste:

9.1: The failure of Board of THFT to successfully secure a multi-million pound contract with the PCT regarding the Transforming Community Services Initiative (50) led to the loss of a significant amount of much needed funding. The Trust submitted its bidding document on 30th April 2010 and on the 7th May the Trust was informed that the bid had reached the final selection stage and it should be ready to submit its amplified, more developed bid by 12th May.

At a private session of the PCT Board on 18th May it was decided not to give the contract to THFT, the Trust complaining that it was given only forty-eight hours to develop its final bid.

The question arising, however, is why the Trust did not begin much earlier the work needed to be successful in this important Government initiative which was published in January 2009? (51) There are many power point presentations of other bids across the country as far back as May 2009. (52) Surely, THFT knew of this important initiative at least a year ago. The fact that the CEO was seconded to another Trust during part of this period may be a pertinent factor.

At the July Board Meeting in 2010, the CEO's report confirmed that Tameside's bid had been unsuccessful and that the Community Health Services in Tameside would be provided by a Community Interest Company (Social Enterprise Co) (53) to be established and managed by Stockport NHS Foundation Trust. (54)

9.2: There was a failure of the Board of THFT to critically discuss the consequences of CIP cuts of £4.4m and their impact upon standards of patient care. At the same time, the Trust has been asked by the PCT to reduce its activity by £5.2m to match an income reduction of the same amount. (55) (Demand Management, PCT initiative).

At the August 2010 Board meeting the FD reported to the Board that a further £136,000 had been identified in relation to nursing costs towards the CIP. The report was approved without question.

9.3: This contrasts with the Board's approval of the use (waste) of the Trust's increasingly scarce resources to hire consultancy firms to advise us on what we already know! Worse still, when recommendations are made by these external consultants, they are usually ignored.

9.4: During the process, the depleted resources of the Trust were further squandered taking the consultants to an expensive hotel for a 'Clinical Leadership Programme', the launch of the Acute Care Unit, etc., instead of conducting these events in the local Post-graduate Centre.

11: Breach of NHS Managers Code of conduct

The high-handed, authoritarian approach characteristically adopted by the Chief Executive (56) at Open Forum – refusing to allow critical questions, intimidating and, indeed, humiliating her employees – constitutes a clear violation of the NHS managers Code of Conduct. (57) which requires NHS managers to show respect for NHS employees at all times.

The Trust Board has been oblivious to the deeply-embedded culture of bullying and intimidation that pervades the Trust. (58) There is no discussion of letters of concerns (59) from senior doctors at the Trust, not even a mention of them, regardless of requests that the concerns raised should be discussed by the Board.

The Royal College Of Physicians Report (January 2009), p.12, Para 13.1 notes that:

We observed a general feeling of unhappiness across many of the medical and non-medical staff... especially newly appointed consultants... a new start is required and senior managers need to look within themselves to see how they can offer genuine support and encouragement... There is a considerable array of talent and expertise the Trust should nurture...'

Moreover, the key principle, fundamental to the Code of Conduct, that the care and safety of the patients must be the managers' first concern has been, frankly, ignored (60) (Example: action by FD to meet CIP delivery, as noted above) and a detailed review of the minutes of the monthly Board Meetings and Board Committees provides ample evidence of this.

12: Failure to negotiate job plans for permanent staff

The Human Resources Director and Medical Director have failed to agree job plans with many doctors, who are working significantly more hours than they are paid for. The HR Director has failed to act as the guardian of the rules and regulations; instead, he has procrastinated with other directors and prolonged the job planning process, in some cases for two or more years. He has also failed to advise middle and senior managers on how job plans are conducted.

The HRD has also failed (61) to negotiate locum pay for in-house doctors, thereby wasting taxpayers' money by employing agency doctors.

He has further failed (62) to agree extra-contractual payment rates with anaesthetic SASs, resulting in the Trust employing agency locums at a rate of circa £70 per hour. Estimated loss to taxpayers is £120k this year.

13: Failure to attract and retain skilled doctors and nurses

The Trust has presided over a failure to retain skilled doctors, many of them consultants, who have left mainly due to dissatisfaction with their working conditions (many recent examples: from Medical Assessment Unit, A&E, Radiology and Medical departments).

This has been compounded by its failure to keep married accommodation for junior doctors. By selling flats which were formerly reserved for married doctors (63), the Trust has rendered itself less attractive to potential candidates for unfilled posts.

According to the Annual Plan, 2008/2009: The Trust also plans to sell a proportion of its staff residences in 2008/2009, which will generate cash for future investment in clinical services. It should be noted that the residences do not form part of the protected assets portfolio.

Yet in the Human Resources Report (64) to the Board for Quarter 1 April to June 2010 it is revealed that:

Quarter 1 saw a 6 per cent increase in expenditure on Medical Locum and Agency Staffing, with over £1.6m spent on such cover. Both emergency Service & Critical Care and Elective Divisions are overspent . . .

There has been a simultaneous failure to retain skilled nurses, over the years, (many examples in file) with many leaving because they felt they could not provide patients with an adequate and safe standard of care. (65)

14: The lack of Transparency and openness – concealment of Facts from Public and Media

The Trust Board has revealed a marked lack of transparency when repeatedly stating to the media that issues of bed capacity occur only in winter, hiding the fact that this has been a continuous problem which culminated in a bed crisis during the summer of 2009, resulting in an Extraordinary Meeting of the SMSC on 7th July 2009. This crisis was followed by another in the summer of 2010.

This lack of transparency extends to denial by the Trust Board of external criticisms and its selective reliance upon only those ratings that reflect its fulfilment of government targets.

Another area in which THFT has been remiss in acting with openness and transparency has been in meeting with its statutory obligations under the Freedom of Information Act. In one instance, when the Trust was asked by members of the public to provide all copies of the correspondence between the Trust Board and Chairman of the SMSC, important documents were omitted by the Associate Information Governance Manager (66), specifically the following:

- 23/1/2009 Letter to CEO, copied to the Chair concerning lack of junior doctors in orthopaedic, use of escalation wards etc.
- 2/6/2009 Letter to CEO, MD, DN with copies to the rest of the Board.
- 9/06/2009 Letter to CEO, copied to the Board, about lack of beds for elective orthopaedic cases and including a request to the Board to visit the wards to see the situation for themselves.
- 19/10/2009 Letter to the Director of Nursing.
- 28/1/2010 Letter to the Chairman, copied to Board, covering 5 main issues:

1. Inability of nurses to provide adequate nursing care;
2. Low number of junior doctors;
3. Low number of beds;
4. Inadequate system of clinical governance;

5. The Trust's preoccupation with finances and other non-clinical objectives to the detriment of the quality and safety of patient care.

• 9/02/2010 Letter to CEO, copied to the members of Board, concerning lack of junior doctors in orthopaedics, use of escalation wards and low nursing staffing levels.

15: The disassociation between Trust Board and Consultant Body

The majority of the consultant body has grown increasingly alienated by the practice of senior management working with a, small, inner circle of highly privileged consultants, whilst the rest of the consultants are, by and large, kept in the dark. It was a concern raised in the recent independent report by KFWM, commissioned by the Trust and Monitor, the Financial Regulator.

Decision-making mechanisms in respect of clinical issues at THFT are not functioning efficiently or effectively, as the Chair and Chief Executive lack the requisite leadership qualities and the Board, its Committees and its Directors fail to understand the consequences of their decisions. A typical example is the complete failure of the 'Right Patient, Right bed' initiative.

The Forums have become a series of 'lectures' and power point presentations from the CEO, MD and various managers with little time for questioning and discussion.

Moreover, Directors rarely attend Divisional Meetings.

16: The Board has not learned from Sudden Unexpected Incidents (SUIs), other incidents and complaints.

This was highlighted in the Monitor Report. The action plan by the Board shows, once again, a lack of understanding of the causes.

The more serious cases are all too often downgraded and therefore not all near misses are reflected in final analysis and there is no feedback to individuals who report incidents, no matter how serious the incident is!

The CEO chairs a group that sits, in camera, to review red incidents, details of which are never revealed in much detail in the reports presented to the Board.
(67)

17: Suppressing Freedom of Expression

When an orthopaedic consultant (68) attempted to highlight the issue of inequality between trusts by writing a letter to the editor of a national newspaper, comparing human resources between the Orthopaedic Department at TGH and an Orthopaedic Department at a neighbouring hospital, he was prevented by the CEO (69) and the DCEO. (70)

The proposed letter to the Editor of The Independent read:

Dear Sir,

Re. Inequality of Human Resources in NHS Trusts

At Tameside Acute NHS Trust, serving a population of 250,000, the Orthopaedic Department is staffed by six Consultants, two Specialist Registrars and one Trauma Co-ordinator Nurse.

A neighbouring Orthopaedic Department, at a Trust serving a population of 350,000, has 16 consultants, seven Specialist Registrars and three Trauma Co-ordinator Nurses. Other junior staff numbers are similar, but within 12 months four junior orthopaedic doctors' posts [at Tameside] will cease.

A Business Plan for a seventh Consultant is being considered and will probably be approved. The British Orthopaedic Association recommended number of orthopaedic Consultants for Tameside is 10.

I recognise that within Greater Manchester, the Orthopaedic Department at Tameside is not alone in lacking Human Resources, but unless these profound inequalities are addressed, we will not be able to compete in what is now a Private/Public Health Market.

Signed

The Human resources at the Orthopaedic department at THFT remain significantly lower than the Trust alluded to in the proposed letter.

SUMMARY

The issues highlighted in this brief report attest to the fact that during the period from 2003 to 2010, the Board has not listened attentively enough to the concerns of patients, their families and staff.

Nor has it learnt from recommendations advanced by numerous bodies, both regulatory and academic.

In addition, the Board has not followed the recommendation from reports of various inquiries and investigation into other failing trusts.

THFT Board has not been operating according to current NHS guidance which promotes openness, transparency and accountability to their local populations, including holding its meetings in public.

Historically Tameside Hospital has been underfunded compared to other Trusts.

For the last seven years the Cost Relief Efficiency Savings (CRES) now called Cost Improvement Programmes (CIP) did 'save' the Trust some £20 million. This report has shown the consequences of these 'improvements'.

The Trust now needs to 'save' £30 million in three years. The Board, unfortunately, has not learned the lessons of the last seven years.

The author of this report acknowledges that the new PFI hospital wing will provide an improvement to services including Children's, outpatients', day-case surgery, medicine and in-patient surgery. However, it will be an added financial burden from October 2010 onwards, year after year for 30 years. On the other hand, the building project (Health Investment in Tameside) will provide the basis for the operational stability of the hospital.

In the opinion of the author of this report, the present Board of THFT will continue to fail to deliver Integrated Governance because it is clear from the Financial Reports to the Board and the Annual Plans that its main priorities are to continue to focus and deliver on Finances and on Targets at the expense of Clinical Governance (safety and care of patients; everyone matters; dignity in care, etc.).

ACKNOWLEDGEMENTS

The author wishes to acknowledge the support of many patients and their relatives when writing this report. In addition, the author is grateful for the support and encouragement from many Nurses, Midwives, Doctors, Physiotherapists, OTs, Radiographers, Clerical Staff, Cleaners, Kitchen and Restaurant Workers, Maintenance Workers, Porters, Security staff, Men of God and Managers and many others. You have worked very hard and battled through many very difficult years. Let us all have hope for a better future.

REFERENCES

1. Korn/Ferry/Whitehead/Mann. Review of Integrated Governance at THFT. June 2010.
2. Milton Peña, Letter to Commission for Health Improvement. (17 page report) copied to CEO and HM Coroner (17.10.2003).
3. Milton Peña, Letter to Chief Executive of the Health Care Commission reporting shortages of Nursing Staff in the Orthopaedic Wards at TGH (22.06.2005).
4. Milton Peña, Letter to the Health Care Commission (07.07.2005).
5. Milton Peña, email to Care Quality Commission requesting an urgent major investigation at Tameside Hospital (07.12.2009).
6. Milton Peña, email to CEO, copy to Directors, non-executive directors and all consultants, regarding capacity crisis (09.06.2009).
7. Dr Foster Hospital Guide 2009.
8. www.tameside.gov.uk/scrutiny/personal/mortalityrates.pdf
9. Chief Executive Officer, Letter to CQC. Re Mortality outlier alert for Emergency Admissions (30.12.2009).
10. Team Brief, October 2010.
11. Francis, Robert, QC. Independent Inquiry into Care provided by Mid Staffordshire NHS Foundation Trust Jan 2005 – March 2009.
12. Medical Director, email 26.10.2010.
13. Royal College of Physicians: Invited Services Review of Acute Medicine at Tameside Hospital. Final Report, 22.01.2009.

14. Lead Consultant Orthopaedic Division, email to CEO, DCEO/DES, MD copied to infection control officer and Divisional managers (24.12.2008).
15. Monthly spreadsheet report listing incidents filed by nurses and doctors.
16. DCEO/DES email to Lead Consultant of Orthopaedic Division (24.12.2008).
17. Milton Peña, email to CEO copied to Board and all consultants explaining that there were 17 patients waiting for a bed on Ward 5 (09.06.2009).
18. Consultant (Medicine for the Elderly) email stating that since his appointment 100 beds have been closed in the Medical Division (June 2009).
19. Minutes of the Board Meeting 26.02.2009.
20. Milton Peña, email to Divisional Nursing Officer, Surgical Division (29.08.2009).
21. Report by Consultant Anaesthetist regarding incident on Ward 46 on 26.03.2009.
22. Data from the Orthopaedic Theatre Register at THFT.
23. Incidents under investigation. Considered possible red incidents.
24. Minutes of meeting of Risk Management & Corporate Governance Committee 23.07.2010.
25. Numerous emails from senior and middle managers to consultant physicians seeking extra ward rounds to discharge patients.
26. Minutes of the Board meeting 02.08. 2010.
27. http://www.thetruthabouttamesidegeneral.co.uk
28. Staffing Level Report forms were introduced by the Trust in February 2003 at the request of the author. They formed the basis of his report to the CHI. From 2009 the nursing staff has been asked to report low staffing levels in 'incident forms'.
29. Incident Reports of shifts with low nursing staffing levels continue to be filed by nurses brave enough to do so. They can be found in the monthly spreadsheet of reported incidents.
30. Letter from Consultant General Surgeon to Divisional Nursing Officer 30.07.2008 copied to CEO, DCEO, ND and MD.
31. Email from senior ward nurse to Divisional Nursing Officer 04.02.2009 explaining that on many occasions one qualified nurse had been asked to care for 17 patients.
32. Email from consultant orthopaedic surgeon to the author, copied to Chair of the Board, DCEO, DN and MD 24.03.2005.
33. Milton Peña, email to Chair of the Board, copied to Board members,

Divisional Nurse Officers and all consultants 28.01.2010.

34. Director of Finance Report to the Board, 02.08. 2010.
35. Minutes of the Board meeting, 02.08. 2010.
36. RISK Management and Health and Safety Report, Quarter 1, Board meeting, 02.08.10.
37. Newburgh Technology, Team Work Report 10.07.2003.
38. Director of Nursing Report, Board meeting 22.10.2003.
39. Royal College of Physicians, Invited Service Review: Tameside Hospital Foundation Trust(Acute Medicine). Final Report 22.01.09.
40. North West Deanery Report 28.05.10.
41. The Junior Doctors' Charter, launched at the Junior Doctors' Forum meeting on 27.03.2008.
42. Email from Nick O'Mullane, senior Consultant Physician to Director of Human Resources 17.07.2009.
43. Email from junior doctor to Nick O'Mullane, attaching Review of Compliance of Charter's 12 points, fifteen months after its launch. (This is a five page document.) July 2009.
44. Milton Peña, email from Chair of SMSC to Nick O'Mullane, copied to CEO, MD, DCEO, DHR and all consultants. July 2009.
45. Email from Chair of the Board to Chair of the SMSC 12.082010.
46. Email from Chair of the Board to Chair of the SMSC March 2010.
47. The Bristol Royal Infirmary Inquiry, July 2001, Chapter 24, Paragraph 32 and 33.
48. CEO email to Chairman of SMSC November 2008.
49. Meeting between the author as Chair of SMSC and CEO, with ND in attendance. 31.10.10.
50. CEO Report, Transforming Community Services, Page 3, Item 3. Trust Board meeting, 27.05.2010.
51. Department of Health, Guidance for Foundation Trusts on Transforming Community Services. 13.01.2009.
52. Power Point Presentation, Transforming Community Services. NHS South Event, March 2009. Available on Internet.
53. Social Enterprise Companies are non-profit organisations competing in the open market.
54. CEO Report, Page 7, Item 7: Transforming Community Services. Trust Board Meeting 22.07.2010
55. The term 'Demand Management' refers to actions taken by the PCTs or nowadays by the Clinical Commissioning Groups to moderate the

demand for health care services.

56. Open Forum at Auditorium Post Graduate Centre (Werner House) February 2010.

57. Code of Conduct for NHS Managers. Department of Health. October 2002.

58. Milton Peña, letter to Chair of the Board, regarding unacceptable behaviour of former MD. 01.12,05.

59. Code of Conduct for NHS Managers: 'Make the care and safety of the patients your first concern.'

60. Milton Peña, letter to CEO, copied to Chair of the Board, ND, DHR, NED and Orthopaedic Consultants 23.01.2009.

61. Email from HRD to Lead Anaesthetic Consultant 08.01.2010.

62. Letter from Lead Anaesthetic Consultant to HRD 22.10.2010.

63. Tameside Hospital Annual Plan 2008/2009, Page 17.

64. Director of Human Resources Report; Agenda Item 9, Quarter 1, Trust Board Meeting 26.07.2010

65. Registered Nurse letter to CEO explaining reasons for leaving the Trust, 04.07.05.

66. Email from Associate Information Governance Manager to Mr W. 06.07.2010.

67. Risk Management and Health and Safety Report, agenda item 10. Board meeting 02.08.2010.

68. Letter to Editor of The Independent 09.09.2008. (Never sent.)

69. CEO email to Milton Peña 11.09.09.

70. Letter from DCEO to Milton Peña 11.09.09.

9. LETTER TO CHAIRMAN AND CEO OF THFT

From: Peña Milton
Sent: 03 February 2012 17:23
To: Connellan Paul; Green Christine
Cc: Jago David; Williams Paul; Dylak Philip; Mahmood Tariq; Corless Robert, NED; Ward Tony, NED; Bates Denise, NED; Anderson Adrian, NED; Kalloo Tricia, NED; Lead consultants, Safety champion.
Subject: Daily struggle to find beds to admit patients/ effect on quality of care and safety/ effect on pledges on Quality Assurance/Everybody matters.

Dear Mr Connellan and Mrs Green,

I was the orthopaedic consultant on call yesterday. I am formally raising concerns regarding the lack of beds which on a daily basis is having a detrimental effect upon the management of my patients and patients in general. My line managers are currently away and, in any case, would be powerless to resolve this matter.

1. Yesterday patient hospital number *****405 with a crushing injury to his right leg arrived at A&E at 10.00am. He was sent to MAU where he remained in a casualty trolley in the corridor until midnight!
2. Yesterday patient hospital number *****661 with a deep laceration to a finger which occurred at 2.00pm was sent to MAU. I found him in the waiting room waiting for a bed, at 7pm. There were several other patients in the male waiting-room waiting for a bed since 9 am.
3. Patient *****570 with a peri-prosthetic fracture of the right femur admitted to MAU. The nurses there tell me that they are a medical ward and have no orthopaedic training.
4. Patient *****225, age 54, previous right hemi paresis and recent fracture of pelvis admitted to Women's Health Ward.
5. Patient *****625, age 96, admitted with fractured pelvis to Women's Health Ward.
6. Daily, patients with fractures are sent home, due to lack of beds, when they should be admitted for operations.
7. Orthopaedic patients of mine (and other consultants) have had operations cancelled due to lack of beds.
8. Patients continue to be admitted to wards which are not appropriate to their condition or illness. (The right patient, right bed policy announced by the MD over two years ago has been regularly flouted)
9. A patient with a serious surgical condition: pancreatitis, age 72, was admitted to the Trauma Unit a few weeks ago. He arrested in the early hours of the morning within 24 hrs of admission. Sadly, he died.

The lack of bed capacity inevitably affects the quality of care and safety of patients. The Trust Board has pledged to uphold the policy, Everyone Matters at Tameside hospital but, looking at two of the three core elements of it:

- *that the patient experience should be excellent at all times.* This it is definitively not the case for many patients on a daily basis; and

- *that the staff experience should be excellent at all times.* This is also not the case for many front line clinical staff, including nurses (I have witnessed nurses under enormous stress first hand in MAU, and other wards, every time I am on call)

Initiatives such as the production of a *Patient Handbook* and the *Behaviours Values leaflet for staff*, although useful, cannot compensate for the lack of a proper clinical environment for each patient which the Board is pledged to achieve. Similarly, the *'Big Conversation'* cannot compensate for the bad experiences (stress, frustration and despair) of staff who receive patients without a bed to admit them.

Following my on-call day yesterday, it has taken me six hours to do a ward round and sort out all the admissions which were scattered across the hospital. My experience is, of course, not unique. I do not mind, in the least, walking; the problem is that because many patients are in the wrong ward, the care is sub-standard. This is no fault of the nurses on these wards - they are not trained to nurse patients with fractures.

This is not the first time I have been obliged to write to you on this matter. Little, however, has changed. As I have said in previous letters, the first step to a solution is to recognise that there is a problem. The continuing lack of capacity is causing poor patient care and sometimes patients suffer adversely. It has a ripple effect on elective and planned admissions, running of theatre lists etc. Some days, the MAU is frantic and so extremely busy that it gives the appearance of bordering on chaotic. I am told that the Nursing officers are regularly informed of the problems.

I have been waiting for an e-mail from Management to acknowledge that there is a problem and an indication of how it is been solved. So far the measures taken have not solved the capacity problem that is clear.

Length of stay is an issue we all are trying to improve. Yet inpatients continue to wait for investigations which could be done in the evenings or weekends, on a regular basis. This will cost but compared to the cost of keeping patients in a ward, is probably cheaper. This has been discussed many times before. This would help, but in my view, it is not enough.

The sad fact is that all those statistics, matrices, calculations and plans of the recent past were not realistic and have failed. The Community and Social Services has not been capable to deliver the prompt discharge of patients, and many beds remain occupied by 'medically fit patients'.

We need more resources.

Some time ago I suggested to Mr Griffiths that the Board should debate and consider making a request to the shareholders of the Consortia (PFI) for a voluntary Donation to the Trust of a percentage of the annual Unitary Payment. I understand it is around £7m a year. If they donate 'back' 10% it would mean £700.000 which the Trust could reinvest in patient care.

I would politely request Mr Connellan to put this item in the agenda of the next meeting of the Trust Board.

Yours sincerely

Milton Peña
Consultant Orthopaedic Surgeon

10. LETTER TO THE CHAIR OF THE PARLIAMENTARY HEALTH SELECT COMMITTEE

Note: *This letter is self-explanatory and was copied to the Health Secretary of State, The Chairman of the Board of Tameside Hospital and relevant regulatory bodies. I am grateful to Mr Dorrell for his helpful response which I received on August 4th 2012. He apologised for the delay and explained that the Committee does not investigate individual cases. However he went on to say: 'Your case does raise important issues around the way in which disputes between clinical staff and the NHS trusts are handled. You have asked the Trust to refer the case to the General Medical Council and/or the Royal College of Surgeons for investigation. I would like on behalf of the Committee, to forward your letter to both bodies to ask for their comments both on the particular issues relating to the case and on the particular principles. I would only do this with your consent, so I would be grateful if you would be happy for me to do so.'*

I replied to Mr Dorrell on August 13th, saying that I was happy for the letters to be forwarded by him to both bodies.

STRICTLY PRIVATE AND CONFIDENTIAL
15th May 2012
The RH Steven Dorrell, MP
Chairman Parliamentary Health Committee
7 Millbank
House of Commons
London SW1P 3JA

RE: REPORTING A VIOLATION OF ARTICLE SIX OF EUROPEAN CONVENTION ON HUMAN RIGHTS AND POSSIBLE MISUSE OF PUBLIC FUNDS DURING TAMESIDE HOSPITAL FOUNDATION TRUST'S INVESTIGATION INTO THE PERSONAL CONDUCT OF THE CHAIRMAN OF THE SENIOR MEDICAL STAFF COMMITTEE (SMSC)

Dear Mr Dorrell,

I am the current chairman of the SMSC at Tameside Hospital, a position to which I was re-elected by my colleagues, after a confidential ballot in May 2010, by a large majority.

In October 2010, at the request of many of my colleagues I called for a vote of No Confidence in the Trust, and in the same year I publicly stated at the Trust Annual General Meeting that I had no confidence in the Board's capability to run the hospital, and I supported the demand by Tameside Hospital Action Group that the Board should stand down.

In June 2011, I took out a grievance against the Medical and Nursing Directors for serious lack of clinical engagement and accountability.

In October 2011, my employer began an investigation into my personal conduct and my conduct as the chairman of the SMSC against the background of the above-mentioned grievances [and the High Court civil action.[OMIT] ·

The Trust contacted the National Clinical Advisory Services (NCAS) in October 2011 and informed NCAS of its intention to appoint an external, independent Case Investigator. On the matter of professional competence, the Trust acknowledged that I am a capable surgeon.

NCAS advised the Trust to adhere to the guidance outlined in Maintaining High Professional Standards (MHPS) and Tameside Disciplinary Policy for Medical Staff.

I was informed of the Trust's intentions at a meeting in October 2011 and later in writing and I accepted the terms of the investigation, although I pointed out to the Trust that neither MHPS nor the local Disciplinary document envisages a case of this complexity and in such extraordinary circumstances.

For at least two years, I have openly and transparently told the CEO and the Board that they are putting finances and targets before quality and the safety of patients and in October 2010, I sent the Secretary of State a thirty page report relating to this matter.

Contrary to what the Trust says, my views are shared by many consultants and senior doctors as is confirmed by my re-election as the Chairman of the SMSC and also by the result of a ballot the SMSC held for a vote of No Confidence in the Board, which incidentally the Trust failed to report to Monitor.

I am writing to the Parliamentary Health Committee for two reasons regarding this investigation into my conduct:

Firstly, on grounds of cost. Whilst the Trust is financially in the red, the charges of the Independent Investigator are £800 per day plus expenses and VAT. The legal fees of the Trust are potentially considerably higher. The Independent Investigator was provided with two bundles bearing the Trust solicitor's name, totalling 985 pages.

Secondly, the Trust has not followed its own Disciplinary Policy and Maintaining High Professional Standards in the Modern NHS (MHPS) during the course of this investigation.

MHPS states: *'The practitioner must be given the opportunity to see any correspondence relating to the case together with a list of the people that the case investigator will interview.'*

I wrote to the Case Manager on 3rd November 2011 and requested copies of all relevant correspondence including from NACS to the Trust and the Trust to NACS, and from the Trust to the Independent Investigator and vice versa. It was not until I made a request under the FOI Act on 20th April 2012, that I received just two documents, one of them the letter of advice from NCAS to the Trust that should have been shared with me six months earlier. I am still awaiting copies of the witness statements and other documents.

MHPS states: *'Personal data released to the case investigator for the purposes of the investigation must be fit for the purpose, not disproportionate to the seriousness of the matter under investigation. Employers should be familiar with the guiding principles of the Data Protection Act.'*

The trust released personal data to the Independent Case Investigator going back to 1997, which has no bearing on the case, some of it very distressing and false, clearly not related to the investigation, and in violation of the Data Protection Act.

On 10th October 2003, I wrote a seventeen page report to the Commission for Health Improvement and sent a copy to the local Coroner. (I had sent a draft of this report to the CEO of the Hospital three weeks earlier.)

One document released to the Independent Case Investigator is a letter written by the Medical Director at that time, dated 24 October 2003, and sent to the Commission for Health Improvement, as a response to my report. Part of this letter reads: *'Mr Peña's motives for writing this document would require the services of a panel of expert psychiatrists.'*

This letter that is full of other false and malicious statements was sent as an enclosure in a letter by the CEO to the Medical Director of the Greater Manchester Health Authority on 10th November 2003. Both these letters along with many other documents, including my current contract have been passed to the Independent Case Investigator in November 2011 and are among the 985 pages contained in the two bundles.

MHPS states: *'...in all cases the purpose of the investigation is to ascertain the facts in an unbiased manner. Investigations are not intended to secure evidence against the practitioner...'*

The witnesses that the Case Investigator deemed relevant do not include a single consultant, other than the Medical Director, although one of the allegations against me is that I have caused conflict between teams, which I completely refute. The list of witnesses was not given to me in advance as in the spirit of MHPS and the investigator has declined to see the witnesses I suggested. Any reasonable, fair-minded person working at this hospital, upon seeing the list, would conclude that there is real likelihood that the investigation is not being conducted in an unbiased manner.

The Trust has declined my repeated entreaties that it should communicate its concerns to the General Medical Council and/or the Royal College of Surgeons and request either of these organisations carry out the investigation.

I would like to have the opportunity to defend myself against all the allegations of the Trust at a fair and unbiased hearing, in accordance with the principles of Article six of the European Convention on Human Rights.

I do not know the Code of Conduct that regulates the work of the external, independent Case Investigator and to which professional body he is accountable.

I respectfully request that the Health Committee investigate the manner in which the Trust has managed this investigation.

Finally, I wish to point out that I have copied this letter to the Secretary of State for Health and the various regulatory bodies, because I am unclear who has the overall responsibility to investigate the manner in which the Trust has managed the investigation against me.

Yours sincerely

Milton Peña
Consultant Orthopaedic Surgeon
Chairman Senior Medical Staff Committee
Tameside Hospital Foundation Trust

Copies to: Mr Andrew Lansley, Secretary of State for Health
Mr Michael O'Higgins, Chairman, Audit Commission

Mr David Bennett, Chairman, Monitor
Mrs Sue McMillan, Regional Director, Care Quality Commission
Mr Firiel Benson, Case Administrator, National Clinical Assessment Services
Mr Paul Connellan, Chairman of the Board, Tameside Hospital

11. LETTER TO REGIONAL DIRECTOR OF CARE QUALITY COMMISSION

Note: *This letter was acknowledged by the CQC, fifteen months later, following the Keogh review, with an apology. Its purpose was to highlight, once again, concerns and inform the regulator of the Investigation into my personal conduct.*

The incidents referred to are, invariably risk-rated 'low' or 'yellow' by the Trust, ratings which, in my view, are nonsensical.

Mrs Sue McMillan
Regional Director
Care Quality Commission
North West Region
16th May 2012

Dear Mrs McMillan,

For your information, I enclose a copy of a letter I wrote to the Chairman of the Parliamentary Health Committee in respect of an investigation into my personal conduct by my employer, Tameside Hospital Foundation Trust. Many of the issues raised by the Trust regarding my conduct as Chairman of the Senior Medical Staff Committee are related to my involvement in serious clinical matters which are within the remit of the CQC, such as:

1. The care of in-patients with Diabetes as co-morbidity;
2. The shortage of radiology consultants at Tameside hospital, made worse by the dis-establishment of an existing consultant post, leaving only seven consultants, the same number that existed in 1999;
3. Avoidable mortality. I have serious concerns that for every one hundred patients that die at Tameside one to two deaths can be avoided with better care. These patients, usually elderly and vulnerable die from a

combination of systemic failures: – admitted to the wrong ward – delays in being seen by a doctor – delays in escalating care – lack of HDU beds – shortage of nurses on a particular shift on a particular ward – shortage of doctors during a particular shift, usually at night;

4. Shortage of bed capacity at the hospital, which on a daily basis directly affects the welfare of patients in many ways;
5. Lack of clinical engagement and accountability by executive directors when making major decisions, such as the swapping around of the Medical Assessment Unit and the Trauma Unit; and
6. Under-staffed shifts. Nurses continue to report shifts that are dangerously under-staffed.

I am aware that the CQC's main role is to monitor the hospital's compliance with the standards of quality and safety which the Trust must meet as part of its registration with the CQC.

I am also aware that in April 2012 Tameside Hospital was found to be compliant on *Outcome 4* – Care and welfare of people who use services, and *Outcome 13* – Staffing.

It is difficult to reconcile the CQC's findings in respect of *Outcome 4* with the sub-standard care that many patients experience on a daily basis. On the other hand, I can understand the limitations of the CQC inspection process.

Below are six random incidents filed by nurses regarding *Outcome 4*:

1. Incident 35032: 10/12/11 Elective Unit. Incident Description: A&E sent patients to ward without informing of their admission, no handover given. Patients did not have treatment sheets – unable to give analgesia. Risk rating – low.
2. Incident 35344: 13/12/11 Fracture Clinic. Incident Description. Poor staffing levels resulting in stress to all members of staff. 70 + patients, long delays in treatments.
3. Incident 36307: 23/02/12 Day Case Unit. Patient admitted for surgery, bed requested. None available. Patient was on ward for 48 hours. Transferred to bed after 57 hours!
4. Incident 36143: 22/02/12 Endoscopy Unit. Patient admitted with headache, currently vomiting and receiving treatment for meningitis!

Inappropriate place to put a patient with meningitis.

5. Incident 36611: 19/03/12 Surgical Unit. Patient arrived by ambulance for admission to ward; no beds available. Patient sat out on wheelchair, needs attended to and toileted; patient waited all day. Bed became available in Trauma Unit, but manager felt it was not appropriate for that Unit. Patient sent home.

6. Incident 36717: 21/03/12 Trauma Unit. Patient was transferred to medical ward at approx. 01.00 hrs. Patient and family upset by this.

Regarding *Outcome 13*, six illustrative Incident Reports filed by nurses:

1. Incident 34791: Date: 25/11/11 Ward: Surgical Unit. Incident description: two qualified nurses for 24 major surgical patients – refused to take any emergency patients. Three immediate post-operative patients, two enhanced recovery patients, one with a complex wound; two with epidural infusions; three confused patients and five 'all care patients'. Risk low (yellow).

2. Incident 35044: Date 02/12/11 Ward Surgical Unit. Incident Description: Patient care compromised, ward unsafe. One qualified staff member for 24 patients: nine all-care patients, one post-operative patient, two poorly patients, three patients with epidural infusions, one patient having a blood transfusion and five patients on intra-venous antibiotics. Risk low (yellow).

3. Incident 35816: Date: 27/01/12 Ward: Elective Unit. Incident Description: Staff member alone working throughout the night; she received five patients from MAU and had to admit two more patients from A&E. Thirteen hours worked without a break. Risk rating: Low (yellow).

4. Incident 35802: Date: 23/01/12 Ward: Day Case Unit. Incident description: patients being sent from A&E and MAU to unsuitable and under-equipped area. Only one qualified staff member on duty. Night Nurse Practitioner was made aware . Risk rating: low (yellow).

5. Incident 35590: Date: 11/01/12 Ward: Surgical Unit. Staff patient ratio was 1:12. Patient care affected, stoma bags leaking, not reviewed in good time. Drugs given late. IV run through, position changes not maintained, post-op observations not done as frequently as per protocol and patients waiting for controlled drugs. Risk rating low (yellow).

6. Incident 36300: Date: 15/02/12 Ward: Surgical Unit. Incident Description: 'Staff nurse was unaware that she was going to be the only

qualified nurse on duty for twenty-four patients. Staff member had never worked on the Surgical Unit before. Risk rating: Low (yellow).

I am sure that you will find it appalling to have one qualified nurse in charge of 24 patients, and the above reports by nurses require checking. I believe they are merely the tip of the iceberg, because many nurses simply do not report understaffed shifts for many reasons: tiredness, fear of reprisals or simply because they believe it will not change anything.

I am not sure if the CQC obtains the electronic information on nursing staffing which is recorded daily, shift by shift and known as Sit Rep (Situational Reports), and whether, this data has any bearing on the outcome of inspections. I would be grateful for a response to this query.

Yours sincerely

Milton Peña
Consultant Orthopaedic Surgeon
Chairman SMSC

12. LETTER TO THE NHS ENGLAND MEDICAL DIRECTOR

Note: *This letter was acknowledged and passed to the Medical Director of NHS North West.*

Private and Confidential
Professor Sir Bruce Keogh
NHS England, Medical Director
10th March 2013

Dear Sir Bruce,

Re: Tameside Hospital Foundation Trust

I welcome the forthcoming investigation into the quality of care at Tameside Hospital where I have worked for the last 16 years. I have read the terms of reference and I would politely ask to be among the clinicians to give written and oral evidence. The Chair of the Trust Board is aware that I am writing to you.

In 2002, I became concerned that many of the nursing shifts were under-staffed and this was contributing to poor care for patients. At that time, Dr Foster's Guide placed Tameside Hospital amongst the worst in the country on many statistics including very high HSMR.

With the full knowledge of the hospital executives, I wrote to the Commission for Health Improvement in 2003 requesting an investigation. After many months, the CHI eventually responded, explaining that it was satisfied with the hospital's proposed Action Plan. Regrettably, for the patients little changed, and nurses continued to report under-staffed shifts, some of them dangerously unsafe.

In 2005, after three years of raising my concerns in writing and at divisional and governance meetings, I became a whistle-blower after one of my patients was put at severe risk as a result of lack of post-operative observations.

From 2002 to 2009, Tameside Hospital remained one of the worst hospitals in the country concerning HSMR. In 2006, relatives of patients who had died and whose care had been criticised in the Coroner's Court formed Tameside Hospital Action Group and together with the local MPs campaigned for better standards of care. I was not involved.

In my opinion, what happened at TH between 2002 and 2009 has many similarities with what happened at Mid-Staffordshire.

Because of pressure from relatives, criticism from the Coroner, the Dame Pauline Fielding Report into care at the hospital and, more recently, inspections by the CQC, the overall nursing staffing has fractionally improved, but insufficient to achieve consistent levels of safe care.

For the last four years, I have been seriously concerned that the Trust has not consistently achieved planned staffing levels - inadequate though these are – on wards across the hospital.

According to the Trust's own metrics, submitted to the Board in January 2013, ten per cent of the nursing shifts take place with fewer nurses than planned. (A twelve-hour shift operates at TH).

A few brave nurses continue to file incident forms, reporting that the wards are unsafe because of under-staffing. The Trust categorises these incidents as of low priority.

I estimate that every year well over one thousand nursing shifts are under-staffed.

In 2010, I was invited to participate in a BBC *Panorama* programme where I gave my opinion that around two per cent of deaths at Tameside are avoidable. I have reported my concerns to the new Chairman of the Board in February 2012 and again just a few days ago.

We are in a financial crisis. From 2002 to 2009 Tameside Hospital made cost efficiency savings which gradually rose from £2.5m to £4m a year. Since 2010, they have risen to £10.5m a year and this will continue for thirty years. The Trust has had three Financial Directors since 2009. This is a clear warning sign.

The 'right patient, right bed' policy that the Trust pledged to the CQC to implement in 2010 never materialised. Forty per cent of patients are admitted to a ward which is inappropriate for their needs. This leads to poor and sometimes unsafe patient care. Furthermore, the lack of bed capacity means that hundreds of operations have been cancelled whilst many patients with fractures needing admissions and operations are sent home to wait for days or even weeks. Cases of patients recovering from serious conditions being sent home too early, only to be readmitted in a worst state, have also occurred in the quest to free up beds.

In October 2010, at the request of over thirty consultants concerned with the standard of care provision, a secret ballot took place regarding a Vote of No Confidence in the Board.

I wrote a report entitled '*A Factual Report on the Systemic Failure of Integrated Governance and Leadership of THFT Board*', which together with the ballot result, I sent to Andrew Lansley, then the Health Secretary. Through his office, it was sent to Monitor and the CQC. I have attached this report and the CEO's response.

Improvements have taken place, but sadly many of the main issues raised have not improved and some, regrettably, have worsened.

I have also attached my letter to the CHI and other documents. I am sorry that they are not in chronological order.

Finally I would be extremely grateful if your secretary could send me the email addresses of the members of the National Advisory Group, so I can copy this letter, with its attached documents, to them.

Yours sincerely

Milton Peña
Consultant Orthopaedic Surgeon

GLOSSARY

GLOSSARY OF MEDICAL TERMINOLOGY AND ACRONYMS

Acute Cholecystitis: Acute and painful inflammation of the gallbladder.

Anatomy: The science of the bodily structure of the human body (also animals and plants).

Brachial plexus: The complex network of nerves on the shoulder that supplies the whole of the upper limb including shoulder, elbow, wrist and hand. Often damaged during motorcycle injuries.

Cauda Equina Syndrome: A surgical emergency, caused by pressure on the peripheral nerves in the lumbar spinal canal, usually due to a centrally protruded intervertebral disc prolapse. The nerves resemble the tail of a horse, hence the name.

CEA: Clinical Excellence Award, equal to £3,000, given to senior doctors after a competitive application process.

Cellulitis: Infection and inflammation of the skin and tissues beneath it, not involving deep tissues.

CEO: Chief Executive Officer.

Ccerebral Palsy: A disorder of posture and movement caused by damage to the developing brain before, during, just after birth or in early childhood.

CHI: Commission for Health Improvement. The regulatory body that existed until 2005. Superseded by the Health Commission and in turn replaced by the CQC.

CIP: Cost improvement programme.

CCG: Clinical Commissioning Group. A group of GP practices that work together to plan and design local health services. They do it by commissioning or buying planned and emergency healthcare from private and public bodies. All GP practices are required to be a member of one of these statutory bodies. They are funded directly by NHS England (NHS Commissioning Board). Serious conflicts of interest may arise if doctors involved in the commissioning have economic links with private providers.

CQC: Care Quality Commission. The current health regulatory body.

DCEO/DES: Deputy CEO/ director of elective services. The most senior executive after the CEO.

Deep Vein Thrombosis (DVT): the formation of a thrombus (blood clot) within deep-lying veins in the leg.

DNO: Divisional Nursing Officer. A senior nurse manager in charge of nursing matters of a hospital division.

Dr Foster: Limited company which analyses data of health care organisations, aiming to improve quality of care. Dr Foster Hospital Guide is one of its many publications.

Embolus: A fragment of material, usually a blood clot that is carried in the bloodstream and obstructs an artery. An embolus can be life threatening if it blocks the blood flow through a vital artery. Or limb threatening if it blocks an large limb artery such as the femoral artery.

Escalating Care: To move a patient to a High Dependency Unit, or higher to an Intensive Care Unit, or higher still to a Specialist Intensive Unit e.g. a Neurosurgical Intensive Care Unit.

Escalation Ward: A ward which normally is permanently closed but is reopened when hospitals are experiencing a capacity crisis. Thus, it does not have permanent nursing, medical or reception staff.

FD: Financial Director. One of the executive directors. He/she submits monthly financial reports to the Board.

GMC: General Medical Council. The body that regulates the medical profession in the United Kingdom.

Governance: In a hospital context is the act of governing or managing in a safe way and maintaining acceptable standards.

Haemoglobin: Protein in red blood cells that carries the oxygen from the lungs to all cells of the body.

HC: Healthcare Commission. The health regulatory body until superseded by the CQC.

HIT: Health Investment in Tameside.

Hospital Division: The stakeholders of a speciality or Department e.g. Division of Orthopaedics. Hence Divisional meeting.

HRD: Human Resources Director. Attends Board meetings but he/she is not executive director

Intranet: A computer network that uses Internet Protocol technology to share information, operational systems, or computing services within an organization.

IVI: Intravenous infusion.

JLNC: Joint Local Negotiating Committee. A small committee composed by senior doctors' representatives and senior managers including the MD and the DHR. It meets regularly to discuss and agree documents and negotiate terms and conditions. A junior doctor representative also attends.

LINK: Local Involvement Network. A community 'watchdog' with powers to inspect a hospital.

LNC: Local Negotiating Committee. A small group of senior doctors led by a Chairman. It represents the interests of the hospital doctors in negotiations with management. It is supported by an Industrial Relations Officer paid by the British Medical Association. The LNC reports to the Senior Medical Staff Committee (SMSC) whose chairman also sits on the LNC.

MAU: Medical Assessment and Admissions Unit. In some reports also referred as MAAU or simply as Medical Admissions Unit.

MD: Medical Director. A senior consultant and one of the executive directors of a Trust Board.

Medicine: The branch of medical knowledge involving management of illnesses and conditions without surgery. Also known as General Medicine or Internal Medicine.

Monitor: The national regulatory body of the financial status of all Foundation Trusts.

MPS: Medical Protection Society.

NCAS: National Clinical Advisory Service. An organisation that advises hospitals regarding doctors professional-competence to practice – and whether they need to be suspended or not.

NED: Non-Executive Director.

ND: Nursing Director. (Also known as Director of Nursing) A senior nurse, one of the executive directors of the Board, with overall responsibility for nursing matters.

NHS England: The Secretary of State for health approved a change of name for the NHS Commissioning Board, to NHS England, to be effective from 1st April 2013. NHS England has the overall responsibility for the £95 billion health budget that passes directly to the Clinical Commissioning Groups. (Not to the Foundation Trusts.)

NICE: National Institute for Health and Clinical excellence.

NO: Nursing Officer (matron). A senior nurse that supervises various wards or clinical areas, such as Out Patients or Accident and Emergencies. Reports to a DNO.

Nursing Shift: A fix period in the working day of a nurse. Presently 12 hours shifts operate at many NHS hospital wards. Other patterns include an early, a late and a night shift to cover 24 hours.

Obstetrics: The branch of medicine that deals with the care of women during pregnancy and childbirth and some weeks following delivery.

Outlier: 1. a statistical result different greatly from others in the same sample. 2. A patient in the wrong ward e.g. a medical patient in an orthopaedic ward.

PALS: Patient Advisory Liaison Services.

Pathology: The science of the bodily diseases.

PARS: Patient at Risk Score is designed to enable nurses to recognise "at risk" patients and to trigger early referral to medical staff.

Paediatrics: The branch of Medicine concerned with the care and development of children and with the prevention and treatment of children's diseases.

PCA: Patient controlled analgesia. A method by which a adult patient control his/her post-operative pain at will by pressing a bell and releasing small amounts of intravenous painkillers from a preloaded syringe.

PFI: Private Finance Initiative. These commercial deals were invented in 1992 by the Conservative government led by Sir John Major, but became widespread under Labour after 1997. The schemes usually involve large-scale buildings such as new hospitals, which would previously have been publicly funded by the Treasury. The projects are put out to tender with bids invited from building firms and developers who put in the investment, build new hospitals and then lease them back. Contracts arrangements for PFI projects are long term, often 30 years or more.

Physiology: The science of the functions of the living organisms and their organs.

Post-Operative Ileus: A disorder in which the muscles of the intestines are unable to contract normally and as a result the intestinal contents cannot pass out of the body. Symptoms include swollen abdomen and vomiting. Commonly follows abdominal surgery.

SAS: Staff grade and Associate Specialist doctors. Senior doctors working alongside consultants.

SitRep: Situational Report. Name given to daily electronic data of NHS activity in a given clinical area, e.g. daily nursing staffing levels in each ward for every shift.

SMSC: Senior Medical Staff Committee. The committee that represents all senior doctors at a NHS hospital. Led by a Chairman. Also known as HMSC (hospital medical staff committee).

Spina Bifida: A congenital defect in which one or more of the vertebra fails to develop completely in the foetus. It varies from being mild and asymptomatic to very severe with the spinal cord exposed and damaged.

SUI: Sudden Unexpected Incident.

Surgery: The branch of medicine that deals with conditions that may require operations. Modern surgery is subdivided into many branches e.g. orthopaedic surgery, plastic surgery, vascular surgery etc.

TH: Tameside Hospital.

THAG: Tameside Hospital Action Group.

THFT: Tameside Hospital Foundation Trust.

THR: Total Hip Replacement.

TKR: Total Knee Replacement.

WLI: Waiting List Initiative. A four-hour session of work outside Job Plan, requested by a manager, to bring down waiting lists and avoid breaches. Usually, done at weekends. At Tameside paid at £300 before tax. Six years ago payment was double, but consultants accepted reduction as a good will gesture in view of financial crisis.

WTE: 'Whole Time Equivalent staff' are calculated by aggregating the total number of hours that nurses are committed to work in a clinical area, i.e. a ward and dividing it by the standard hours per week (37.5 hours for nurses). In this way part time staff are converted into equivalent of whole (full) time staff.

Unitary Charge: The annual payment that a trust must pay for buildings under a PFI contract. Usually, over a period of thirty years. It is a kind of non-negotiable rent. It includes all the service charges for the building.

GLOSSARY OF MOUNTAINEERING TERMINOLOGY

Anchor: Any combination of pitons, nuts, ice screws and the like that secures a stance from which a climber can securely assist his partner to climb or descend.

Bivouac: To spend the night on a mountain on the open without a tent

Cache: hoard of supplies left buried in the snow.

Crampon: A metal plate with 12 sharp spikes (two at the front), which is fixed to a boot, for walking on ice or climbing ice walls.

Crevasse: A deep crack or fissure in the surface of a glacier. A crevasse may be rendered all but invisible after a bridge of snow closes the crack and disguises it.

Glissade: A controlled slide down a steep slope of snow or ice, sitting and facing down with support of an ice-axe.

Jumar: A metal device that grips the rope under a downward pull but slides easily upwards, it is used to climb fixed ropes. The word derives from the first mechanical ascender, introduced in 1960.

Névé: An expanse granular snow accumulated in high mountains and subsequently compacted into glacial ice.

Penitente: Name for a large lump of ice in the Andes which resembles the shape of a person in penitence. Can be several metres tall and in large numbers they form a difficult obstacle.

Over Boot: Thick neoprene garment worn over the plastic boots.

Plastic Boot: Heavy mountaineering boots used for high mountains to prevent frostbite. They have an insulated thermal inner boot. Neoprene over boots are applied over the plastic boots and are a must for Mount McKinley.

Serac: A very large pinnacle of glacial ice, the size of a tower or building, found between crevasses, the surface of a glacier or mountain slope. Particularly dangerous because it can break and collapse without warning.